SCIENCE FICTION TV

The first in the Routledge Television Guidebooks series, *Science Fiction TV* offers an introduction to the versatile and evolving genre of science fiction television, combining historical overview with textual readings to analyze its development and ever-increasing popularity.

J. P. Telotte discusses science fiction's cultural progressiveness and the breadth of its technological and narrative possibilities, exploring SFTV from its roots in the pulp magazines and radio serials of the 1930s all the way up to the present. From formative series like *Captain Video* to contemporary, cutting-edge shows like *Firefly* and long-lived popular revivals such as *Doctor Who* and *Star Trek*, Telotte insightfully tracks the history and growth of this crucial genre, along with its dedicated fandom and special venues, such as the Syfy Channel. In addition, each chapter features an in-depth exploration of a range of key historical and contemporary series, including:

- *Captain Video and His Video Rangers*
- *The Twilight Zone*
- *Battlestar Galactica*
- *Farscape*
- *Fringe*

Incorporating a comprehensive videography, discussion questions, and a detailed bibliography for additional reading, J. P. Telotte has created a concise yet thought-provoking guide to SFTV, a book that will appeal not only to dedicated science fiction fans but to students of popular culture and media as well.

J. P. Telotte is a professor of film and media studies and former Chair of the School of Literature, Media, and Communication at Georgia Tech. He is the author of more than 100 scholarly articles on film, television, and literature, and has published eleven books, including *The Science Fiction Film* (Cambridge, 2001), *The Essential Science Fiction Television Reader* (Kentucky, 2008), and *Science Fiction Film, Television, and Adaptation: Across the Screens* (Routledge, 2012).

Routledge Television Guidebooks

The Routledge Television Guidebooks offer an introduction to and overview of key television genres and formats. Each guidebook contains an introduction, including a brief history; defining characteristics and major series; key debates surrounding themes, formats, genres, and audiences; a videography; questions for discussion; and a bibliography of further reading.

Science Fiction TV
J. P. Telotte

Forthcoming:
Sports TV
Victoria Johnson

SCIENCE FICTION TV

J. P. TELOTTE

Routledge
Taylor & Francis Group

NEW YORK AND LONDON

First published 2014
by Routledge
711 Third Avenue, New York, NY 10017

and by Routledge
2 Park Square, Milton Park, Abingdon, Oxon OX14 4RN

Routledge is an imprint of the Taylor & Francis Group, an
informa business

Library of Congress Cataloging in Publication Data
Telotte, J. P., 1949-
Science fiction TV / J.P. Telotte.
pages cm. — (Routledge television guidebooks)
Includes bibliographical references and index.
1. Science fiction television programs—History and criticism.
I. Title.
PN1992.8.S35T45 2014
791.45'615—dc23
2013032536

ISBN: 978-0-415-82581-8 (hbk)
ISBN: 978-0-415-82582-5 (pbk)
ISBN: 978-0-203-53877-7 (ebk)

Typeset in Joanna
by Swales & Willis Ltd, Exeter, Devon, UK

Printed and bound in the United States of America by
Edwards Brothers Malloy

TABLE OF CONTENTS

LIST OF ILLUSTRATIONS

FIGURES

ACKNOWLEDGMENTS

As is usually the case, this book's completion reflects the efforts of many contributors, several of whom deserve special mention. Foremost among them are Leigh and Gabby who have enjoyed—or silently endured—a good many episodes of science fiction television, ranging from the best of *Doctor Who* to the stumbling efforts of early *Captain Video*. While our tastes did not always coincide, their reactions were consistently instructive and helped shape my own comments. At Georgia Tech a number of colleagues have encouraged my work in science fiction, among them Lisa Yaszek and my Chair, Richard Utz, while Jacqueline Royster, Dean of the Ivan College of Liberal Arts at Tech, provided crucial support with a research grant that allowed me to finish this project in a timely manner. My students at Tech, especially those in my courses on Film Genres and on Science Fiction Television, have, as ever, proven to be an invaluable resource, sharing their knowledge and insights, while suffering my own enthusiasms. While this group is numerous, let me give special thanks to Josh Andrews, Emily Davidson, Tyler Delaney, Amy Elliott, Joe Murphy, Andrew Silva, Alexis Taylor, and Lori Vaughn. Finally, I am especially grateful to the editorial group at Routledge for their encouragement and enthusiasm in the launch of the Television Guidebooks series. Erica Wetter, as senior editor, provided strong and constructive feedback in the project's formative stages, while editorial assistant Simon Jacobs was consistently encouraging, attentive to all publication details, and helped to push the volume to completion. I very much enjoyed working on this project, and part of the pleasure I had was due to the professional editorial team at Routledge.

INTRODUCTION: WHY SCIENCE FICTION TELEVISION (SFTV)?

I.

Science fiction television (SFTV) today has become big-time. That status should be fairly obvious to anyone who surfs cable/satellite television on which a typical week of viewing possibilities will serve up several dozen different science fiction (SF) series. Of course, a number of these are the seemingly perennial reruns, such as the various flavors of *Star Trek*, the original *Twilight Zone* (or one of its later reboots), or shows with a dedicated cult following like *Farscape*, *Stargate SG-1*, and *The X-Files*. Moreover, there are many shows—older ones such as *Buffy the Vampire Slayer* and *Angel*, as well as newer ones like *Do No Harm*, *The Fades*, and *Grimm*—that because of their fantasy focus are near kin to SF, as well as a variety of Japanese anime programs, the great majority of which are framed in a science fictional context. The key point is that there is a lot out there, new and old, more SF than at any time since the early days of American television programming. Then, with only four broadcasting networks and a far smaller television viewership, one could choose from series like *Captain Video*; *Space Patrol*; *Tom Corbett, Space Cadet*; *Rocky Jones, Space Ranger*; *Buck Rogers*, and *Rod Brown of the Rocket Rangers*—to name just a few among the space opera types—as well as packaged SF film serials alongside far more serious fare, such as the early anthology shows *Tales of Tomorrow* and *Science Fiction Theater*.

I was prompted to that rather informal survey and to begin considering the whys behind this resurgence for several reasons. One is that the undergraduate students in my science fiction film classes repeatedly demonstrated more familiarity with and enthusiasm for SFTV than they did for cinema. They generally knew more about it than I did and seemed eager to bring it into our genre conversation. If the rather rabid population at my university was any indication, I knew there must be something interesting going on in SF broadcasting—and if so, there was almost certainly an equally eager audience for writing about what was happening. Another is that, at about the same time, I had been struck by a rather curious assessment I read in one of the few academic books on the subject. In this work entitled, appropriately enough, *Science Fiction Television: A History*, and bearing the relatively recent imprint of 2004, the author described what he saw as the "maturity (and perhaps exhaustion) of the genre of science fiction television" (Booker 192). That point was obliquely echoed in one of the few other books that claimed to offer a historical view of the form, a work entitled *American Science Fiction TV*. While not quite suggesting that we had already reached a state of "exhaustion," it offered a cognate but equally striking notion: that the genre faced a very difficult future, because many of its staple themes—space travel, robotics, genetic manipulation, social engineering—"are now science, not fiction," and that this situation posed a problem for the form, a challenge as to whether it would ever be able to move beyond this new, everyday, highly technologized world and to visualize an even more speculative—or spectacular—vision of what the future might hold (Johnson-Smith 2). And this challenge would, it was suggested, be a key test for the genre, since media SF (a term I shall use throughout this text to denote both television and film and, for convenience's sake, to distinguish those forms from literary SF) has from its inception drawn much of its appeal from its ability to offer a striking vision of what our science and technology hold in store for us (Figure I.1). Of course, if either one of those assessments was very accurate, then creating a class on the subject might be little more than an exercise in recent cultural history—and writing a book like this one might not be such a good idea.

However, I find it as difficult to buy into those visions as it seemed for my recent students to bracket off SFTV from our discussions about SF cinema. If SF was "exhausted," or even nearly so, then why would the CW and Fox

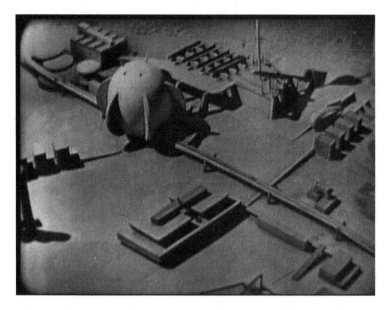

Figure I.1 Visualizing the future from 1950: *Space Patrol*

networks be adding multiple new SF/fantasy shows to their prime-time line-ups? If that audience was waning, then the Syfy Channel with its all-SF-all-the-time-except-for-the-one-night-of-wrestling programming each week was in big trouble, as was that venerable television institution, the BBC, which at various times over the last decade has invested heavily not only in resurrecting with an unusually large budget its old hit of the 1960s, 1970s, and 1980s *Doctor Who* (now celebrating its fiftieth anniversary), but also in fashioning a set of connected series, such as *Torchwood* and *The Sarah Jane Adventures*, that were all designed (by Russell T. Davies) to synergistically support each other, and in devoting entire nights to new fantasy line-ups, featuring shows like *Being Human*, *Paradox*, *Primeval*, and *Orphan Black* (a Canadian series), while also rerunning a number of syndicated American programs, such as *Battlestar Galactica*, *Star Trek: The Next Generation*, and *The X-Files*, all of which it has offered in marathon sessions, 24 hours of back-to-back episodes. And other, newer outlets, such as the Science Channel, have adopted similar programming strategies, offering day-long marathons of *Fringe*, *Firefly*, *Dollhouse*, and *The Twilight Zone*, while also developing a range of intriguing hybrid shows that bring together science fact and science fiction, and which we might, mindful of the paradox, hereafter refer to as *science fiction reality* shows.

Then too, the *real-ization* (that is, the presenting as potentially *real*) of our SF as science—or as history—had never posed a problem before. Certainly, one of the great pleasures of looking back at early SF—in both film and television manifestations—is seeing how accurately or inaccurately the genre has managed to take the measure of *our* world; for there are always hits and misses to be found. Numerous SF films of the 1930s, after all, would forecast television's role as an essential part of everyday life in the future, as well as its rather disturbing potential for intrusion, surveillance, even possible danger. And personal communications devices—typically envisioned as wrist- or belt-mounted radios rather than cell phones—were frequently seen on the horizon, as in the case of the *Dick Tracy* comics and movie serials. But then, just as many films and early television series predicted that we would, well before the twenty-first century, have reached an age of easy travel via personal rockets and enjoy great personal leisure thanks to our ubiquitous robot workers/servants. Despite such hits and misses—or in some cases because of them—SF has continued to flourish and to find new concerns, new issues, and certainly new *science* to depict and evaluate, and just as importantly to inspire *fiction*, in effect, relinking those two key terms that Johnson-Smith, observing the rapid pace of development, worried were becoming completely disconnected.

Ultimately, that very flourishing—and a corresponding body of evidence that the public increasingly takes SF narratives rather seriously, not as the childish entertainment of the early space operas—begs a questioning of why SF is such a popular part of the television landscape today and certainly seems to have a solid future, one worth chronicling and studying. So by way of a quick diagnosis I want to suggest three very simple reasons that might help explain that popularity, and in turn, reasons why we should be paying closer attention to, even studying, its history and characteristics through texts like this one. Why, then, are we doing more—and arguably better— SF on television? An easy answer is because people want it, but that reason simply avoids the three underlying ones. The first, and perhaps still a bit superficial an answer, is because we *can* do it; funding and technology have both changed, allowing for the genre's proliferation. A second is because we *have* to do it; science and technology, it seems, keep getting in the way of our lives, popping up in full view and practically *forcing* us to take notice. And a third is because we simply *should* do it; it makes sense and helps us *make sense*—of ourselves, our world, and our futures. But let's consider those answers in a bit more detail.

We *can* do more and better SFTV for a number of reasons, not the least of which is the sheer availability of outlets, all needing programming, now that we have moved beyond the simple major networks broadcast over the public airwaves. The previously mentioned Syfy Channel is probably the most important of those emerging venues, but the rapid proliferation of cable/satellite channels also means there is an increasing number of broadcast slots, as well as potential money available for new series development. If you have an idea for a show that might have an audience, and if you know the right people, you can get a hearing; if you're convincing and have skill, you could get seed money for a pilot; and if that pilot is any good, there is a strong chance for an airing before a national audience, for at least a try-out. But even smaller ambitions—and smaller resources—also stand a chance of reaching fruition and finding an audience in an age of iPhones, laptop-loaded editing tools, and YouTube. "Broadcast yourself," in fact, is the come-on for YouTube, suggesting both the easy ability to make films (and making them available to a large audience), and the alluring possibility of almost instantly showcasing the self and speaking directly to an audience of millions, as was envisioned in the early H. G. Wells-scripted SF film *Things to Come* (1936).

And I am already suggesting another and equally important reason why we *can* do SF on television, one that would seem to follow from the very nature of the form. SF film and television are not only *about* technology, but also, and in a way that is not true in the same way for SF literature, *driven by* technology. That is, audiences have tended to gauge film and television SF in terms of their technologically driven ability to give life to those visions. In fact, Michele Pierson has suggested that this link is quite natural, and that media SF, like other types of fantasy, serves a very particular need. She argues that there is "a cultural demand for the aesthetic experience of wonder" that SF, better than any other popular genre, has helped us to satisfy (168). And the technology involved in the production—as well as the budget—determines how well we can satisfy that "demand." In the early 1950s *Captain Video and His Video Rangers* made do—and even created a sense of wonder appropriate to its era of live broadcasts, low-definition televisions, and undemanding new audiences—with an effects budget of only $25 per week. More than a decade later a show like *Star Trek* was still having to work its visionary magic within a very constrained budget, drawing as much as possible on its audience's imagination. Thus the famous transporter "effect" was developed as a way of avoiding having to build shuttlecraft models and sets, and then film their take-offs and landings every time the *Enterprise* crew—including the ubiquitous expendable crew member—had to descend to a new planet for exploration or to reach a neighboring ship.

But now we simply can do so much more, in part because SF attracts far larger budgets than in those early days, but also because the computer technology we now regularly use to create those effects is relatively cheap and widely available, and the viewing experience so much more *movie-like*. Consider a recent and highly praised series like *Battlestar Galactica* with its host of spaceships of varying types, transporting all that remains of humanity to a promised land named Earth. These are relatively simple digital creations, constructed in the computer, sutured into the story, and then saved for later use in other episodes. And replicating them, or even creating vast space battles between the motley fleet of humanity's ships and the fleets of pursuing Cylon vessels, is the next step, allowing a show like *Battlestar Galactica* to look almost as impressive as the early entries in the *Star Wars* film franchise with their extensive—and expensive—model work and computer-controlled cameras. Certainly, as we move further into the digital realm, as more shows are designed for HD broadcast and with a wide-screen format—or the newer Ultra-HD format with four times the resolution of HD broadcasts—and as we begin to create 3D effects for home 3D viewing, we should see the distinction between the theatrical and televisual SF experiences become ever less marked. In any case, today we can do much more—and so we do.

I have also suggested that we almost *have to* do more SF on television. That perhaps strange assertion comes from the simple recognition that we live in a highly technologized society, in a world where we just cannot get away from technology, as well as the science that creates it and the reason that conceives it. In fact, that triadic relationship—of reason, science, and technology—is one that we live with, that informs all that we do today, and that consequently seems to find its way into so many of our stories. So while I am not suggesting that most of our television stories are in some way science fictional, I do think it is important to recognize how the elements of science and technology invariably show up more and more, working their way into our narratives just as they are worked, almost imperceptibly, into our everyday lives. And of course we need only note how often science is becoming woven into so many of our popular shows, as in the examples of fictional programs like CSI and House, as well as in reality-type programming like Modern Marvels, How Do They Do It, and Rocket City Rednecks.

In this context, it might be useful to point to a recent series like Eureka, one that could well serve as a metaphor for this pervasiveness of the forces of technology, science, and reason. It is a series about a small town in the Pacific northwest where almost everyone knows everyone else, and it is patrolled by a likeable, down-to-earth, Andy Griffith-like cop, Sheriff Carter (Figure I.2). But initial appearances are a bit deceptive, as it is also a rather special town, one full of geniuses working on various government and industry projects that often produce unexpected, at times absurdly amusing, but sometimes disturbing and even deadly outcomes. As a result, it consistently surprises its sheriff—and the audience—with its sudden appearances

Figure I.2 Eureka's small-town sheriff briefed on the latest scientific mishap

of flying robots, dimensional displacers, particle decelerators, genetic mutations, and so forth. That sense of surprise comes about because *Eureka* so carefully lodges all of its fantastic developments in a world that, at first glance, *looks* so very normal, even Mayberry-ish. But this situation is not so different from the world we live in today, where big-time science is constantly developing big-time—and sometimes quite dangerous—technology just out of our everyday view, and like Sheriff Carter, we cannot help but run into it—and be surprised by it. And that's the case for television too; it seems that the medium cannot help but run into it.

However, I would also suggest that this sort of inevitable encounter is a good thing, and it helps give reason to my perhaps even stranger-sounding third suggestion that we *should* be doing—and consequently also studying—more SFTV. That "should" has almost a moralizing ring to it, as if it were implying that SFTV were somehow *good* for us. But it may well be. At least if we accept some of the previous premise, that we are going to keep tripping over science and technology anyway, then it follows that we should try to understand it for our individual mental health *and* for our larger cultural health. Genre stories, I have always tried to emphasize for my students, typically serve as important cultural highlights *and* problem-solving devices. Through their central concerns those stories echo our own cultural anxieties, and through their conventions—and familiar, conventionalized presentations—they also help us make sense of those things. The more popular genres in any period have that status, that level of popularity, I would argue, largely because their trappings are best suited for helping us make sense of, better understand, or simply find some way of being reconciled to the culture of the period. And here I might point to a recent British series, *Torchwood*, which presents viewers with a new multicultural and forward-looking Britain, a country that, on the surface, seems to be flourishing, even regaining a position of leadership in world events and prospering economically. Yet the series underscores that the country is constantly under assault from forces that most people never see, in fact, that there is a space–time "rift" running right through the center of England (or more precisely, Cardiff), through which all sorts of alien menaces keep appearing, and only the ability—and courage—of the secret Torchwood group, who capture and use those alien technologies for Earth's defense, allows the country to remain safe. It is a view into the very real cultural situation of England, a snapshot of a country that today fundamentally feels that it *does* occupy a very precarious position and is always in danger of being pulled apart by newly opening rifts in its increasingly complex social fabric (of very different political ideologies, of racial mixtures, of varying religions); and it can only be saved by the strength of its people, and to some extent by the new technologies that are themselves a part of the problem. That show speaks, and in an important and supportive way, to its British viewers, and it suggests why we should create such programming, in fact, why we might even need the subtle sort of help shows like *Torchwood* can provide.

As a sign that at least some people are recognizing that element of the "should," we might note that in 2006 the longest-running of all SFTV series, *Doctor Who*, won the BAFTA award for Best Drama Series on British television, as would another SF show *Misfits* in 2010—and here we need to emphasize that these awards were not just for the best SF series on British television, but for best *dramatic* series. And that sort of recognition is not simply another British oddity—or at least not *only* a British oddity. For after all, in the United States *Lost* also won an Emmy award for the Outstanding Drama Series, while another popular SF show, *Heroes*, garnered the prestigious Television Critics Association award for Program of the Year. And there are many other awards that might be mentioned, ranging from those of various SF and fantasy associations (e.g., the Hugo and Nebula awards) to technical societies, recognizing for an ever-broadening audience the expertise, timeliness, and indeed the weightiness of today's SFTV.

Finally, the various cans, musts, and shoulds that we have noted above also suggest another important fallout from today's wealth of SFTV. As my own experience has suggested, and as a number of editors have indicated, SF film and television fans generally also tend to be *readers* and *thinkers*, which is a good reason for books such as this one. But that fact is important simply because we do not have nearly enough *readers* and *thinker*. SFTV—*good* SFTV, anyway—tends to lure some of those fans to the books that we write about their projections and fantasies, it draws these works and those readers/viewers into a serious discourse, and, most importantly, it situates that subject matter—the role of science and technology in our fast-evolving culture—into another level of popular discussion, thereby helping to make us aware of how these things are impacting our lives. So SFTV—it is simply a good sign and one to which we ought to pay attention.

II.

One of the key functions of this book, of course, is to help us pay that necessary attention, or rather, as the title for this series suggests, to "guide" our attention in some useful and valuable directions, specifically as a kind of roadmap to the evolving world of SFTV, at least as it has operated in the context of American television—our focus. As a way of contextualizing that subject, we might first give some consideration to the general practice and context of television studies. On the one hand, it is, as the very title of a recent text like Lincoln Geraghty's *American Science Fiction Film and Television* (2009) readily suggests, work that has seemed to grow quite naturally out of and to share many of the assumptions of other media, but especially film studies. That linkage is not just because of their shared approach to entertainment, or as John Ellis succinctly explains, since "the entertainment film can be broadcast on TV . . . it seems as though there is little real difference between the two media" (*Visible* 24). Rather, there are numerous shared elements between film and television that seem to suggest we should see the latter as little more than an extension of the former. Film and television, after all, have shared many industrial components, ranging from early—and abortive—efforts by several Hollywood studios to broadcast television into their studio-owned theaters; to a similar and in some cases combined "star system"; to the use of the same production facilities, as relatively early television shows like *Commando Cody* and *The Twilight Zone* illustrate; and, as this and other volumes have often noted, to a reliance on similar narrative conventions and generic formulae. These and other common features of film and television production might seem to suggest that there is little point in distinguishing between the two regimes.

However, as Ellis and others have begun to stake out the landscape of television studies, they have noted quite a few distinctive territorial features, several of which bear directly on the study of televisual SF. Because modern television is driven by the series format, that is, by connected narratives, working together over entire seasons or even groups of seasons, it is often referred to as *long form* narrative—thus distinguishing it from the relatively *short form* (ninety minutes to two hours) of the usual feature film. And that notion of the long form reminds us that the typical television series is almost always something more than a succession of stand-alone episodes. Even in several of the early space operas, most notably *Rocky Jones, Space Ranger*, episodes were linked to form more complex *narrative arcs* that allowed for more ambitious story-telling, while also giving audiences further reason to tune in week after week. And in some cases that notion of the long form has extended to the entirety of the series, as in the case of *Babylon 5*, a program that creator, writer, and producer J. Michael Straczynski envisioned from its inception as a five-year narrative. That length, as Sherryl Vint has observed, capitalized on television's often untapped capacity "to tell complex stories and to allow characters and situations to change with time" (247), much after the fashion of the ancient epic or sprawling nineteenth century novel. If we are to study such series properly, then, we have to take into account those ambitions of development and change, considering, among other things, the links between episodes, the ways that characters rise and fall in importance (or are written out of or into narratives on the basis of casting issues), and how themes build to support a larger thematic structure for the entire show. In short, we have to be aware of what that long form allows and how the series addresses—or fails to address—those allowances.

That long form is often described as taking two distinct approaches to narrative organization, as it assumes the form of the *series* or the *serial*. As Ellis explains, the notion of "serial implies a certain narrative progression and a conclusion; the series does not: whether documentary, drama or everlasting soap opera, it has no end in view. The series always envisages its own return" (*Visible* 123), and thus the ongoing flow of life that it depicts. With its emphasis on discrete stories, each usually wrapped up within the length of a single episode, the series has generally become the standard for broadcast television narrative. William Shatner's opening voice-over introduction to the original *Star Trek* show, announcing that "These are the voyages of the starship *Enterprise*," demonstrates the guiding principle for the series. While the characters and starship setting remain the same, each show represents a different "voyage" or mission on behalf of the United Federation of Planets, and each mission usually reaches its climax within the episode's allotted time frame. That approach is, as we might suspect, highly flexible, allowing for a great variety of situations and stories, but it does not necessarily make maximum use of the long form's possibilities.

In contrast, the principle of seriality emphasizes episodic continuity and thus an ongoing and coherent time-line for a show's events. To reinforce that sense of continuity—while also helping viewers who might have missed an episode to orient themselves—the serial program often feels compelled to do more by way of contextualizing its narrative: it might offer a more complex title sequence that visually (or aurally, through a voice-over) reintroduces characters and their relationships; a show like *Farscape* is paradigmatic in this regard. In the tradition of the movie cliffhanger, a show's opening scenes might repeat concluding action from the previous episode or offer a brief reprise of events; *Roswell* often resorted to this tactic. Or the characters might simply refer to prior events or circumstances— probably the most common tactic for producing continuity. Because of their roots in the cinematic serial tradition, early space operas like *Captain Video* and *Commando Cody* closely followed the film model, but even more recent series such as *Battlestar Galactica*, *The Walking Dead*, and *Revolution* also depend heavily on that sense of episodic connection as they work towards resolutions for their various calamitous situations. By understanding the difference between the principles of series and seriality—or, in some cases, recognizing how a show might at various times and for specific narrative reasons draw on both impulses—we can gain a better sense not only of how a narrative is constructed, but also how that narrative works on us, how it seeks to compel audience involvement in its events.

Another key concept that is related to narrative organization is that of flow. First articulated by media theorist Raymond Williams, flow designates a sort of blurring that, he suggests, characterizes broadcast television's typical mode of presentation. As he explains, what the typical channel offers on any given night is not simply "a programme of the published sequence of programme items but this sequence transformed by the inclusion of another kind of sequence, so that these sequences together compose the real flow, the real 'broadcasting'" (91). This sense that programming easily dissolves distinct series or shows into a constant stream of dramatic shows, news, and commercials signifies much more than the recognition that certain channels, like the Syfy Channel, the Science Channel, the Disney Channel, or BBC America, tend to program in groups of similar shows with similar narrative approaches. Rather, it draws on the theory that broadcast television forms a continuous cultural experience, such that while "the items may be various the television experience has in some important ways unified them" (96). While that approach has often been challenged, it remains a useful vantage, suggesting that despite their ostensible differences in subject, themes, and even purpose (as in the case of commercials versus dramatic programs), all of the shows on a given day might be viewed through the framework of a dominant ideology, all forming part of what Williams describes as a "cultural set" (85). And in considering programs as if they constituted such a "set," as when the Syfy Channel offers dramatic series like Continuum and Lost Girl back to back with a reality SF show like Face Off, we can gain a better awareness of how those programs commonly address audiences, fashion a reality illusion, and support a particular ideological vantage.

Working from that context of flow theory, commentators have also described a different sense of the audience's relationship to the individual program. Ellis notes that television has traditionally offered viewers an experience that is visually inferior to the cinema, while also presenting them with many segments that form into a stream of similar texts. As a result, the "regime of vision is less intense . . . it is a regime of the glance rather than the gaze" (Visible 137). That formulation derives from the belief that the cinema engages spectators through an objectifying "gaze," one that produces "an unbridgeable gulf between the seer and what is seen" and that "permits the spectator to maintain a particular relation of power over what he or she sees" (Visible 45), whereas the "glance" of television implicates a more casual, less-involved relationship, one that recognizes the almost inevitable distractions involved in the domestic viewing experience and that thus tends to rely more heavily on dialogue/talk than the complex image to complete the narrative experience. While that glance theory downplays the possibility of the sort of engaged spectatorship that we often associate with the film experience, Catherine Johnson has offered a counter view, theorizing that SFTV and fantasy, thanks to their greater reliance on visual spectacle, challenge that regime of the glance. In fact, her question—"To what extent does the visual representation of the fantastic in telefantasy encourage or even demand attentive viewing?" (12)—not only reminds us of the increased resources that are today being allotted to the *real*-ization of televisual fantasy, but also suggests how our SF works might constitute a most fertile territory for interrogating a number of these foundational concepts in television studies.

One of the advocates for a rigorous approach to television studies, David Bianculli, complains that many people, including many in the industry itself, simply do not take television very seriously. Because it is so pervasive, or as he puts it, "our most common language, our most popular pastime, our basic point of reference" (5)—a kind of imaginative environment in which we spend very much time—we often take its presence for granted, treating it with no more consideration than we do the real environment in which we live—something else that we have often and manifestly taken for granted. However, Bianculli urges that we not overlook the medium as we have our physical environment, and that we recognize how television, like many of our more time-honored arts, "has done its part, like fairy tales and classic literature, to satisfy certain needs and explore certain themes" (285). In the particular case of SFTV, as we have already noted, it addresses a "need" for that "experience of wonder," while it also explores certain key themes surrounding the roles of reason, science, and technology in our lives. So studying how television continues to do "its part," by focusing our attention on this particular genre, in part through the theories and language of television studies, can only further advance our initial question of "why science fiction television?"

III.

Over the course of this book we explore that question broadly, staking out a variety of signposts that are historical, conceptual, and cultural in nature; and these signposts will serve to remind us that, as Jason Mittell observes, there is a "variety of discourses surrounding and running through a given genre," such as SF, that "are *themselves* constitutive of that genre" (*Genre* 14). The following chapter begins to take us along this path by focusing on the history of American SFTV, tracing its roots in other media, such as the pulp magazines, popular radio programs of the 1930s and 1940s, and the film serials that provided program material, as well as narrative models, for some of the most popular early SFTV shows. In the course of setting out this historical context, we describe the gradual emergence of specific narrative approaches to a televisual SF; recount the form's efforts at imitating the cinema, especially through the development of ever more elaborate special effects; and chronicle the emergence of SF into the mainstream of television production and viewing habits. As this variety of goals should suggest, the aim of this first chapter is not to offer a single account that will explain SFTV's evolution, but rather to provide a useful historical framework within which readers might situate the subsequent discussions of more than sixty years of SF programming.

As part of this background chapter—and as a forecast of the format that the subsequent chapters all follow—we shall also discuss in detail a key series. In this first instance the discussion focuses on the pioneering SFTV show, *Captain Video and His Video Rangers* (1949–55), a program that not only modeled an early and dominant mode of SFTV—the space opera—but also one that can provide some insight into the development of a SF viewership. For the special mode of audience address pioneered here, including its incorporation of commercials into the narrative structure, its use of direct address to the audience, and its framing of serial episodes that were a part of each show, point up how this series, like much other early SFTV, not only sought to tell stories and entertain its audience, but also was engaged in constructing that audience for the genre, in effect, in showing audiences how to engage with the new SF narratives that would become so popular in the 1950s.

The next chapter focuses on some of the key narrative models or subgenres that have emerged over the sixty-plus years of American SFTV. Each chapter, as readers will quickly note, is pointedly linked to the preceding one, and here that linkage is accomplished through a brief opening discussion of the space opera, as pioneered by shows like *Captain Video*, *Space Patrol*, and *Tom Corbett, Space Cadet*, and as later updated in more recent series such as *Farscape* and *Firefly*. Following this introduction and necessarily drawing more attention are the anthology shows, such as *The Twilight Zone* and *The Outer Limits*, which both recall the earlier world of the pulp magazines with their emphasis on the short story and shock endings, and suggest an ongoing effort to find alternative modes to the early dominance of the space opera formula. Additional consideration is given to various forms that fantasy narratives typically take—the marvelous, the fantastic, and the uncanny—as well as to comic or parodic forms. Ultimately the chapter acknowledges that we are still finding new models for SF series, new ways of telling those necessary stories.

As an acknowledgment of its seminal place in the larger development of media SF, this chapter is accompanied by a commentary on what is arguably the most influential of SF series, and one that explored the wide variety of narrative possibilities open to SFTV: Rod Serling's original *Twilight Zone* series. In the course of its five-year run (1959–64)—a run later extended by revivals in 1985–89 and in 2002–03, as well as a 1983 film version—this series explored a great many of the narrative modes found in later SF, such as the mystery, the psychological thriller, the shock story, and so forth, and in the process helped to open up the form for further exploration and development, and ultimately for more ambitious undertakings. While *TV Guide* recently rated *The Twilight Zone* as the second best series in the history of SFTV (following *Star Trek*, see Roush 14), in light of its pioneering of so many narrative modes that would impact the entire history of SFTV, as well as its continuing to play in syndication today, rating it as the most important of such shows, as my students have typically done, seems well justified.

The third chapter similarly connects to its predecessor, in this case by emphasizing one of those many legacies of *The Twilight Zone*; namely, its treatment of some of the key cultural issues of its day. Indeed, many consider this dimension of the series at least equally as important a development as its narrative explorations, since prior to its time many critics saw media SF as essentially escapist or children's fare. For example, one of the key discussions of the genre, Susan Sontag's famous essay "The Imagination of Disaster," charged that cinematic SF especially tended simply to "perpetuate clichés about identity, volition, power, knowledge, happiness, social consensus, guilt, responsibility" (228), and that it was characterized by "above all . . . an inadequate response" (227) to the most pressing social issues of the day. Yet in contrast to that oft-cited opinion, and as this chapter illustrates, our SF series have increasingly provided an important space for such cultural critique, from the racial and cultural explorations of the original *Star Trek* series, to the political issues examined in *Babylon 5*, to the gender considerations of shows like *Battlestar Galactica*, *The Sarah Connor Chronicles*, and *Dollhouse*.

To further this discussion, the chapter concludes with a discussion of the rebooted *Battlestar Galactica* of 2004–09. An unusual follow-up to a similarly titled series of 1978-80, the new *Battlestar Galactica* would explore a wide variety of the cultural issues that were only hinted at in the original. In the course of chronicling a devastated humanity's search for a new home planet, a mythic place called "Earth," the series managed to unpack and examine much of the cultural baggage that, it suggested, we might continue to carry with us far into humanity's future: our fixations on racial difference, our gender prejudices, our nationalist leanings, and our most violent tendencies as a species. More than simply a rebooted space opera, exploiting the possibilities of the latest digital technologies, then, it became a kind of national soul searching, conducted in the shadow of the terrorist attack of 9/11. Examining actions and attitudes from all angles, it demonstrated the extent to which SF could provide an effective stage on which to dramatize, and hopefully better understand, a number of deeply rooted social and political issues that continue to haunt us.

In contrast to the previous chapters' emphasis on content, the following section assesses the general appeal of SFTV, focusing on the genre's audience as well as that audience's changing nature. This focus seems both appropriate and necessary because the SF audience, as has long been suggested, is rather different from that for most mainstream film and television. It is interested in ideas, in speculation—thus the alternative term often used for much SF writing and production today, that of "*speculative fiction*" (i.e., another version of "SF" and an explanation of why that abbreviation is so often used). Like no other form, SFTV is concerned with how our science and technology function *and* with the implications of that functioning. Yet as the proliferation of SF series in recent years suggests, SF has also become very much mainstream, attracting not so much the children's audience that was devoted to early series like *Captain Video*, *Space Patrol*, and *Tom Corbett, Space Cadet*, but a broad cross-section of the American television audience. Moreover, that audience has demonstrated a marked and powerful passion for its shows, as was early on evidenced by the famous audience mobilization against NBC's precipitous cancellation of Gene Roddenberry's milestone program *Star Trek*. When NBC brass announced the cancellation of the series after its second season, a grassroots letter-writing campaign rescued the show and resulted in a third season—and eventually a long history of syndication, sequels, film adaptations, reboots, and so forth. Moreover, that flexing of audience muscle demonstrated the potential of a mobilized viewership, and that effort at involvement has, since then, been repeated multiple times—successfully and unsuccessfully—in campaigns to save such SF shows as *Farscape*, *Firefly*, *Jericho*, and *Roswell*.

The power of the SF audience thus seems worth examining, and we shall trace out that audience heritage in one of those beneficiaries of a cult-like enthusiasm, *Farscape*. It is a series that *TV Guide* has ranked number four among the top cult series of all time and one that faced a fate similar to that of *Star Trek*. Canceled after its fourth season and with a cliffhanger ending for that season leaving its audience with no narrative resolution, *Farscape* was brought back in a miniseries format, as *Farscape: The Peacekeeper Wars* (2004), a narrative that brought some closure to the series' story about a wandering American astronaut trying, as he says at the start of each episode, simply to "find a way home." Yet that picaresque tale of wandering and amazing encounters rather reflexively speaks to the sort of relationship that audiences often find most appealing about such series and that may best account for this show's enthusiastic viewership and its enduring cult status.

One of the frequent characteristics of such cult works is that they often seem to challenge the conventional boundaries of narrative, as if they were hybrids, unusual mixtures of several generic forms. And that pattern has proven especially true in the case of SFTV, as some of our more popular series—*Lost*, *The X-Files*, *Firefly*—seem to attract audiences in part because of their very ability to cross borders, to open up new territory, to ally the familiar conventions or trappings of SF with other elements. It is a pattern that has worked to the benefit of other generic forms, such as the mystery, as *The X-Files* most prominently demonstrates, but also, and perhaps surprisingly, in a form that seems rather far afield from SF, the teen melodrama, as has been shown through such series as *Smallville*, *The Powers of Matthew Star*, and *Roswell*. But in the process it has profited SF as well, imparting to its usual generic trappings new or unexpected attractions, while also demonstrating the adaptability and flexibility of the typical SF narrative. Perhaps because

SF is, as we began by noting, so much a part of our contemporary cultural environment, it seems to have provided a most hospitable platform for hosting or staging other generic elements, resulting in some of American television's most effective hybrid programs.

As we shall see in our accompanying discussion for this chapter, this hybrid pattern shows to special prominence in a recent series like *Fringe* (2008–13). This program, much like the earlier *X-Files*, seems at least as much a crime thriller or police procedural drama as it does SF. Also concerned with a special FBI division, *Fringe* links its standard investigative activities to the exploration of events that keep spilling over from a parallel universe and even another time-line, constantly challenging—and frustrating—efforts to make sense out of mysterious events that keep cropping up in our world. And yet, as its very title advertises, the real appeal of this series lies precisely in the way it is always opening up new—or parallel—possibilities, in its constant efforts at playing at the "fringe" of our narrative expectations, in its crossing and recrossing the narrative borders to which we might have become accustomed, as a variety of other recent series have also tried to do.

This fringe-like development also points to a key direction for the further development of SFTV—and an appropriate conclusion for this text. For even as we see the genre stretching, expanding what genre theorists would describe as its "supertext," we also see it increasingly exploring new forms, allying itself with other media, reaching out to other audiences. As our more traditional visual media—that is, film and television—have entered into a digital age, and as blogs, vlogs, video podcasts, Twitter, and other on-line or social media phenomena crowd into our daily lives, in fact, as the television experience itself has changed to a highly portable, variably screened, and time-shifted mode, our SF texts have—and only naturally, given the form's technological thrust—responded as well. For the new media and new media experiences have begun to play an important role in providing viewers with an expanded relation to SFTV, in the process contributing their own distinctive impact on the proliferation of SF fan cultures. The conclusion, consequently, will sketch this new horizon of SFTV—a horizon that sees television not as a characteristic and genre-defining experience, but more as another textual source, to be downloaded, called up, and viewed on-the-fly, as well as one to be continued in other realms, as fan cultures blog about the latest series episodes, tweet their immediate responses to others—effectively producing a new electronic community experience, a different kind of fan culture—and even produce their own "episodes" (or "webisodes") of their favorite shows, readily available for download, for commentary, and for inspiring other efforts in the same vein.

The conclusion for this "guide," then, is actually a reminder of the seemingly infinite horizons that are rapidly opening up for the form and for our experience of SFTV. And yet, that potential should be no real surprise for fans of the genre. SF has inevitably been a technology-conscious form, and in its media manifestations—film and television—especially so. As Annette Kuhn notes, these forms of the genre have been particularly marked by their "mobilization of the visual" (6), that is, by their self-consciousness about visual media and their tendency to foreground that consciousness, offering audiences a wealth of reflexive images such as screens, surveillance devices, holograms, scanners, radar devices, and so forth, all of which underscore that, within these narratives, we are dealing with mediated, highly technologized visions of our world. But reflexively they also call our attention to that process of creation and construction, practically compelling us to consider our own roles as producers, consumers, and even the products of these constructive practices.

Media SF, consequently, increasingly serves an important cultural function. For in that reflexive tendency, one driven by those ubiquitous images of technological imaging and construction, it not only helps us better see a world that always seems to be disappearing into the technological landscape of modern life, but it also enables another, and ultimately more important envisioning: letting us see ourselves as inhabitants of that increasingly strange—or as cultural critic Paul Virilio puts it, "derealized" (University 24)—landscape, and thus better understand our needs in this "brave new world." Hardly as some commentators have suggested an exhausted form, nor one bound—and bounded—by the rapid pace of technological change, then, SFTV today serves a quite vital function. In its best instances it has itself become a kind of guidebook for us all that gives reason to this and indeed to ongoing study.

1

A BRIEF HISTORY OF AMERICAN SFTV

While SF has a long history in literature, on radio, and in the movies, all predating the advent of television, SFTV has had a significant impact on the shape, popularity, and potential of the genre, in part because of its own implicitly science fictional nature. Indeed television, much like early radio, was initially presented to audiences in a science fictional mode, that is, it was usually framed as a powerful sign of the future and a recurrent icon of the genre. In fact, in the United States the first public television broadcasts originated from the grounds of the 1939 New York World's Fair, an exposition with the title "Building the World of Tomorrow" that readily evoked thoughts of SF. However, long before television broadcasts were a common part of our cultural experience, the medium had already become a regular feature of SF discourse and a signpost of that "tomorrow." It was constantly featured in the various popular science magazines early in the century; it was a common fixture in the literature of SF; and in SF films and serials of the 1920s and 1930s, from Metropolis (1927) to The Phantom Empire (1935) to Things to Come (1936) to S.O.S.—Tidal Wave (1939), television was depicted as a ubiquitous, intrusive, and in some cases even dangerous technology (as a title like Murder by Television [1936] dramatically suggests). In light of this ubiquity, Joseph Corn and Brian Horrigan suggest that in the decades leading up to the development of regular television broadcasting, "the idea [my italics] of television in our future heated the popular imagination as few technologies ever have" (24). It signaled progress, technological modernity, and indeed, as the World's Fair suggested, a world of the future—and given the impact of the Great Depression and World War II, it was a future that very many people eagerly anticipated.

In the context of that sense of cultural anticipation, it seems only appropriate that some of the first efforts at public television broadcasting involved stories precisely about the world of tomorrow. In the United Kingdom, for example, the BBC produced several ambitious adaptations of classic SF literature focused on the future, including versions of Karel Capek's R.U.R. in both 1938 and 1948, and of H. G. Wells' *The Time Machine* in 1948. However, the intrusion of World War II, with its insistence on a devastating *now* and its prior claim on technical resources needed to expand broadcasting capability and produce television receivers for the public, pushed the development of American SFTV television into the late postwar period when three types of programming would bring the genre into homes on a regular basis: the film serial, the anthology show, and the adventurous space opera. These shows would quickly establish the popularity of SF with the new audience for television, and they would provide models for the genre's continued development.

The first two of these types are largely important for the way they helped demonstrate the range of potential SF programming. The serial had long been a popular staple of the film industry and a key place-holder for that industry's SF efforts, as is evidenced by the prewar *Flash Gordon* (1936, 1938, 1940) and *Buck Rogers* (1939) films, as well as postwar serials such as *Superman* (1948), *King of the Rocket Men* (1949), and *Flying Disc Man from Mars* (1950). These cliffhangers flashily displayed the adventurous possibilities of SF by mixing rockets, robots, and ray guns with plenty of more conventional fistfights and high-speed car chases. Typically created in 15–20-minute installments, the serial episodes lent themselves to early television programming needs and were among the first products of the American film industry to be sold to both local stations and the fledgling networks for regular broadcast. By 1948 both the ABC and Dumont television networks were devoting blocks of prime-time programming to various sorts of film shorts, including serials, and many local television stations were using public domain serials to produce their own programming (Barbour 234). And since these films were the products of studios like Universal, Columbia, and Republic, they brought to the small screen the sorts of elaborate sets and special effects that film audiences were both accustomed to and practically expected from the genre.

A second type of influential early programming was the SF anthology show, such as *Out There* (1951–52) and *Tales of Tomorrow* (1951–53). Because of their format, these shows, as Mark Jancovich and Derek Johnston explain, had to walk a difficult line in early broadcast television, between the more prestigious single-shot dramatic presentation and the supposedly more formulaic series: "As weekly shows rather than single plays, they could build audience loyalty, and by presenting a different story each week they avoided being seen as standardized and low quality" (75). Although neither show ultimately found great success, both offered audiences adaptations of some key literary works in the genre, such as *Frankenstein* and *20,000 Leagues under the Sea*, while also providing opportunities for up-and-coming SF writers like Ray Bradbury and Arthur C. Clarke. More important, the very variety of their stories recalled popular radio programs of the 1940s and early 1950s, series like *Escape*, *Inner Sanctum*, and *Beyond Tomorrow*, all of which opened onto a broad spectrum of speculative narrative, while they also suggested the possibility for addressing a more adult audience than was typically attracted by the serials or, by this time, the spate of new space operas.

It is this third type of programming, the space opera, that would have the most significant impact on the early trajectory of SFTV. Introduced in 1949 with *Captain Video and His Video Rangers*, the live-action space opera adapted many of the conventions of the film serial—in fact, *Captain Video*, the most popular of these shows, both incorporated serials into its regular broadcast slot and was itself eventually adapted as a big-screen serial—and it would quickly come to dominate early SF broadcasting, so much so that one contemporary commentator noted of these shows, "if you haven't watched the spacemen on TV, you haven't lived in the future" (Robinson 63). For slightly more than six years, that future was solidly linked to the exploits of the Captain and a long line of imitators who sought to capture his success with what was predominantly a children's audience. In addition to *Captain Video* (1949–55), we might especially note these created-for-television followers: *Tom Corbett, Space Cadet* (1950–55), *Space*

Patrol (1950–55), Captain Z-Ro (1951–56), Rod Brown of the Rocket Rangers (1953–54), Rocky Jones, Space Ranger (1954), and Captain Midnight (1954–56), along with new television versions of both Buck Rogers (1950–51) and Flash Gordon (1954–55). Operating from Earth but quite easily and frequently venturing into the far reaches of space, these futuristic tales not only offered audiences the familiar thrills of the space opera, with its simplistic characters and conventions, adventuring focus, and well-worn, often overblown plots, but they also gave audiences at least a taste of what Lincoln Geraghty refers to as "the aesthetics of technological innovation and visualizations of the future" (American Science Fiction 27) with their constant invoking of new and intriguing inventions, such as Captain Video's Opticon Scillometer and Mango-Radar, or Tom Corbett's Paraloray Gun, along with their cheaply done but visually intriguing sets.

Of course, that visual excitement—an element that, as we have noted, viewers already associated with cinematic SF—was somewhat qualified by these series' minimalist special effects. As John Ellis reminds us, the early television experience was characterized by a "radically different" weighting of the image than we are used to in the cinema, as we are also accustomed to today with our digital, high-definition, even 3-D home theater systems (Visible 127). With its small screen, often live-action presentation, and limited camera work, these television adventures were for the most part distinctly "pared down" (112) visual events. But those experiences offered audiences another sort of pay-off. For with their repeated depictions of video screens and video monitoring devices, with their stylistic reliance on reaction shots and looks of outward regard, and with their embedding of commercials that frequently used the series' stars in character as product spokesmen, these shows also demonstrated a level of self-consciousness about television story-telling. It is as if they were all engaged—and trying to engage us—in another sort of SF adventuring and exploring: exploring how SF narrative might best function in this new medium and how audiences, especially the children's audience at which much of this early work was aimed, might best relate to the medium.

Some of this same impulse would be further developed in the next major wave of SF programming, a return to the earlier anthology format that would, according to M. Keith Booker, mark "the maturation of science fiction television as a genre" (*Science* 6). Shows like the Ivan Tors and Maurice Ziv-produced *Science Fiction Theatre* (1955–57), which began each episode with the assurance that it would "show you something interesting"; Rod Serling's justly famous and expensively produced *The Twilight Zone* (1959–64), which promised to "unlock . . . another dimension of space and time"; and the more special effects-oriented *The Outer Limits* (1963–65), which told viewers to "sit quietly and we will control all that you see and hear"—these all directly addressed an implicitly adult audience, promising them something new, something that would capitalize on the new medium's (as well as the genre's) immense possibilities. And with their generally first-rate scripts, written by such figures as Jack Finney, Ivan Tors (*Science Fiction Theatre*), Richard Matheson, Charles Beaumont, Rod Serling (*The Twilight Zone*), Joseph Stefano, and Harlan Ellison (*The Outer Limits*), they consistently provided SF drama that competed well with the more conventional theater-like dramatic productions that were so popular on American television in the 1950s and 1960s, shows like *General Electric Theater*, *Kraft Television Theater*, and *Playhouse 90*.

Arguably the most important of all SFTV shows, and one that would subsequently be revived twice (1985–89 and 2002–03), *The Twilight Zone* appeared at a time when the Western had replaced the SF space opera as the most popular programming for younger audiences. In fact, when it premiered in 1959, nine of the top twenty national series were Westerns. But *The Twilight Zone*'s success with an older audience helped counter a growing sense that the genre, as it had been embodied in the early space operas, was both moribund and essentially "a subliterary form of culture designed to appeal to children or to . . . lowbrow plebeian tastes" (Booker, *Science* 8). Its critical and popular success was due not only to its higher budgets, talented writers, and obvious parallels to the highbrow live-action dramatic anthology shows—for which Rod Serling himself had previously labored—but also to its rather different style (Figure 1.1).

The Twilight Zone was shot on film, and used the various set, prop, and costume resources available at the MGM movie studio where most of the episodes were created. Furthermore, it was photographed by veteran cinematographers like George T. Clemens and directed by established Hollywood directors, including Richard Donner, Don Siegel, and Jacques Tourneur.

Figure 1.1 Creator Rod Serling introduces his groundbreaking *The Twilight Zone*

Moreover, *The Twilight Zone* often foregrounded that same emphasis on video and technologies of reproduction that was commonly featured in the space operas. As a result, Jeffrey Sconce's description of the show as a kind of "perverse 'unconscious' of television" (134) might well be extended to suggest that it represented a cultural unconscious as well, as it pointed to the already media-haunted nature of contemporary America, an America that, in light of the ongoing space race and the international tensions of the Cold War, was very much primed to look at the future more seriously and with a bit more anxiety than had audiences for the earlier space operas.

Not only was *The Twilight Zone* a more serious SF effort, but it also fully exploited its anthology format, opening the door to a variety of narrative possibilities. For the series, much like the best of the period's SF magazines, ranged across the spectrum of narrative types that had become identified with the genre: stories of space adventuring, of utopian and dystopian societies, of alien encounters and invasion, of time and dimensional travel, of extraordinary inventions, of alternate worlds or dimensions, as well as comic takes on many of these story types. As a result, The Twilight Zone also helped spur a revisioning of the space opera, an effect that would show most notably in two of the most important and influential of subsequent SF series, both of which debuted in the 1960s: the British Doctor Who (1963–89, 1996, 2005–present, and first appearing in American syndication in 1978) and Star Trek (1967–69). Both series have obvious roots in the earlier flood of space operas, with Doctor Who, the longest running of all SF series, clearly recalling a show like Captain Z-Ro (1951–56) with its educational tales of travels to real historical events in each episode, and Star Trek, which has generated more spin-offs than any other series, exploiting the potential of those previous adventure shows by emphasizing the infinite wonders of "space, the final frontier," as its epigraph weekly announced.

Both of these series also underscored the larger promise that was starting to be realized for the television medium, what we might refer to as their tele-visuality. For Doctor Who, with the Doctor's TARDIS as his iconic travel vehicle, literally opened up a new dimension for audiences. The Doctor's surprised companions when first introduced to the vehicle repeatedly observed, "it is larger inside than out," and they would then exit the TARDIS to encounter a new time and place, indeed a different reality; and in the process they would echo the similarly amazing experience that the series' audience was supposed to enjoy with each episode. Star Trek's own iconic vehicle, the starship Enterprise, with its panoramic viewing screen—which pointedly had a wider aspect ratio than any television screen of the period—always seemed to be positioning viewers not only to go "where no man has gone before," as its introductory narration promised, but also to see what (and as) no one had seen before, at least on network television (Figure 1.2). While these shows were justly praised, like The Twilight Zone, for taking on topics that were not commonly expressed or explored on broadcast television—issues involving racism, women's rights, and social prejudice—they also provided viewers, and in a way that previous SFTV had not, an immediate visual correlative to what Michele Pierson and others have identified as one of the SF genre's key appeals, an "aesthetic experience of wonder" (168).

These series' visual appeal was certainly significant; in fact, the Enterprise quickly became a highly recognizable element of SFTV and fan culture,

Figure 1.2 The iconic starship *Enterprise* explores another new world in *Star Trek*

as did dialogue that was redolent of that "experience of wonder," such as "Beam me up, Scottie" and "Warp speed, full ahead." However, *Star Trek* might be most significant because it was the brainchild of another of the most influential figures in the form's development, Gene Roddenberry. Like Rod Serling, an experienced writer for television, Roddenberry pitched the concept for *Star Trek* in terms of one of the most popular Western series of the time, referring to it as "*Wagon Train* in space." While the resulting adventures of the *Enterprise* in the 23rd century would in its initial network run on NBC prove only moderately successful—it ranked 52nd among all series in its peak season (Brooks and Marsh 1119)—it demonstrated the power of the new medium to attract a loyal and vocal audience when fan protests cut short the network's decision for its early cancellation. And even following its three-year run, it found a constant audience in syndication, inspired a series of feature films, spawned an animated series (1973–75), and provided the seed for a host of even more ambitious and better-rated spin-offs: *Star Trek:*

The Next Generation (1987–94), Star Trek: Deep Space Nine (1993–99), Star Trek: Voyager (1995–2001), and Star Trek: Enterprise (2001–05). Trying to explain this longevity and continued appeal, Roddenberry would claim that the primary reason for the show's impact, and indeed for the success of the entire franchise that it gave birth to, was Star Trek's willingness to offer the sort of social commentary that seemed out of place in the earlier space operas. As he offered, he found that by focusing on "a new world with new rules, I could make statements about sex, religion, Vietnam, unions, politics and intercontinental missiles" (quoted in Fulton 429). But just as crucial to its reception was its optimistic vision, or as M. Keith Booker terms it, a "compelling (and heartening) future image" (Science 51), one that suggested that humanity's problems could be worked out, that technology would prove a truly useful rather than an inherently dangerous servant, and that humanity is not alone in the universe. For a culture steeped in Cold War anxieties and, by this point, growing concerns over the continuing war in Vietnam, this affirmative sense of wonder was quite compelling.

Yet Star Trek's importance to the development of SFTV is due to more than just the affirmative and liberal vision that, through his series, Roddenberry articulated for American viewers. In pursuing his original theme of "Wagon Train in space" he effectively set out a narrative formula that has had a dominant impact on the genre to the present day. The key injunction offered in its well-known opening epigraph—that the "voyages of the starship Enterprise" were intended "to boldly go where no man has gone before"—not only readily evoked a new kind of frontier, but also easily differentiated the show from a somewhat similar and similarly popular show from the same period, Irwin Allen's Lost in Space. For the Enterprise was never truly lost; rather, the starship was engaged in what might be described as purposefully picaresque travels through space, with its racially and even species-diverse crew tasked with exploring and mapping part of the universe as representatives of the United Federation of Planets, bringing with them the Federation's message of peaceful cooperation and assistance. The adventuring, interactions of a wide variety of characters, and strong sense of purpose or promise would prove to be a significant evolution of the space opera formula and a strong legacy to the SF genre.

With its ability to take viewers anywhere and to immerse them in almost any sort of narrative, a show like *Star Trek*—as well as *Doctor Who*—also points to the larger trajectory of SFTV in this period. For the 1960s ushered in a great many other series about extraordinary explorations or travels of various types (*Lost in Space* [1965–68], *The Time Tunnel* [1966–67], about extraordinary technology (*Voyage to the Bottom of the Sea* [1964–68]), and about extraordinary encounters (*The Invaders* [1967–68], *Land of the Giants* [1968–70]), as well as series that afforded a different perspective on the genre itself. In this last category we might especially note the sudden rise in comic science fiction, as marked by shows like *My Favorite Martian* (1963–66), *My Living Doll* (1964–65), and *It's About Time* (1967-68), as well as animated versions of the genre, such as *The Jetsons* (1962–63), *Space Angel* (1962–64), and *Jonny Quest* (1964–65). Inflected by the space race of the era and by the appearance of such big-budget SF films as *Fantastic Voyage* (1966), *Planet of the Apes* (1968), and especially *2001: A Space Odyssey* (1968), these series demonstrate the extent to which SF had become highly popular programming in the United States and elsewhere. As SF had gained an increased respectability, it also offered the broadcast networks, as Lincoln Geraghty observes, "a chance to experiment, gambling with the bigger budgets needed for special effects and large sets using colour to attract new audiences" (*American Science Fiction* 43).

Helping to develop and exploit the genre's new profile was another key figure in the history of SFTV, Irwin Allen. An Academy Award-winning director, writer, and producer, Allen created four key series in the 1960s and, like Rod Serling, brought a highly cinematic sensibility to the medium. His most successful show, *Voyage to the Bottom of the Sea*, was adapted from his own hit film of the same title, and it, in turn, established a popular formula for scientific adventure, usually centered around a piece of extraordinary technology, such as, in this case, a submarine, a flying saucer (*Lost in Space*), or a time machine (*The Time Tunnel*)—all the sort of spectacular images that were commonly featured in cinematic SF. The success of *Voyage to the Bottom of the Sea* led Allen to create in quick succession *Lost in Space*, *The Time Tunnel*, and *Land of the Giants*. While he would later become known as the "Master of Disaster" because of his blockbuster disaster movies, Allen was already anticipating the sort of spectacular narratives that would become his hallmark. And while he seldom explored the kinds of cultural issues that were associated with Serling's work on *The Twilight Zone* or Gene Roddenberry's on *Star Trek*, he gave his signature visually spectacular narratives a basic human focus, exploring how people respond when faced with unusual or extraordinary circumstances, and that human focus appealed to a viewership beyond that which usually watched SF. At the same time, Allen's series, with their larger budgets, bigger casts, and the use of film-like special effects (often simply intercut from some of his feature films), brought a big-screen look to SFTV—and with that, larger audience expectations for the genre. While they have received scant critical praise, Allen's spectacular, effects-heavy series did have an impact on viewers' expectations for SFTV, leading them to anticipate seeing the sort of images and effects that heretofore had been the province of film.

Allen's work also paved the way for another element of media convergence, and indeed what we might see as a kind of identity struggle for SFTV that would occur during the next decade. Following the lead of a film adaptation like *Voyage to the Bottom of the Sea* were several efforts at copying other big-screen hits. And here we might consider two series for which there were clearly high expectations, although both proved to be major failures. Both *Planet of the Apes* (1974) and *Logan's Run* (1977–78) drew heavily on big hit films, the former even using some of the film's original cast members and striking make-up effects, and the latter employing left-over models, sets, and costumes from its cinematic original. However, *Planet of the Apes* lasted only thirteen episodes on CBS and *Logan's Run* fared little better, managing just fourteen episodes on the same network. The main, yet still moderate successes of this period were two linked series, both of which explored a new area for SF, that of biotechnology, while again trying to emphasize how individual humans responded to extraordinary circumstance. *The Six Million Dollar Man* (1975–78) and its spin-off *The Bionic Woman* (1976–78), arguably the most successful SF series of the 1970s, both told stories about government employees who, after suffering serious injuries, were reconstructed by scientists and turned into real-life superheroes. While anchored in rather fantastic extrapolations of the latest science and technology, each series was, as Lincoln Geraghty notes, ultimately "just as much a crime or detective series as a science fiction drama" (*American Science Fiction* 63), although in keeping with other SF programming, they effectively foregrounded various media effects—slow motion, special sound effects, and point-of-view shots—to emphasize the activated super-powers of their protagonists. However, their real-world context, evoking the current headlines scientists were making in this period with the creation of various human prostheses (including the first artificial heart), along with their more commonplace crimefighting/spyfighting plots, represented a marked shift from the fantastic worlds of shows like Planet of the Apes and Logan's Run, and suggested a genre that was trying to establish a new identity and to stake out a more realistic arena within the cultural imagination.

Given the cultural impact of contemporary SF cinema—a cinema that saw the advent of a series of big-budget, effects-intensive films near the end of the decade—that identity struggle would, at least for a time, not result in the sort of turn to real-world concerns and contemporary science forecast by a show like The Six Million Dollar Man. Instead, the phenomenal success of George Lucas' Star Wars (1977) and its sequels, of Steven Spielberg's Close Encounters of the Third Kind (1977), of Ridley Scott's Alien (1979), and the appearance of Star Trek—The Motion Picture (1979) would prompt television to re-emphasize fantasy and space adventure. As examples of this influence we might consider such series as Battlestar Galactica (1978–80), Buck Rogers in the 25th Century (1979–81), and the British Blake's 7 (1978–81). All were highly ambitious, having fairly large budgets—in fact, that for Battlestar Galactica was reportedly the highest to date for a prime-time television series (Brooks and Marsh 93)—big casts, elaborate special effects, and epic plot trajectories that in various ways recalled the Star Wars universe that Lucas had firmly implanted in the popular imagination. The first of these series detailed the epic wanderings of a space fleet, bearing all of humanity's ancestors following the destruction of their home planets by Cylons, a rebellious race of robots who aim to exterminate the human race. Buck Rogers in the 25th Century, while nominally an updating of the early comic strip, radio series, film serial, and 1950–51 television series, clearly modeled its protagonist on Star Wars' Han Solo and even gave him a comic robot assistant, Twiki, whose character was a combination of the film's R2D2 and C3PO. And Blake's 7, in its chronicling of the efforts of a small group of rebels to subvert the dominant Federation, similarly echoed Star Wars' saga about an alliance of planets trying to resist the repressive regime of the galactic Empire. Moreover, the large scope of these series was matched by their efforts to further push the boundaries of television effects and model work—a point underscored by the fact that John Dykstra, who had been responsible for many of the innovative effects used in the first *Star Wars* film, was recruited for *Battlestar Galactica*. In these series—and others that would soon follow their model—we see the full flowering of a development in SFTV that Jan Johnson-Smith has characterized as a definitive shift "from a predominantly verbal medium into a predominantly visual medium" (61).

That convergence of cinematic and televisual models of SF would be furthered throughout the 1980s, as a spate of highly successful films that were focused on themes of alien encounters and alien invasion—works like E.T.: *The Extra-Terrestrial* (1982), *The Thing* (1982), *Aliens* (1986), *The Hidden* (1987), *Predator* (1987), and *Alien Nation* (1988)—found their reflection in a group of television series about alien invasions or encounters. These programs include *The Powers of Matthew Star* (1982–83), *V* (1984–85), *The Tripods* (1984–85), *Starman* (1986–87), *War of the Worlds* (1988–90), *Alien Nation* (1989–90), as well as the situation comedy *ALF* (1986–90) and a reinvigorated *Doctor Who*. As was the case in the large group of listed films, the aliens depicted in these series would prove to be both threatening and benevolent, even comic in the case of *ALF*. They would lend new possibilities to various familiar narrative forms, as in *Alien Nation*'s revisioning of the police drama with its two "buddy cops", a hardened Los Angeles detective and a "newcomer" alien, and *The Powers of Matthew Star*'s rendition of the high school student/teenager not only as a stereotypically alienated character, but as a real alien—a concept that would be explored in far more detail in the later and far better received *Roswell* (1999–2002) and *Smallville* (2001–11) Moreover, these series, with their constant threats of alien invasion or observation, would give repeated testimony to a growing cultural paranoia and a general sense of insecurity, attitudes that would later come into much sharper focus with the long-running *The X-Files* (1993–2002).

Yet arguably more influential in this period was another sort of encounter with aliens and a frontier that, as those various alien portrayals underscored, remained "out there." It was that found in Gene Roddenberry's return to television with his reformulation of *Star Trek* as *Star Trek: The Next Generation* (1987–94). As Jan Johnson-Smith observes, Roddenberry was very mindful of the positive impact of his original series and that he did not want to risk upsetting its "established audience dynamic" (108), a dynamic that had resulted in the creation of a dedicated cult following of "Trekkers" who were already immersed in the *Star Trek* mythos, celebrating it in dedicated national conventions (the first major *Star Trek* "con" occurring in 1972), and following it through syndication on cable broadcast. So the new series, while set 80 years beyond the events of the original program, did not diverge far from its predecessor. While the crew was new, it had much the same sort of multiracial and multispecies make-up as the original, and their interactions followed a similar dynamic. Under the guidance of a wise and strong captain—Jean-Luc Picard—they carried out their interstellar explorations in an updated starship *Enterprise-D*. And thanks to a larger budget—reportedly $1.3 million per episode, the largest for a one-hour television series at that time—the new show sported first-rate special effects, of the order that audiences, steeped in the SF cinema of Lucas and Spielberg, were coming to expect from television as well. Most importantly, as in the original series, *The Next Generation* deployed its rather more convincingly realized futuristic settings and situations to explore contemporary social and cultural issues, as well as larger philosophical questions, especially ones clustered around androids, artificial intelligence, and cybernetic beings. With the introduction of the cybernetic organisms collectively known as the Borg, *The Next Generation* not only foregrounded key cultural issues raised by the increasingly close relationship of humans to technology and computerization, but also introduced a tag line that quickly entered into the popular consciousness, the Borg's warning that "Resistance is futile."

If it has never been quite as self-conscious of its status as a media product as many other science fiction series, *The Next Generation* did develop another dimension of self-referentiality—one that attests to its transcendence of conventional television narrative. Exploiting the new dynamic of television consumption that derived from the development of cable—and later satellite—broadcasting, which resulted in a demand for more product for syndication, *The Next Generation* would soon spin-off other series, producing narrative lines that would allow for cross-series character appearances, cross-referencing of key events, and a more elaborate, even historical development of key issues. Before *The Next Generation* finished its original run, and notwithstanding Gene Roddenberry's death in 1991, another syndicated effort was launched in 1993, *Star Trek: Deep Space Nine* (1993–99), and it was eventually followed by additional series, *Star Trek: Voyager* (1995–2001) and the prequel narrative *Enterprise* (aka *Star Trek: Enterprise*, 2001–05). These series would elaborately expand on the established *Star Trek* mythos, not only by the sort of cross-referencing noted above, but also by tracing out a history of the United Federation of Planets and the work of its Starfleet, and by elaborating on a number of the most popular motifs or plot threads, such as the ongoing menace of the Borg to assimilate all "biological and techno-logical distinctiveness" into their collective identity, or the intense racially themed conflict between the Cardassians and the subject Bajorans, that are woven throughout many of the series. While at times, as Jan Johnson-Smith observes, these sequels and prequels seemed to become "backward- not forward-looking" like the original series (109), as they sought to develop the larger *Star Trek* story, the overlap and continuity they generated helped contribute to what M. Keith Booker has described as "an unprecedented period of richness and innovation" (*Science* 108) in SFTV, as they generated a new level of audience involvement in their material. Moreover, these and other series of the 1990s demonstrated the medium's new-found ability to generate, largely independent of the film industry, a powerful and compel-ling narrative world that could flourish in the new distribution environment that was already anticipating the appearance of the dedicated Syfy (origi-nally Sci-Fi) Channel that would premiere September 24, 1992.

Taking a new approach to the broad SF mission of exploring what Jeffrey Sconce has termed the "electronic elsewhere (92)," and launched by one of those new distribution outlets, was the Fox Network's enormously successful and influential *The X-Files* (1993–2002). Rather than taking viewers on explor-atory interstellar voyages and envisioning what might lie out in deep space, this series argued, as one of its protagonists Fox Mulder repeatedly asserts, that there is a crucial "truth" in our world, just waiting to be seen, if only we look carefully enough and behind various efforts at covering it up. The series also little resembled anything then available on the film screen, as it brought together a wide variety of fantasy concerns, including horror, supernatural phenomena, and urban legends, binding them within the series' larger focus on investigating government cover-ups of alien activity. The two central char-acters of *The X-Files*, FBI agents Mulder and Scully, effectively personify two sides in the public debate about UFOs and other unexplained phenomena, with Mulder, because of earlier events in his life, being cast as a firm believer in such things and Scully, a trained forensic scientist, always providing a kind of narrative balance, expressing her skepticism about the incidents they are assigned to investigate. It was a dynamic that was clearly designed to suggest the conflicted public attitudes towards such phenomena, as well as towards the government, as, in show after show, it is implicated at various levels in knowing about and even conspiring with a shadowy alien presence.

While that dynamic would eventually seem to move towards a resolution when Scully is abducted by aliens—there becoming an X-file case herself—the series still retains its character as what Lincoln Geraghty effectively terms a "metanarrative of secrets and concealment" (*American Science Fiction* 99). For even when *The X-Files* shifts from discovering monstrous figures and psychopaths to laying bare an elaborate alien plot for Earth's conquest, the investigation never proves to be simple, never reaches completion. Rather, the series repeatedly takes audiences towards that "truth" only just as insistently to swerve off or pull back from any final revelation. If the show's contemporary setting, FBI agent protagonists, and police procedural actions often made it seem more like a detective mystery than SF, its foregrounding of what M. Keith Booker describes as a "postmodernist mode of epistemological skepticism" (*Science* 142) and its emphasis on an unfolding approach to narrative—coupled with an increasing level of self-consciousness—would prove highly attractive. Its success would lead to two feature film versions (1998, 2008), generate a short-lived and even more self-conscious spin-off series about conspiracy investigators, *The Lone Gunmen* (2001), and help it build a cult following of "x-philes," as fans called themselves, that nearly rivaled the following for the various *Star Trek* films and series.

Given its tendency towards narrative convolution and its overarching skeptical/paranoiac vision, *The X-Files* did not immediately inspire many imitators, save for NBC's *Dark Skies* (1996–97), a short-lived effort about insect-like alien invaders and government cover-ups that lasted just nineteen episodes. However, *The X-Files*' postmodern influence, and especially its fantastic take on the criminal investigation narrative—that is, as an investigation whose complexity seems to stretch across the galaxy—would eventually translate into a string of SF-inflected investigation and conspiracy series. Among many broadly similar shows we might note the following: *Taken* (2002), *Lost* (2004–10), *Invasion* (2005–06), *Eureka* (2006–12), Life on Mars (British series 2006–07, American series 2008–09), its sequel *Ashes to Ashes* (2008–10), *Terminator: The Sarah Connor Chronicles* (2008–09), *Fringe* (2008–13), *Dollhouse* (2009–10), and *Warehouse* 13 (2009–14). In these series a realistic, mostly present-day setting provides the unexpected context for mystery narratives that involve time travel, dimensional travel, teleportation, or simple unexplained occurrences, often associated with either real or suspected alien activity or artifacts.

These series' amazing narrative amalgam, of the everyday and the fantastic, of the familiarly real and the strangely science fictional, almost invariably involves a mixture of tone as well. For episodes in most of these shows, but especially series like *Eureka*, *Fringe*, and *Warehouse* 13, freely slide into a comic or absurd register that, as was sometimes the case with *The X-Files*, seems to correspond to one of those signature characteristics of the postmodern—a widespread suspicion of reality itself, either as it is commonly perceived or as it is typically presented by the government, by the media, and by everyday culture. And that sense of suspicion, along with its accompanying absurd inflection on the real, has become part of an attractive narrative formula, one that, as Lincoln Geraghty suggests, "attracts fans familiar with many different genres . . . who do not necessarily understand it as one particular genre over another" (*American Science Fiction* 117). Simply put, that mixed tone and gaming of the real create a context wherein genre conventions can freely mix and narrative boundaries frequently blur, opening the shows up to a diverse audience and providing them with widely varying narrative pleasures.

Yet while these paranoid investigations of reality, with their implicit investigations of the very medium used to present these series, have become a dominant mode of SFTV in the early twenty-first century, an earlier narrative model has continued to prove a powerful vehicle for the cultural imagination. The model developed in the various *Star Trek* series, with its more conventional tone and greater emphasis on visualizing the future and showing viewers what might lie "out there," continues to flourish in the new viewing environment of cable and satellite television with their increasing ability to "narrowcast" or target specific audiences. Of particular note are shows like the syndicated *Babylon 5* (1994–98) and *Stargate SG-1* (1997–2007), the

longest-running SF series on American television and, like *Star Trek*, the pro-
genitor of several spin-off series—the animated *Stargate Infinity* (2002–03),
Stargate Atlantis (2004–09), and *Stargate Universe* (2009–11); the Syfy Channel's
Farscape (1999–2003), and the Fox network's *Firefly* (2002), both of which
have developed dedicated cult followings that recall *Star Trek*'s "Trekkers";
the computer-animated *Star Wars: The Clone Wars* (2008–13), a continuation
of George Lucas' SF film epic; and the ambitious reboot of *Battlestar Galactica*
(2003–09), which has, in the best SF tradition, used its updated tale of
apocalyptic conflict between humans and their Cylon creations as a way
of metaphorizing and exploring contemporary gender and racial issues, as
well as the American political dynamic. All of these series are in the updated
space opera mode of the *Star Trek* franchise, all depend heavily on digital
special effects, and, apart from *Stargate SG-1* and *Star Wars: The Clone Wars*, all
seem more indebted to television traditions than to the cinema. In fact,
the ability of these "postmodern space operas," as Gary Westfahl allusively
terms them ("Space" 207), to attain great popularity at the same time as
the more reality-bound, contemporary-set investigation series attests to the
great health and ongoing popularity of the form on television.

All of them also have made great capital from the television industry's
increased ability to offer relatively inexpensive special effects that, at least
on the home screen, seem to rival the work of the cinema. But in her assessment of the state of contemporary SFTV, Jan Johnson-Smith also notes a
consequence, even a possible pitfall of that ability: "as broadcast technology
has advanced and increased, so have our expectations, and we demand so
much more" (252). Certainly, the contemporary shows cited above lend
some credence to that assessment. These are, after all, very ambitious series,
both narratively and technically. Series like *Babylon 5* and *Battlestar Galactica*
especially were designed on what might well be described as an epic scale
(Figure 1.3). They tell sweeping stories that project human wanderings,
ambitions, and destinies across the vastness of the universe, much as ancient
cultures did with their stories of the known world in works like *The Iliad*,
The Odyssey, and *The Aeneid*, and all are impressively realized. Tapping into the
latest—and an increasingly affordable—digital technology, many of these
contemporary series have managed to effectively visualize other worlds, to
evoke other, highly complex, even similarly self-conscious species, and to

Figure 1.3 *Battlestar Galactica*'s digitally fashioned and sexualized Cylons

present us with armadas of spaceships, space stations, and other advanced technology, all by way of providing audiences with a portion of that generic pleasure that, as we have noted, is part of the larger aesthetic experience of wonder.

Yet at the same time, the best of these series—and here we might single out not only *Battlestar Galactica*, but also shows like *Farscape* and *Firefly* with their complex characters and scripts—seem to recognize that their technological empowerment, their ability to show us something wondrous is not enough, not simply what, as Johnson-Smith says, "we demand . . . more" of. These series, and others like them, also ask important questions about the current world, such as how different races and cultures might peacefully and productively coexist. Following the tradition of *The Twilight Zone* and *Star Trek*, they are using the future, space, other dimensions, alien figures, and arresting technology—including the technology of representation—as tools for interrogating our own nature and our own condition, particularly as we confront an age in which history seems to have lost much of its relevance, the future seems by turns mysterious and absurd, and our humanity is often perceived as just a construct of various forces beyond our full understanding or control. These are all very large issues, the stuff of mainstream fiction and film, and SFTV's ability to address them, not only with but in some cases *despite* its emphasis on the spectacular, helps explain the genre's increasingly important place in contemporary media culture.

In keeping with this turn, we are also seeing a new type of SF show that, while also posing some of these "big questions," very pointedly backs off from that technological thrust, simply refusing to go down the path of a purely technological "more." For one of the most popular new show types, the reality show, has given birth to a variety of popular series that explore both subjects and themes familiar to SF fans, while opting for a kind of pared-down visual field that, for the typical reality audience, serves as the very badge of its truthfulness. Series like UFO Files (2004–07), UFO Hunters (2008–11), Ancient Aliens (2010–13), and Chasing UFOs (2012–13), produced by and for such unlikely sources as The History Channel, the Science Channel, and National Geographic Channel, have taken our fascination with—and apparently a popular desire to believe in—the familiar stuff of SF, such as alien civilizations, advanced technology, and space travel, and situated them as subjects of realistic scrutiny, in effect, bracketing off the "fiction" component of "science fiction." While they capitalize on the same fantastic appeal that has driven our space operas, insofar as they all tease us with the promise of showing something spectacular, of discovering mysterious artifacts, or of retrieving candid photos or film of something simply unearthly, these shows also mobilize that same skepticism and mistrust of governmental or institutional voices—the voices that many believe are obscuring or covering up "the truth"—that are central to paranoiac series like The X-Files, Lost, and Fringe. But these reality series are closely allied to others that mix the real with dramatizations or re-enactments of real events, such as director Ridley Scott's documentary show about great SF artists, Prophets of Science Fiction (2011–12), produced for the Science Channel; the Discovery Channel's Weird or What? (2010–11), hosted by Star Trek star William Shatner; Dark Matter: Twisted but True (2011–12), the Science Channel's series, dramatizing bizarre scientific experiments, hosted by John Noble, star of Fringe; and The History Channel's Mysteryquest (2009). In their mix of fact and narrative, of truth and mystery, these shows effectively draw together the two most popular strains of SF programming, while underscoring the extent to which SF has become fully a part of mainstream consciousness, part of the way in which we think about our world—and other possible ones—today.

They also represent a significant development on which we might appropriately conclude this brief survey. For these reality shows, with their re-enactments of eye-witness accounts, their computer-generated images (CGIs) of possible aliens and alien technology, and their examination of common SF subjects and themes, suggest a level on which the real and the science fictional have begun to merge, as our own world seems to have become ever more fantastic. As a further example of this element of convergence, we might consider the relationship between a reality show like *Stan Lee's Superhumans* (2010–12) and mainstream television narratives such as the award-winning NBC drama *Heroes* (2006–10) and the Syfy Channel's *Alphas* (2011–12). All are series about people with unusual characteristics, even superhuman powers, although the first simply puts on—rather spectacular—displays of *real* people with unusual traits or abilities, while the latter two fashion narratives around slightly exaggerated versions of similarly "super" people, using those abilities in the service of narrative. What these series commonly underscore is the fact that, just like our popular genres, humans today too seem to defy traditional conceptions and limitations, to have what might even be termed a science fictional identity.

Given that blurring of lines, the slogan for the cable-broadcast Science Channel probably does not strike its viewers as surprising. As a key part of its advertising, the channel reminds us to "Question Everything." It is a reminder that readily recalls Mulder's repeated comment on *The X-Files* that "The truth is out there," and it is also the sort of injunction we might well expect to hear on a number of other pointedly fictional shows, as the skeptical attitude that has always been a part of the scientific method intersects with the contemporary political and philosophical skepticism that empowers our paranoiac investigative series, as well as the quest for the wondrous that has always driven our space operas. This convergence may prove to be only a relatively brief pattern in the overall history of SFTV, but it seems both important and promising. For in it we can clearly see some of the ways in which SF has become an important tool for interrogating our world and ourselves, and of helping us not only to envision the future—as the genre has always sought to do—but also to prepare for it, to live with and in it.

KEY SERIES: *CAPTAIN VIDEO* AND
THE DEVELOPMENT OF A SFTV AUDIENCE

Viewed today, an early television space opera like *Captain Video* seems a bit quaint, even surreal. For regularly in the midst of an episode involving heroic adventures in space or on other planets, the Captain or his Video Ranger assistant will suddenly turn on a video monitor, the "Special Remote Carrier Beam," as it is termed, so that audiences can watch the exploits of some of the Captain's "special agents"—usually scenes from a Western serial of the 1930s or 1940s.[1] More than just a sop to youngsters who, as one commentator suggested, "might otherwise pine for TV cowboys" (Robinson 63), that strange interruption/eruption brought with it a certain self-referential baggage, as if *Captain Video*—the show—was suddenly taking stock of itself, reflecting on its potentially transportive power, and offering a kind of lesson in watching. Yet *Captain Video* was hardly unique in this regard, for its many imitators, the various space operas that colonized American television screens between 1949 and 1955 (and then suddenly disappeared from those screens when the real-life science of a burgeoning space race overtook science fiction), also seem conscious of the new medium, and particularly of the role they were playing in constructing an audience for early television.

While still relatively new to American audiences, television—and by extension the televisual experience—was something that, for many years, had been presented as a futuristic, science fictional device. Popular SF films of the 1920s through the 1940s repeatedly depicted television as a technological development that, when it finally arrived, might in various fantastic ways change our lives. But even as it became more familiar—or domesticated—the medium was unable to shake off elements of that earlier character. As William Boddy notes, various "anxieties and conflicts . . . accompanied the postwar launch of commercial television in the United States," and those attitudes still show traces of that science fictional character and of "a profound cultural ambivalence about the television set as an object, television viewing as an activity, and about television's relation to the ideals of post-war domesticity" (*New Media* 45). That ambivalence made it essential for television to find ways of modeling a proper audience attitude, of suggesting how both television and its viewers might function. And as John Ellis has shown, television quickly followed this imperative, developing "distinctive aesthetic forms to suit the circumstances" (*Visible* 111): an emphasis on short, discrete narrative segments, a heavy reliance upon dialogue, and a kind of dislocated viewer gaze, or as the Introduction noted, a "glance" (112). And with SF invested in visual spectacle and already tied to a postwar prominence of science and technology, the new medium also located a narrative model that could support a proper viewership, countering those free-floating cultural "anxieties and conflicts" by letting us see them "in a different way."

Shows like *Captain Video*, *Tom Corbett, Space Cadet*, *Space Patrol*, and others played an important role in this development, helping to turn audiences into proper viewers, right-*seeing*, as well as right-*thinking* members of modern American society. What did it mean to be a television viewer in the late 1940s and early 1950s, to be involved with this new technology that was suddenly linking our homes to another sort of "outer space," to the larger world "out there" somewhere? How were we supposed to respond to this new space that was just a window away yet beckoning to us, especially with its commercial pitchmen who regularly "beamed in" *to us*, directly addressing us in our homes? A show like *Captain Video* especially demonstrated the rather different manner of seeing that its audience would have to learn in order to cope with this brave new scientific and technological world.

Of course, constructing the spectacle of technology—much less conveying that spectacle—was no simple task for shows that found much of their narrative inspiration in the cheaply made serials of previous decades and that suffered under the minimalist budgets of juvenile television. *Captain Video* accomplished its futuristic vision with just a $25 per episode effects budget. In fact, in surveying the many toys and kids' products created to promote and profit from the series, one discussion of this pre-eminent space opera archly suggests that the products "inadvertently recreated some of the cardboard feel of the sets for the program" (Corn 26). Another critique noted that "sponsors and licensees could credibly claim that the guns, rings, and uniforms for sale at the local store were the same ones that were used on the set" (Weinstein 149). And most of the other space operas similarly relied on a narrative pattern of cheapness, intercutting small, crudely crafted rocket miniatures with many interior dialogue scenes.

Moreover, even while most of the space operas were set far in the future—*Captain Video* in the 22nd century, *Tom Corbett* in the 24th century, and *Space Patrol* in the 30th century—little effort was actually made to depict that future. For doing so would have required far more than the few miniatures of rockets and spaceports that these series typically used to denote their future eras. Instead, these series relied on limited, broadly suggestive sets, with most of the action limited to interiors. Thus Lucanio and Coville note how *Captain Video* "was earthbound" for many months in its early run, with most of its action taking place at Video Ranger Headquarters (*Science Fiction* 96) where audience point of view could be carefully framed and constructed, directed towards effects like the Special Remote Carrier. The more thoughtful *Tom Corbett, Space Cadet*, with its primary emphasis on character relationships, would use its central characters to suggest futuristic spectacle—a technique remarked upon in a review of the very first episode, which describes "a rocket crash sequence, in which light flickered on the faces of the watching cadets to give the impression [my italics] of the ship in flames" (*Variety* Oct. 4, 1950). While the far more expensively produced *Space Patrol* promised at the start of each episode "high adventure in the wild vast reaches of space," the interior of Commander Buzz Corry's rocket ship was usually the location of much of that action with Buzz, Cadet Happy, and others reacting to events, peering through the eye-like windows of the ship, or monitoring action on television-like screens. When land-based action occurred in any of these shows, it was most often keyed by crudely painted backdrops. And the lack of a concerted focus on the usual fascination of media SF, that is, on wondrous spectacle, is itself telling, reminding us that, as Ellis suggests, a televisual "glance" was enough to gauge those future realms.

Besides emphasizing the *seeing* of and *reaction* to spectacle rather than spectacle itself, all of these series offered another sort of wonder, as they larded their narratives with various futuristic gadgets, used not only to defend the solar system, galaxy, and/or universe, but to connect to the largely *suggested* or crudely depicted realms out there. *Captain Video* was the template in this regard, since the Captain in each episode used a number of such devices, all with highly scientific-sounding names, such as: the Opticon Scillometer that let him see through solid objects; the Mango-Radar for eavesdropping on conversations anywhere on the planet; the Ultraplanetary Transmitter, a galactic communication device; and the Discatron, a portable video screen and intercom. Such devices not only attested to the Captain's status as, the show's narrator often intoned, "Master of Science," but they also modeled a properly futuristic way of interacting with the world, using technology to extend the reach of our senses. In fact, a contemporary commentator argued that the show "derives it appeal" precisely from its constant use of such "fancy gadgetry" (Gould 9). And that argument is not far off the mark, since those strangely named props suggested that, in the future, we would interact with our world largely through technology—technology that would allow us to see, hear, and even control the world in ways that had never before been possible. They hinted, in effect, at the very power of new technologies of surveillance and control such as television itself. So when, in each episode, the Captain or a Ranger would turn to the Special Remote Carrier, the video screen centrally placed in a wall of the Ranger Headquarters, always looking back at us, that reflexive connection, as well as the true import of the Captain's name, became explicit (Figure 1.4). The camera would dolly in to the screen while one of the Rangers directed our attention with a phrase like, "What do you say we beam in Captain Video's Western agents?" It is an invitation that effectively frames another sort of adventure within the following short, discrete narrative segment, that establishes our role as passive viewers (and consumers) of the ensuing narrative, and that prepares us for other sorts of direct address that would ensue, easily interrupting our "glance" relationship to the screen to afford other, equally appealing relationships.

The key other relationship is seen in those instances when Captain Video's own adventures would often and suddenly be framed on that same video screen by one of the Rangers, who would then segue into a commercial for a sponsor's products, such as Post's Sugar Crisp cereal or Power House candy bars. The resulting *mise en abyme* created by this narrative shift, a typical camera track back, and transitional comments such as, "Suppose the Ranger and the Captain don't come through all right?" or "Things couldn't be worse for Captain Video and the Ranger," situated viewers not in the sort of narrative immersion common with classical Hollywood films of the period, nor even in the cliffhanger circumstances

Figure 1.4 Captain Video and the Video Ranger on another dangerous mission in *Captain Video and His Video Rangers*

of the adventure serials. Rather, they constructed a realm of discrete narrative segments that easily shift from one narrative level to another, and from narrative to commercial, in fact, blurring the lines between the show's various "levels," while also both underscoring and suspending our relationship to the narrative—a double move that would prove essential to the further development of commercial broadcast television with its constant negotiation between the dual imperatives of story and advertisement.

With *Captain Video*'s primary space opera imitators, many of these audience characteristics would find further development. However, in few cases were there the sort of enforced narrative breaks associated with watching the Captain's "Western agents," since that show had so quickly and effectively demonstrated the primary appeal of the space opera itself, and especially of its stalwart futuristic heroes, who were clearly attractive in their own right and, as Lucanio and Coville note, were even invested with "enough mythic quality to compel a considerable number of adults to take notice" (*Science Fiction* 9). A series like *Johnny Jupiter* (1953–54) did feature a young inventor, Ernest P. Duckweather, who, we are told at the beginning of each episode, "invented a television set unlike any ever known before, for on this set he was able to tune in the planet Jupiter." With it he would converse with two of that planet's inhabitants, Johnny Jupiter and his robot companion B-12 (both hand puppets), who could see Ernest even without a camera. Thus at various points in each episode the action would break as Ernest contacted his planetary neighbors for advice or help on his latest Earth-bound dilemma. And as with *Captain Video*, these television-breaks-on-television would also provide the opportunity for another re-framing—or re-monitoring—as the show would pull further away from the action to directly address the audience, urging them to buy the sponsor's product, in this case M&M candies. That link between the television as a source of advice and power and as product appeal, though, only makes more explicit the connection that *Captain Video* had already firmly established and formularized.

The more famous and longer-lived space operas, particularly those that derive most clearly from the *Captain Video* mold, such as *Tom Corbett, Space Cadet* and *Space Patrol*, offered few such narrative shifts, reserving their self-referential breaks solely for the commercials, typically featuring Tom or other space cadets in the former and, in the latter, frequently Commander Buzz Corry himself (originally Kit Corry), the leader of the Space Patrol that policed the galaxy, keeping peace in the name of The United Planets. In both cases, the principles would directly address the "boys and girls of the audience," looking directly into the camera as they urged them to "wear Red Goose shoes" (*Tom Corbett*)—which came with a free "space cadet identification bracelet"—or to hear a "special message" from Commander Corry, one that urged members of the Patrol to "get supercharged like I do" by eating such Ralston/Purina cereals as Rice Chex and Wheat Chex, or to enjoy Nestlé's chocolate candies (*Space Patrol*) so they would be properly "fueled" for their own adventures.

That easy shift of the central characters from their narrative immersion to the hawking of sponsors' products and back again is consistent both with Jeffrey Sconce's description of early television's "uncanny electronic space capable of collapsing, compromising, and even displacing the real world" (18), and with the new medium's reliance on dialogue. And in fact, it reminds us of the extent to which, for all of their adventurousness, these shows were more invested at every level in talk and character reactions than in real action. As an example, we might consider "The Runaway Rocket" (1954) episode in which Tom Corbett and his fellow cadets on board the *Polaris* spaceship must track a new test rocket. Their task is largely that of visual and telemetric observation, as Tom and fellow cadet Astro spend much of the episode simply looking out through the viewport and towards the audience, describing their actions, while their companion, Roger Manning, watches on a telescopic device and later on the ship's long-range scanner. In fact, most of the show's action is measured in their visual and verbal reactions as they watch—electronically—the test ship malfunction, veer off course and out of control, and head towards the sun. Even their ensuing rescue of the "Runaway" is played as a series of cross-cut scenes between the cockpits of the two rockets, during which their ship pulls alongside the other and nudges it away from danger, while the crews of each rocket observe from their seats. Here and elsewhere, space—both *outer* space and the physical space in which action typically occurs—has indeed been collapsed into dialogue and framed by the act of looking, as the on-screen characters in their watching and talking effectively construct the typical SF spectacle.

This construction affords much narrative economy and serves the series' primary focus on character, as a remarkably similar episode, "The Pursuit of the Deep Space Projectile" (1955), illustrates. Much of this show's plot derives from the introduction of cadet Monroe, a specialist who helped design a rocket sent to collect information on the planet Sirius. Monroe quickly comes into conflict with the *Polaris* crew, Tom, Astro, and T. J. Thistle, as he questions their navigation and flying ability, as if they were not able to "see" properly—either electronically or physically. Tensions rise when they are unable to locate the "deep space projectile," and those tensions play out against a background of anxiously looking into scanners, watching radar screens, and inspecting a large, wall-mounted plotter. In fact, one extended scene emphasizes the strain surrounding their search by superimposing a radar screen over close-ups of the various characters. When the rocket is eventually located, all must work together to retrieve it before it can fall into Sirius' sun. In this episode, models of the *Polaris* and the smaller projectile help to depict their docking, but Tom largely *describes* that activity as he watches, as Astro attends to various monitors, and as Monroe, now fully integrated into the crew, helps by plotting a safe course. With the rocket successfully retrieved, the show ends with the crew again seated and happily looking out towards space, like their audience, looking towards their next adventure. Like the larger narrative, the ending is a commonplace one, but it also points up how much of the series is spent not in *action*, but in *inaction*, with the cadets, like a proper television audience, *watching* events, talking about them, seated before a spectacle that unfolds on their screens, scanners, or other technological tools. And its satisfying resolution, marked by unity and good fellowship, suggests the sort of benefits that this unmistakably *televisual* situation can produce.

While running in approximately the same period as *Captain Video* and *Tom Corbett*, *Space Patrol* differentiated itself by emphasizing production values through the use of models, matte paintings, and complicated exterior sets. In fact, we see a measure of its reputation for placing more emphasis on such visual spectacle in a singular event: the show's participation in a first demonstration of 3-D television broadcasting during the height of the cinematic 3-D craze of 1953. Reviewing this landmark event, *Variety* termed *Space Patrol*'s participation a "wise choice of space and dimension as a rocket ship goes forth in quest of the 'fourth dimension.' Some of the shots actually conveyed depth" (*Variety* Apr. 30, 1953).[2] But more than that, its appearance here, even in what was generally seen as a *failed* demonstration, suggests how much *Space Patrol* benefited from a quickly developing sense of the televisual. For while its earlier episodes were dialogue heavy and prone to showing how the television audience should see this future world—in reclining seats, watching on monitors, and as part of a nearly "domestic" group (modeled by Buzz Corry, his young cadet Happy, the Commander's love interest Carol Carlisle, and the male and female supporting figures of Tonga and Robbie Robertson)—*Space Patrol*, later in its run, became far more action driven with its characters involved in events that threatened to upset that almost familial grouping.

Yet even fairly late in the series we still see traces of that effort at properly constructing and situating the television viewer. As an example, we might consider an episode from approximately the same period as that 3-D experiment, "The Laughing Alien" (Mar. 28, 1953). While it begins with elaborate establishing model work that shows the *Terra V* voyaging in space, dramatic music keys a cut to the rocket's interior where Commander Corry looks out and begins seeing strange images, first of Cadet Happy, bound and in pain, and then of an unfamiliar "laughing alien," both of which we subsequently see in subjective shots, as figures superimposed on the dark spacescape. However, only the Commander can see them and he admits to Major Robertson how strange this vision is—"I know it sounds like I'm space happy"—and that feeling returns when, back at the base, Buzz again begins "seeing images." But in an elaborately furnished medical lab where he uses a Brain-O-Graph machine, Buzz broadcasts his visions to a monitor and even produces a copy of the alien's face. We eventually learn that the alien, evocatively named Muzak, is a telepath, able to project images and thus dominate "weak-minded" races. However, the Commander's own unsuspected telepathic abilities—developed in a prior confrontation with such types—eventually overcomes Muzak and saves Cadet Happy.

While visually quite rich, thanks to its extensive model work, its varied sets (including several rocket interiors, the Space Patrol headquarters, and the lab), and technology like the Brain-O-Graph, "The Laughing Alien" episode also points up that concern with audience construction seen in the other space operas. Throughout the episode there is much sitting and looking into space, talking about what is being seen (or not seen), and monitoring or looking at things through electronic gadgets. Moreover, the show thematizes the televisual experience, presenting Buzz, Major Roberston, and Happy all initially as passive consumers of broadcast (telepathically) images who are challenged to resist their controlling power. And in his ability to turn the tables on the alien wielding this power, Commander Corry demonstrates for his audience their own proper relationship to such projective technology; he reassures them that they ultimately had little to fear from those broadcast images.

Of course, in the postwar period of the early space opera's popularity, we were already entering into a new regime of vision. We were beginning to craft new sorts of "sight machines," as Paul Virilio has termed them (*War* 2), that would ultimately insist on a new relationship to our world. Television was just one of these emerging and decidedly science fictional technologies—"machines" like the communications satellite, the spy satellite, the jet or rocket-propelled reconnaissance vehicle, all of which would, as Virilio prophesied, permit "eyeshot" to "finally get the better of gunshot" (2). And those machines were entering into the home, insinuating themselves as a part of the postwar domestic regime and the modern technological culture that was taking hold.

In these efforts of the space operas of the 1950s—and their early depictions of television and the televisual experience—we can begin to sense how important it was to inculcate a proper televisual attitude, to frame our relationship to the new visual environment, in effect, to teach us how to see. Francesco Casetti has suggested that in the first half of the twentieth century film "gave form to the modes of vision of its time, negotiating ongoing cultural processes" (5); and in the second half of the century television managed a similar feat. Before we could move culturally into the New Frontier of science and technology, before we could begin "to scrutinize outer space as an attainable technological possibility" (Lucanio and Coville, *Science Fiction* 116), and before science entertainment could be placed in the expert hands of Walt Disney's "Man in Space" shows (1955, 1957) and Frank Capra's *Bell System Science Series* (1956–64) with their rather different emphasis on what was termed "edutainment," we first had to learn how to be good television viewers. The space operas of the 1950s, with their repeated invitations to "beam in" and "take a look," with their demonstrations of domestic-like group watching, with their emphases on the power and even necessity of broadcast images and visual surveillance, taught that lesson well and in the process helped us to prepare for SFTV's world of tomorrow.

NOTES

1 Lucanio and Coville in their *American Science Fiction Television Series of the 1950s* explain that the parent DuMont network had purchased a package of old Westerns with the original intention of using the Captain Video character as a host who would introduce the films. Despite the change in format to a science

fiction adventure, the network decided to go ahead with the generic combination, since "DuMont wasn't about to waste the broadcast rights to all of those old Western movies" (99).

2   Unfortunately, this test presentation was almost comically unsuccessful. A polarized light system was used and polarized glasses issued to viewers, but only some time into the broadcast was it discovered that the "polarization had been reversed" on the broadcast, which required the viewers to then "turn their glasses upside down" in order to see the space images in their intended depth. See the *Variety* review of Apr. 30, 1953.

2

SFTV: INDUSTRIAL AND NARRATIVE MODELS

While we might think of telling stories as a very simple, even intuitive act, there are a number of factors in every medium that impact such telling. Among them, this chapter focuses on the nature of broadcast television programs and on the generic conventions that have helped to shape the formal and narrative possibilities of SFTV. Specifically, I first want to consider a number of what we might term *industrial models* commonly in use—in early American broadcast television and still often employed today—and then turn to a variety of aesthetic models that might be used in describing SF story-telling practices. Of course, not one of these models, descriptions, or categories adequately takes the measure of our SFTV experience, but the variety of narrative considerations surveyed in this chapter will serve to remind us that SFTV does not simply provide us with a pleasurable and, at its best, thought-provoking experience (or as some commentators on the genre have put it, a "thought experiment"), but also imposes specific patterns on its expressions and our experience. So if we are to be more than just consumers of televised SF, we need to be able to recognize some of those industrial and aesthetic patterns or limitations, to think about how they produce what we have earlier termed an "experience of wonder," and to consider why that experience affects us as it does.

ANTHOLOGIES, SERIALS, AND SERIES

As SF first made its way to television in the late 1940s and early 1950s, several of those industrial models for presenting its work were already well entrenched and familiar to SF audiences. At this time the radio was still the key domestic form of entertainment, and since the mid-1930s the radio industry had found some success in presenting SF scripts on the popular anthology-type shows that dominated much of radio broadcasting in that era. These programs were each essentially unique broadcasts, as each week (and in some cases several times a week) a live cast, with the aid of music and sound effects, would dramatize a new story, typically adapted from a novel or short story. Easily the most famous case of such an anthology-type SF broadcast was Orson Welles' adaptation of H. G. Wells' *The War of the Worlds*, done for his *Mercury Theater on the Air* program in 1938. Presented on Halloween and amidst the ongoing war rumblings in Europe, this show touched popular anxieties, inciting a public panic in some areas and a subsequent media uproar. In the process it not only demonstrated the potential power of SF in the media, but also showed that there was indeed an adult audience for SF programming. The reception for this sort of sporadic anthologizing of SF would eventually make possible more specialized shows in the 1940s and 1950s, series like *Suspense* (1940–62) and *Inner Sanctum* (1941–52), that were devoted to the fantastic in its various forms, and eventually dedicated SF radio series such as the tellingly titled *Beyond Tomorrow* (1950), *2000 Plus* (1950–52), and *Dimension X* (1950–51).

All of these early anthology shows employed a generally similar format, offering an atmospheric introduction that established the mysterious, fantastic, or science fictional context for the ensuing narrative, while the stories themselves, whether written expressly for the radio or adapted from previously published work, tended to be highly dramatic in nature, were typically salted with elaborate and atmospheric sound effects, and often provided an ironic or twist conclusion. Yet within this simple format, anthology radio provided for a great deal of flexibility and even sophistication, since each episode could open new doors for listeners, introduce new characters and situations, and give opportunities to some of the leading SF writers of the period, including Isaac Asimov, Ray Bradbury, Frederik Pohl, Robert Heinlein, and Clifford Simak, most of whom would eventually find similar opportunities in television. In fact, one of those writers, Theodore Sturgeon, would help develop one of the earliest television anthology shows, *Tales of Tomorrow*, in 1951.

With this format already in place and with an audience for such programming well established, it was only natural that television would readily adopt the anthology approach. Thus, as we noted in Chapter 1, several of the first efforts at an adult-oriented SFTV followed this pattern, shows like *Out There* and *Tales of Tomorrow*, and it would remain a major component of American SF programming for several decades thanks to such popular programs as *Science Fiction Theatre*, *The Twilight Zone*, *The Outer Limits*, *Night Gallery*, and *Ray Bradbury Theater*. However, a more recent effort to revisit this format in the Syfy Channel's series *Welcome to Paradox* (1998) lasted just thirteen episodes. All of these series would draw effectively on the chief attractions of this format, particularly its capacity for *variety* and its outright sense of *difference*. For each episode, much like a short story found in one of the popular SF magazines of the day, was something quite new, and apart from the recurring and typically atmospheric introductory commentary by the likes of Truman Bradley (*Science Fiction Theatre*), Rod Serling (*The Twilight Zone*, *Night Gallery*), and Vic Perrin (*The Outer Limits*), each required that the audience immerse itself in a process of cognitive orientation and mapping: finding its way in whatever mysterious situation was being presented and trying to understand what—if any—laws governed this realm, this time.

The anthology shows' narrators only underscored this audience task— and pleasure—by reminding viewers that these strange experiences and these other worlds were indeed different from their everyday reality. The attraction was fairly obvious, for each show suggested at its start—and often underscored the point at the end, as a kind of *coda*—that there were indeed special thrills and/or pleasures to be found in exploring that sense of difference, in experiencing the new, the unknown, or "outer limits" of our world. In this way the anthology shows were just drawing upon— and underscoring—a key element of the genre's lure, offering audiences a format equivalent for what Brooks Landon has described as SF's inherent "agenda of change" (7), although in truth much of their appeal also lay in their ability to provide audiences with the simple *frissons* that were not to be found in most other television programming of the time.

However, two other formats were—and have remained—more dominant, both of which mined another sort of attraction, that of familiarity or continuity. Both serials and series had a long tradition in literature, radio, and film, and while the SF subject matter on which they drew for their stories provided some of that sense of difference noted above, they sought to frame that sensibility in a known context by providing viewers with a stable narrative base of characters, situations, and ongoing story arcs. The serial form (or chapter play), particularly as it had become well known in the movies during the 1930s and 1940s through films such as *Flash Gordon* (1936), *Captain America* (1944), and *King of the Rocket Men* (1949), offered a limited narrative arc, one typically defined by accomplishing some fantastic feat or defeating a mysterious enemy, as when Flash Gordon must thwart Ming the Merciless' plans to invade the Earth. While each episode would bring a new and exciting challenge or menace, the events were very much the same from one episode to another and usually involved fistfights, chases, and a seemingly deadly end for the hero or one of his or her friends—thus allowing each episode to end with a cliffhanger or suspended menace, from which the imperiled figure would, at the next episode's start, miraculously escape so that the narrative process could then begin again. Usually moving along at a fast pace (to help distract from the sameness of the episodes), serials were exciting and at times surprising—since often the villain's identity was a mystery throughout the narrative—while allowing audiences the comfort of knowing that their overall narrative arc would end satisfactorily.

As noted in Chapter 1, film serials were among the first properties of the film industry to be sold to television as programming, either as stand-alone television shows or, as *Captain Video* demonstrated, as material that could be incorporated into another show. But that format also provided a useful and proven narrative model for the television industry as it sought to create new programs. Thus, a number of serials were adapted as television shows—*Flash Gordon* (1954–55), *Buck Rogers* (1950–51), *Commando Cody* (1955)—while others would adopt to one degree or another the basic principles of serial storytelling, such as short but complete narrative arcs, physical action (in place of the more expensive special effects), cliffhanger situations to link episodes, and so forth. While far less given to action or visual spectacle than any film serial, largely because of its small budget, *Captain Video* relied heavily on serial principles and, thanks to its popularity, would become the only early television space opera to make the journey to the big screen when it was adapted to a film serial as *Captain Video, Master of the Stratosphere* (1951). *Rocky Jones, Space Ranger* would also follow the serial format, with most of its stories unreeling as three-chapter arcs. Later, the most successful of all SF shows, the British *Doctor Who* (which ran regularly on American television starting in the early 1970s), also adopted this narrative approach, although its narrative arcs would vary in episode numbers, depending on the complexity of the story, and physical action was largely replaced by dialogue. Irwin Allen's *Lost in Space* (1965–68) too would follow this general pattern, but with a far higher budget and more emphasis on special effects and various sorts of monsters or aliens. While the serial model allowed for a degree of narrative flexibility, as a full story could be played out in some complexity over multiple weeks, when followed too slavishly it has tended, much like its cinematic kin, to descend into formulaic story-telling and repetitious action, and as a consequence it has had little presence in contemporary SFTV.

Rather, the long-running series with its emphasis on stand-alone episodes, suggesting the continuing adventures or encounters of a set of familiar characters, has become the dominant industrial format for SFTV. To sketch the nature of this familiar approach, we might turn to John Ellis' influential explanation of television aesthetics, in which he sought to differentiate between cinematic and televisual narrative:

> Broadcast TV narration has a . . . dispersed narrational form: it is extensive rather than sequential. Its characteristic mode is not one of final closure or totalizing vision; rather, it offers a continuous refiguration of events. Like the news bulletin series, the broadcast TV narrative . . . is open-ended, providing a continuous update, a perpetual return to the present. Since closure and finality [sic] is not a central feature . . . it follows that the hermetic nature of the cinema narrative, with its patterns of repetition and novelty, is also absent.
>
> (*Visible* 147)

He adds that the typical series does depend on one sort of repetition, "the repetition of a problematic" (154), that is, it will repeat from week to week (or episode to episode)—and draw a large part of its narrative complexity out of—a particular situation, ongoing event, or case of character conflict, as in the series *Revolution*'s ongoing efforts at discovering why the power has gone out all over the world. Furthermore, these elements of extensiveness, continuity, openness, and recurrence are bound to a "segmented" presentation because of the usual (in the case of broadcast or network presentation) industrial requirement for commercial breaks and, as Ellis argues, because of the different sort of "attention span that TV assumes of its audience" (148). The result is that while each episode of a series typically functions in a stand-alone fashion and provides its audience with a level of satisfaction in that mode, its narrative is geared to a number of segmented beats or emphases per episode that have a somewhat similar function to the serial cliffhanger, as a plot segment reaches a point of anticipation that is typically postponed by a commercial break.

As an example of these characteristics, we might consider an episode from one of the most influential of SFTV series, *Star Trek*. "The Corbomite Maneuver," a first-season show broadcast on November 10, 1966, and written by veteran television scriptwriter Jerry Sohl, details an encounter between the starship *Enterprise* as it is mapping an unexplored section of the galaxy and a massive and powerful alien spacecraft. An introductory segment shows First Officer Spock and a junior officer going about the routine activity of "star mapping" when suddenly an unknown, cube-shaped object comes directly at them and blocks their path. Unable to maneuver around the massive object, Spock orders an emergency alert and calls Captain Kirk to the bridge; and on this point of obvious emergency, the narrative breaks for a title sequence, cast credits, and brief commercial. A second narrative beat begins with a serial-like reprise of what has happened, delivered by Kirk in voice-over, through the narrative device of one of his entries in "the Captain's log," as he explains that he was in sick-bay undergoing his annual check-up. That scene, shown in flash-back, puts Kirk's physical nature on display, as we see him shirtless, pedaling a device, and working up a sweat, prior to grabbing a towel and moving swiftly—but still shirtless—towards the bridge when he is summoned. After assessing the situation and making several unsuccessful attempts to break away from the alien object, Kirk orders the Enterprise's phasers to fire, which results in a violent explosion and another narrative break. That melodramatic and explosive suspension of events results in the next narrative beat starting with another pay-off commentary, as Kirk takes stock in another log entry, noting "the cube has been destroyed, the ship's damage minor," and assessing his next line of action. When an even larger object appears, locks the Enterprise in a tractor beam, and announces it will destroy the starship, Kirk reassures his crew and attempts to communicate with the object. The monstrous alien face that appears on the ship's viewing screen notes that the Enterprise will be destroyed in several minutes, and on that point of impending, seemingly inevitable doom another break occurs.

The following segment begins with Kirk and Spock discussing their dire situation, as Spock notes that they have apparently been "checkmated" and that he can offer "no logical alternative." With a reference to the game of poker, Kirk then plays a bluff, telling the alien that the Enterprise incorporates the element "Corbomite" that ensures the destruction of any attacking force, and challenging the alien to strike. While the bluff postpones the ship's destruction, this segment again concludes with the Enterprise in danger, as another ship begins towing it to a planet where it will be destroyed and the crew interned. While the Enterprise manages to escape the towship, Kirk learns that the stresses of breaking free have damaged the alien ship, but rather than escape, he determines to follow his prime directive, "to seek out and contact alien life," and so boards the alien vessel to try to help those on board. Once there, he finds that the monstrous face they have seen was just that of a dummy and that the alien himself is a small, child-like figure who was testing their intentions with a distress call. On this note of relief and even fellowship—as the alien observes, they are "very much alike"—the episode concludes with a shot of the Enterprise moving through space, continuing its mission.

Each narrative segment, as we have noted, is a carefully developed piece of action, yet also one that anticipates something more to come, in fact, linking to that something more with a suggestion of danger or even destruction and providing an immediate pay-off as the next beat begins. Giving importance to these beats are the characters and situation with which the audience is already familiar—Kirk, Spock, the other crew members, and the general exploratory mission of the *Enterprise*. And all of these beats serve the presentation of what Ellis terms the "problematics" of the series, that is, the ongoing issues with which audiences were already familiar: how will the *Enterprise* crew, especially Captain Kirk and Spock, work together to meet the challenges of space; how might Kirk outwit a technologically superior alien culture; how can communication and peaceful relations triumph over hostility and a common suspicion of others (and of *otherness*)? The repetition of such problematics, as well as the variation on their solution, provides one of the constant sources of both interest and pleasure for the audience, as does the rather open-ended return to exploration on which this episode concludes, as it reminds viewers, often through another log entry, that this sort of satisfying experience can be reprised in a subsequent episode.

STORY TYPES

Like the anthology show and the serial, the long-form series, which has become the dominant form for SFTV, draws much of its narrative shape—and satisfaction—from the industrial imperatives of broadcast television. All of these forms draw on earlier models (from other industries) with which audiences were already familiar, thanks to literary, radio, and filmic forebears, while they have also adapted those models to the conditions surrounding television production, presentation, and viewing, that is, to the imperatives of such things as standardized time segments, limited budgets, commercial breaks, and patterns of viewer attention, particularly as they became standardized in the early rise of television during the 1950s and 1960s. Yet most of what we have been describing does not speak directly to these shows' science fictional character, and thus to their special generic appeal. To address that other level of narrative, we need to consider the types of stories that have dominated most of SFTV, that recur across forms like the anthology, serial, and series, and that exercise their own lure on audiences, providing them with different versions of that *sense of wonder* that has so often been described as the true appeal of SF throughout its various media manifestations.

Working on the basis of subject matter, SF historian Edward James has identified three broad types of tales that have largely dominated the genre, or as he puts it, "determined membership" in it: "the extraordinary voyage," "the tale of the future," and "the tale of science" (*Science Fiction* 13). While acknowledging that "there are numerous cases of overlap" and that these titles refer more to subject categories than to distinct narrative forms (13), James manages to provide us with a useful start to considering the science fictional dimension of our television narratives. For while each of these categories attempts to name what a story is *about*—and how that *about*-ness makes it science fictional—each also, at some level, implicates a certain kind of story-telling. For example, in the extraordinary voyage story, whether the trip is under the sea (as in *Voyage to the Bottom of the Sea*), through time (as in *The Time Tunnel*), across the universe (as in *Stargate SG-1*), or to another dimension (as in *Fringe*), the narrative is typically structured around the events of that travel, or at least, given the episodic nature of most SFTV, around a singular event (Figure 2.1).

A tale of the future, as James observes, often involves the discovery of some utopian, dystopian, or apocalyptic world (as depicted in shows like *Babylon 5*, *Logan's Run*, and *Jericho*). Such shows usually build their stories around the exploration of various dimensions of those futuristic worlds and commonly involve the revelation or stark recognition of how some facet of that world parallels our own world or its conditions. The tale of science, concerned with marvelous inventions or discoveries, would not seem to lend itself readily to any sort of prescriptive structure. Yet shows as varied as *Eureka* (perhaps the most obvious tale of science), *Warehouse 13*, *The Six Million*

Figure 2.1 The technological "extraordinary voyage": the futuristic submarine *Seaview* surfaces in Irwin Allen's *Voyage to the Bottom of the Sea*

Dollar Man, and *Roswell* do at least hint otherwise, as they each week explore either a new or recurring consequence of a specific invention/discovery or, as is the strength of both *Eureka* and *Warehouse* 13, confront their continuing cast of characters with some new invention/discovery that they must cope with or corral. Thus in *Eureka*'s final episode one character fittingly notes, "Wow! Wormholes, cyborgs, endless possibility. No wonder you guys love this place." In effect, these categories not only help us to see the science fictional character of many series, but they also imply a certain narrative trajectory for their shows.

Elsewhere, and in trying to approach the cinematic forms of the genre, I have suggested that we might adopt another approach to SF narrative, particularly that provided by the critic Tzvetan Todorov in his discussion of fantasy narratives (Telotte, *Science Fiction Film*). For Todorov not only recognized that SF readily sits within the realm of fantasy, but also argued that the character of fantasy resides just as much in its "syntax," that is, in its form, as in the *things* on which it focuses—and which James' categories tend to emphasize. Thus he reminds that, in approaching the fantastic text, "we are concerned here as well to describe a configuration" as we are "to name a meaning" (*The Fantastic* 95), as fantasy in its various forms always implicates certain structures. Even as he identifies three distinct categories of fantasy—the *marvelous*, the *fantastic* proper, and the *uncanny*—then, Todorov also sets about explaining how each typically functions as a narrative principle. The marvelous, as he says, "corresponds to an unknown phenomenon" (42), to that which contravenes our normal laws of reality and requires that they be revisioned—as would be the case in any alien encounter. The uncanny tale emphasizes the mind's ability to produce seemingly inexplicable events—and thus the mind's own power to construct, explain, or alter reality. The fantastic proper is in effect an intersection of these other modes, a story whose very focus is on what he terms a "hesitation" (41) between the seemingly inexplicable and the psychological projection, between a strangeness that exists "out there" and an equally unsettling strangeness that exists within the self. And all three modes posit a challenge to the status quo, resulting in a narrative that typically introduces something or some event "which cannot be explained by the laws of this . . . familiar world" (25), involves the investigation or exploration of that phenomenon, and details its effects, either temporarily or permanently, on our "familiar world." Or as he more simply describes, all involve an equilibrium that is upset, resulting in a state of disequilibrium, which is then countered to produce a new, but different equilibrium.

While Todorov's discussion is not concerned with SF proper, his categorizations—much like James'—can be useful for differentiating between the various sorts of stories that crowd the world of contemporary SFTV and for better understanding how those stories work upon us. To these ends it might be helpful to consider how several shows might be approached from the vantage of this conceptual framework.

The Marvelous Tale

One of the more popular space-oriented series, *Farscape* begins from the premise that an American astronaut John Crichton, in attempting to prove his theory about super-speed flight, is shot through a wormhole in space and exits, as he says at the start of each episode, "in some distant part of the universe." In the course of this extraordinary voyage type of story Crichton encounters bizarre life forms (including the living space ship *Moya* and a humanoid plant species exemplified by a fellow traveler Zhaan), he finds himself in the middle of interstellar warfare, he becomes the subject of various experiments, including the implantation of a neural clone; and he quickly learns what it is like to be considered an "alien," an intruder, and a guinea pig for experimentation. While constantly trying, as he says, simply "to get back home," Crichton is forced to measure both his sense of self and "home" against this always new and indeed *marvelous* world, resulting, as Jes Battis describes it, in a process of learning "to question just who the 'aliens' are in this story, and, by extension, to question and explore the multiple versions of humanity available to him" (3) (Figure 2.2). The result is a continuing narrative that, in the best tradition of the marvelous, forces both the audience and Crichton, who is situated as the embodiment of our point of view, to confront a very different version of the universe—a difference effectively embodied in the use of sophisticated muppets, created by co-producer Brian Henson, for the characters of Pilot and Rygel. That "new" universe is also driven by rather different impulses (as in the series' sense

Figure 2.2 John Crichton tries to map the "marvelous" world of *Farscape*

that there are multiple realities), and in the face of its apparently infinite variety, humanity represents only a very minor and not-very-well-thought-of race.

Yet precisely because of its *marvelous* thrust, *Farscape* insists on bringing the impact of Crichton's (and our) confrontation with this universe to bear on our previously limited laws of reality. Thus it presents us in each episode with new languages and new challenges to communication—challenges that Crichton meets by constantly picking up new words (such as "arn," "frell," and "microt") that become part of his regular vocabulary and that demonstrate the ability to adapt to others and become a part of other cultures. It offers a very different vision of sexuality and sexual identity, not only through a character like Zhaan who is both a plant-species and someone with a reputation for, as the character D'Argo notes, "a very flexible morality," but also through the female Peacekeeper Aeryn Sun, who is stronger than her eventual mate Crichton and sees sexual activity as essentially a "recreational" thing; through Chiana who, as Battis offers, apparently "operates on the pleasure principle," freely using sex "to escape potentially threatening situations" (33) and to express her feelings at any given moment; and even through Crichton himself and his "unstable masculinity"

(Battis 68), which often has him crying, being comforted by both males and females, and admitting his weaknesses. And *Farscape* continually interrogates a traditional sense of nationality, particularly when, in the initial episode, Aeryn resists joining with the crew of *Moya* because of her identity as a Peacekeeper, only to be told by Crichton that "You can be more!", and when Crichton rejects his father's urging to give his knowledge about wormholes and possible wormhole weaponry to the United States for "defensive" purposes, and instead rejoins his companions on *Moya*. As Jan Johnson-Smith nicely observes, *Farscape* repeatedly demonstrates—especially in those episodes wherein Crichton manages to return briefly to his home planet—that "no one on Earth has any concept of the 'bigger picture,'" that is, the universe (165). It is this sort of understanding that *Farscape* and similar series, through their *marvelous* pattern, provide audiences, thereby prompting them to think more carefully about the "laws" or "rules" that control much of our lives, in effect, limiting our very notion of what constitutes our reality.

The Uncanny Tale

As an example of an *uncanny* narrative we might consider a more recent— and ultimately less successful—series, Joss Whedon's *Dollhouse* (2009–10). Broadcast for just two abbreviated seasons, the show chronicles the activities at a secret Los Angeles "Dollhouse," a private facility run by a world-wide medical research corporation that houses human "dolls," individuals whose original memories have been erased and replaced with programmed personalities. The Dollhouse "rents" out these operatives (or Actives, as they are termed) to wealthy clients or companies, who use them as they see fit: for romantic/sexual engagements, for bodyguards or companions, for criminal activities, for undercover investigations, and so forth. Many of the episodes simply focus on this base activity, that is, on how one of the various Actives at the Dollhouse is programmed to be someone else and thus to live out a dangerous and kind of ghostly existence, one in which her or his real personality always seems to be struggling to the surface or the memory imprint proves faulty. Other episodes translate this same schizophrenic play to a larger, cultural level of action and concealment, as FBI agent Paul Ballard investigates rumors of the Dollhouse's existence, while the facility's staff tries to maintain its shadowy status by keeping the Actives under control, by dealing with a rogue Active, Alpha, who has been imprinted with forty-eight personalities and is using his/their skills to kill other Actives, and by working to thwart a Senate investigation of the parent corporation's imprinting technology. In every instance, the real focus is on the potentially destructive relationship between a new, mind-altering technology and the psyche—a relationship that holds out the promise of easy knowledge and exciting experiences through mental programming, but at the cost of thought manipulation, behavioral conditioning, and ultimately a complete surrender of the self, imaged in the series' conclusion wherein the mind-wiping technology has become widespread, producing a population of virtual and uncontrollable zombies.

While the central science fictional aspect of *Dollhouse*, that mind-wiping, mind-altering technology and its uncontrolled use, is not (quite) part of our contemporary experience, its speculated existence does not really challenge or overturn any of our laws of reality. Rather, it simply extrapolates from ongoing research in mind control, developments in artificial intelligence, and a cultural tendency to abdicate from moral responsibility. In fact, that is part of the power of this series—its ability to seem so much a part of our world, and its troubling developments to seem like a very possible result of current technological and cultural trends. As Todorov explains, a natural thrust of such uncanny narratives is always the development of what he terms "themes of the self" (107), and here, thanks to the focus on mind control and an almost willing self-enslavement, a host of such "themes" are explored: the all-too-easy objectification of the self, the ethical implications of human experimentation, the extent to which the self is always a construct of various forces, even the very nature of human consciousness. Focusing on the increasingly precarious state of the mind in a postmodern, technological society, *Dollhouse* well illustrates the appeal of such uncanny SFTV, although its relatively short lifespan might also suggest the difficulty in sustaining those sorts of uncomfortable investigations.

The Fantastic Tale

To illustrate the workings of a fantastic text—that is, one that operates between the realms of the marvelous and the uncanny, effectively linking them—I would like to turn to one of our most popular SF series, *Lost*. Running from 2004 to 2010, *Lost* is a show that won numerous awards, including an Emmy for Outstanding Drama Series, a Golden Globe Award for Best Drama Series, and a Saturn Award from the Academy of Science Fiction, Fantasy, and Horror Films. It also built a large fan base, and prompted a number of popular and academic studies, but it has confounded many commentators who struggled to fit it into a generic niche. For its central plot line about the crash of an Oceanic Airlines flight on an unknown tropical island and the struggles of its various survivors to deal with life in a primitive environment, the appearance of a hostile group of other inhabitants (known as "The Others"), the discovery of a mysterious scientific research project on the island, the appearance of rescuers who are not really rescuers, and the strange disappearances and reappearances of members of the group all result in a narrative that is full of mysteries and marvels, but they do not necessarily add up to SF, nor do they—*necessarily*—radically upset our view of reality. In fact, much of what occurs in the series could well be interpreted as the traumatic interpretations of different characters, individual or group hallucinations prompted by this calamitous event that has left them all so totally "lost." Yet the island does seem to produce miraculous recoveries from injury and illness; the mysterious "hatch" that is discovered hints of great destructive powers that might be unleashed (including the ability to knock planes out of the sky); there is a "smoke monster" that—sort of—manifests itself at various times, and there are numerous instances of time travel, to the past, to the future, and to a parallel time/reality (Figure 2.3). All are elements that might well seem at home in any SF narrative, and together with a larger mythic thrust that repeatedly surfaces in the story, they do challenge our worldview, as well as that of the survivors, leaving us, at various times, also cognitively "lost."

What I am describing, of course, is a work that puzzles and frustrates precisely because we, like so many of the series' critics and commentators, want to fit things into a simple category, want to *explain* it. But like other texts of the fantastic proper—and we might especially point to a similar show like *The X-Files* with its often repeated and very telling tag line, "The truth is out there"—*Lost* resolutely remains *speculative* and indeed derives much of its appeal from the sense that there does remain more "out there," more to be

Figure 2.3 The "fantastic" realm of *Lost*: investigating the mysterious metal hatch

accounted for, more to be learned. On no firmer ground than the characters in the series, the audience needs to find its own way off of this puzzle of an island. Thus throughout the series' run the characters, our stand-ins, engage in the key activity of any truly fantastic text, the exploration and attempted explanation of what *might be*. But it is this effort that empowers a number of series that Lincoln Geraghty sees as fundamentally reflective of the contemporary cultural climate, series that are "infused with a sense of unease—the audience doesn't know and cannot guess the outcome of stories, and it is as if the writers and producers don't really know either" (*American Science Fiction* 117). In short, the fantastic, with its various speculations on what might be, is more common than we might expect and seems very much a sign of our times.

Other Story Types

While these fantasy models can help us to isolate basic story concerns and better understand their appeal, critics also frequently refer to other types of SF narrative, generally drawn from earlier literary models, that we have already mentioned in passing and that merit further discussion. Certainly the most popular of these, as its dominance of the first wave of SFTV in the 1950s suggests, is the *space opera*. Drawing on the early stories of Hugo

Gernsback, E. E. "Doc" Smith, and Edmond Hamilton, the space opera—a term that points both, disparagingly, towards the "horse opera" or hackneyed Western, and, hyperbolically, towards the overblown situations of "grand opera"—is essentially about daring exploits in space, often with the fate of entire worlds in the balance. While it frequently has an almost epic feel, as is clearly the case with a series like the recent *Battlestar Galactica*, it is also often patterned along familiar storylines; as Gary Westfahl observes, because of its usual emphasis on our encounter with the vastness of space, space opera narratives have typically drawn from "genres dealing with frontiers, such as the ocean, criminal underworld, and Wild West to introduce the universe to readers in reassuring fashion" ("Space" 199). The flexibility that derives from this mixture is probably a large reason for its ability to generate new, popular series decade after decade, and for their ability to range from the melodramatic to the broadly comic, as evidence titles like *Star Trek*, *Buck Rogers in the 25th Century*, *Farscape*, *Enterprise*, *Battlestar Galactica*, *Blake's 7*, *Space: 1999*, *Babylon 5*, and *Red Dwarf*. Moreover, we should note that this story type benefits from media SF's emphasis on visual effects, so given the increasing availability of cheap digital effects, the space opera is likely to continue to have an influence on the growth of SFTV.

Another common story designation, already implicit in James' reference to "the tale of the future" and also subsumed in Todorov's category of the fantastic with its abiding concern with what *might be*, is the utopian/ dystopian narrative. It is a type of story with a long lineage, including as it does Plato's *Republic* of the fourth century BC, Sir Thomas More's *Utopia* of 1516, Tommaso Campanella's *The City of the Sun* of 1602, and Francis Bacon's *New Atlantis* of 1627—all works that predate what we generally think of as SF. Such narratives typically explore the possible shape of another, idealized culture, particularly emphasizing such elements as its architecture, science, economic and political structures, and general social dynamics (such as gender, racial, and familial relations), and that culture may be situated in some other, distant location, in another dimension, or, more commonly, in a far-off future. In fact, distance of one sort or another seems one of its prerequisites, for as Carl Freedman observes, in its positive form it usually designates an end point of development, "the promised land that can only be attained by means of exodus" from our current place, time, or situation (65).

In both film and television, though, the dystopian (or negative) version of such narratives has been more common, in part because it allows for more dramatic possibilities because of the conflicts that inevitably emerge between individuals and a society that seems to fall short of or even to repress their needs or desires. Among the key instances of such narratives on SFTV are *The Prisoner* (1967–68), *Planet of the Apes* (1974), *Logan's Run* (1977–78), *Earth 2* (1994–95), the anthology series *Welcome to Paradox* (1998), and *Revolution* (2012–present). Tellingly, few of these series have attained great popularity, even in the cases of shows like *Planet of the Apes* and *Logan's Run* that had the advantages of successful cinematic predecessors and the use of sets, costumes, and prosthetic effects from those originals. However, it is a type that also holds out much potential, since in this dystopian form—and the utopian to some extent—this sort of narrative allows for dramatizing and commenting upon the latest cultural concerns, as evidence a show such as *Revolution* with its explorations of what life might be like without the benefits of readily available power, and thus in a world where there are no buffers against the everyday stresses of climate, population growth, and the struggle for resources, including such givens as food and clean water.

An often allied but rather less common story type is that of the alternate history, that is, a tale in which, as Andy Duncan explains, "history as we know it is changed for dramatic and often ironic effect" (209). While not inherently science fictional, alternate histories draw upon many of the basic principles of SF. A key is their ability to highlight differences from the historical continuum with which we are familiar; another is their creation of a sense of wonder precisely through the highlighting of those differences. However, the alternate history is not common in SFTV, save for those "extraordinary voyage" series that are focused on time or dimensional travel—among them, *Doctor Who, Primeval* (2007–11), *The Time Tunnel* (1966–67), and *Fringe* (2008–13)—and that thus often put their characters in a position of influencing history or encountering another version of the self, acting in a different timeline. However, as Christine Mains has observed, a number of very popular SF series, such as *Star Trek: Deep Space Nine* (1993–99), *Smallville* (2001–11), and *Stargate Atlantis* (2004–09), have constructed episodes or whole story arcs around alternate histories, based on the dreams or hallucinations of central characters, all as part of the shows' larger emphasis on foregrounding "the impossible storyworlds of SFTV" and affirming their ability to "teach the viewing audience to question reality" (157). In fact, it is with this thrust, this fundamental note of interrogation, that the alternate history narrative probably best demonstrates its link to the science fictional, as well as its key attraction. For to derive satisfaction from such an episode, audiences must hold its events alongside their own understanding of the past or present and, like time or dimensional travelers themselves—or companions to the Doctor of *Doctor Who*—consider the implications of the differences they observe.

Finally, we should note that SFTV, for all of its seeming seriousness, has often adopted other modes, such as the comic. In fact, any survey of SFTV will find a number of successful SF situation comedies, parodies, and comic-themed narratives. Among them we might note *My Favorite Martian* (1963–66), *Mork and Mindy* (1978–82), *The Hitchhiker's Guide to the Galaxy* (1981), *3rd Rock from the Sun* (1996–2001), *Red Dwarf* (1988–93, 1997–99, 2009, 2012–13), as well as animated series like *The Jetsons* (1962–63, 1985–87), and *Futurama* (1999–2003, 2010–13). The lure of this combination for broadcast television is fairly obvious. As Lincoln Geraghty sums it up, network executives often calculate that "science fiction could reach a far wider audience by offering comic variations on typical generic tropes and settings such as aliens and the future" (*American Science Fiction* 61). That broadened appeal, though, comes at a price. We might note that while there are also many examples of comic literary SF, notably Douglas Adams' *Hitchhiker's Guide to the Galaxy* novels, Stanislaw Lem's comic robot stories, *Cyberiad*, and Harry Harrison's *Stainless Steel Rat* books, most histories of the genre generally avoid addressing this kind of hybrid. The problem is that, in its parodic mode, the comic SF tale often seems to be making fun of SF and that general sense of seriousness we have noted, as it sends up the many character types, stock motifs, and futuristic trappings on which the form has long drawn for its popularity. As a result, series in this vein also run the risk of turning off some of the usual SF audience.

Yet the tendency for SF to surface in a comic mode (or as some would put it, for comedy to adopt/adapt SF's trappings) speaks to both the popularity

Figure 2.4 SFTV in a comic mode: *My Favorite Martian*

of SF and its larger influence. Both *My Favorite Martian* (Figure 2.4) and *The Jetsons* would appear amidst the space race of the 1960s, along with *Lost in Space* (1965–68), which in its later run often centered its episodes on the comic machinations of the scientist Dr. Smith; all sought to capitalize on the audience's current fascination with space, science, and technology. But as the long-lived *Red Dwarf* and *Futurama* might attest, the general popularity of SF has simply made it a consistently useful platform for comic and satiric efforts. And indeed, part of that popularity has to do with our sense of the genre's serious purpose, an issue Brooks Landon has addressed in his description of SF as "the new realism of technological society" (xiii). As such, it constitutes one of our key tools for seeing our world—and *seeing through* its own convention-bound reality, even subverting that reality. It is, in essence, the same subversive impulse that is fundamental to the mission of comedy, as it constantly pokes holes in the conventional, challenging us to perceive our world differently. So a comic SF might be seen as tracing out the intersecting agendas of both comedy and SF by drawing on the strengths of both forms. In fact, that sense of intersecting agendas might help explain why so many of our SF series—*Doctor Who, Firefly, Farscape, Warehouse 13, Eureka*, and others—regularly, and quite successfully, incorporate comic elements and scenes into their episodes.

As a cap to this discussion, I would like to return to one of this chapter's starting points, the notion that SFTV narratives have to be considered from both industrial and aesthetic vantages. In a pioneering piece on television study, Jane Feuer observed that television genres "tend to be *historical*," that is, rather than following from a prescriptive notion of what constitutes a particular genre and how it should function, they have been more reliant on "industrial or common-sense usage" (115). Taking her lead, we have here noted a number of those industrial factors: scheduling blocks, commercial (or other) breaks in the time slot, viewer positioning, other media models—all of which impact how we can tell our stories. But we have also spent considerable time outlining how SF narratives might be categorized, in terms of subjects, the mechanisms of fantasy, and certain familiar story types, usually based in an earlier literature. Working in a "common-sense" fashion, as Feuer suggests, we can use all of these descriptions and categories to help us better understand not only how SFTV tells its stories, but also how those stories work so effectively upon us, that is, how they help to satisfy what Michele Pierson has described as our "cultural demand for the aesthetic experience of wonder" (168).

KEY SERIES: *THE TWILIGHT ZONE* AND THE PLASTIC ANTHOLOGY MODE

As this book's Introduction suggested, *The Twilight Zone* has arguably been one of the most influential series in the history of SFTV. That influence, at least partially measured through its five-year initial run, subsequent revivals in 1985–89 and 2002–03, and its adaptation as a feature film, speaks to a number of the show's hallmarks: the scripts produced by such important writers as Richard Matheson, Charles Beaumont, and producer/writer Rod Serling himself; the contributions of established film stars like Burgess Meredith, Agnes Morehead, and James Whitmore, as well as such relative newcomers as William Shatner, Inger Stevens, and James Coburn; the recruiting of talented film directors, including John Brahm, Mitch Leisen, and Jacques Tourneur; and its polished, expensive look as a result of being shot on film and with all of the resources to be found at the MGM studio. Just as significant, though, was *The Twilight Zone*'s anthology mode, an approach that gave the series great narrative flexibility, allowing it to explore a wide variety of story types, while also demonstrating—to audiences, sponsors, critics, and network executives—the SF genre's own flexibility and its potential for addressing a broad range of popular concerns.

Of course, neither the genre nor Serling was a stranger to the anthology format. Starting in the 1920s, the SF pulp magazines, most notably *Amazing Stories*, *Astounding Stories*, and *Wonder Stories*, regularly offered readers a variety of new stories and reprints of classic tales by Jules Verne, Edgar Allen Poe, H. G. Wells, and others. And by the mid-1930s SF narratives had begun appearing on many of radio's popular dramatic anthology programs, perhaps most memorably on Orson Welles' *Mercury Theater on the Air*, which featured the panic-inducing adaptation of H. G. Wells' *The War of the Worlds*. The 1940s and 1950s would see a proliferation of fantasy-specific anthology shows being produced for the radio, including *Inner Sanctum*, *Escape*, and *Beyond Tomorrow*—all of which would soon find their first television counterparts in such series as *Tales of Tomorrow* (1951–53), a live dramatic show that offered adaptations of classic SF mixed with contemporary tales, and *Out There* (1951–52), an anthology show that featured the work of well-known SF writers, including Ray Bradbury, Robert A. Heinlein, and Theodore Sturgeon. However, the more significant kinship for a series like *The Twilight Zone* was the serious dramatic anthology, as embodied in such critically praised programs as *Fireside Theater* (1949–58), *Kraft Television Theatre* (1947–58), *Playhouse 90* (1956–60), and *The United States Steel Hour* (1953–63). For here not only did writer/producer Rod Serling first air his own acclaimed stories "Patterns" (*Kraft Television Theatre*, 1955), "The Rack" (*United States Steel Hour*, 1958), and "Requiem for a Heavyweight" (*Playhouse 90*, 1956), but he also located a format through which SF could reach a mainstream audience and be taken seriously.

By the time that Serling launched *The Twilight Zone* in 1959, the dramatic anthology show had clearly established itself as one of the most popular television types of the era, as well as a primary source for sophisticated television entertainment. And as Mark Alvey has chronicled, by the late 1950s the major ratings services had begun "offering demographic breakdowns" of television audiences to broadcasters, with the result that "the networks were gaining a growing appreciation of reaching the 'right' audience in prime time" (19). What Serling offered to the CBS network in 1959 was an interesting combination that might capitalize on that information, for his series' focus on fantasy and SF promised to attract a fairly young and increasingly affluent audience, while its format, his own critical standing, and a promise of other top talent being involved would allow it to compete with the popular live drama anthology shows. Moreover, that anthology format would set in motion the exploration of a broad spectrum of narrative possibilities, with scripts ranging across all varieties of the SF genre: space adventures, utopias/dystopias, alien encounters and alien invasions, time and dimensional travel, tales of extraordinary technology, alternate worlds, as well as comic takes on conventional SF forms. As Horace Newcomb neatly sums it up, The Twilight Zone "as narrative was open to a huge range of topics and plot configurations" (296), and thus to a correspondingly large potential audience.

To understand the series' place in the development of SFTV, we might do well to consider it from this vantage of narrative possibility. By framing it in the context of Raymond Williams' notion that broadcast television consists of a kind of "flow" of programs that often seem to blur together (91), and Jeffrey Sconce's suggestion that The Twilight Zone represented the "perverse 'unconscious' of television" (134), we can gain a better appreciation of its story-telling accomplishment. As much as any series, The Twilight Zone's distinctive character owes much to the way it embodies the spirit of television, with its many types of narratives all bound together within what Sconce evocatively terms "an occult space" (135), one in which each show was discretely marked off by Rod Serling's opening narrative and the episode's typical twist endings, but also easily dissolved into the "flow" of programming, the televisual collective "unconscious" wherein different narrative forms all seem to dissolve into the larger media experience, or in this case the larger SFTV experience.

As an example of this effect, we might briefly consider The Twilight Zone's special take on a familiar sort of narrative that had previously dominated SF programming, the space adventure. Five episodes, "And When the Sky

Was Opened" (Dec. 11, 1959), "Third from the Sun" (Jan. 8, 1960), "I Shot an Arrow into the Air" (Jan. 15, 1960), "The Little People" (Mar. 30, 1962), and "Probe 7, Over and Out" (Nov. 29, 1963), all scripted by Serling, involve various groups of intrepid space explorers. Their adventures typically involve them in discovering other worlds, even other races; several depict a desperate struggle for survival, while two others describe the possibility for escaping from the problems of Earth and starting life over on another world. And the props in several of these (and other) shows—space suits, ray guns, and spaceship models—were taken from MGM's lavish cinematic space opera, *Forbidden Planet* (1956). Yet that adventuring plot is invariably brought up short, and the grand scale of the universe becomes a kind of bounded nutshell, as the spacemen find themselves back where they started in "I Shot an Arrow into the Air"; on another planet named "Earth" that seems primed to repeat humanity's history in "Third from the Sun" and "Probe 7, Over and Out"; or doomed by events and forces beyond their control in "And When the Sky Was Opened" and "The Little People." The familiar story has, very simply, been defamiliarized by binding it up with the sort of inner explorations of inevitable human faults and cultural failings that were the stock-in-trade of the dramatic anthology shows on which Serling had first made his reputation.

Reversing that narrative direction, and working more clearly in the mode of what we have termed the marvelous narrative, *The Twilight Zone* frequently offered stories about aliens coming to Earth. Episodes such as "The Monsters are Due on Maple Street" (Mar. 4, 1960), "The Invaders" (Jan. 27, 1961), "Will the Real Martian Please Stand Up?" (May 26, 1961), "The Gift" (Apr. 27, 1962), and "Black Leather Jackets" (Jan. 31, 1964)—among others—recall one of the era's most popular story types, the alien invasion narrative, as seen in feature films like *Invaders from Mars* (1953), *It Conquered the World* (1956), *War of the Worlds* (1956), and *Invasion of the Saucer Men* (1957). However, in every instance *The Twilight Zone* revisions the cinema's generally formulaic approach to such narratives. In his survey of the alien invasion film, Patrick Lucanio describes the relatively common pattern found in these films: there is a report "of a sighting" or "unusual occurrence," an "alien invader makes its presence known by waging war—in most cases against society," but a "strong leader" comes forward, and "a battle is fought and society eventually emerges victorious" over the invaders (25). Such an easy, even archetypal formula, though, is nowhere to be found in these Twilight Zone episodes. In fact, we seldom glimpse aliens, and when we do they seem almost indistinguishable from humans, looking like a typical businessman (but with a third arm hidden beneath his trenchcoat) in "Will the Real Martian Please Stand Up?", like motorcycle-riding teenagers in "Black Leather Jackets," and just like us in "The Monsters are Due on Maple Street." In "The Gift" the alien "invader" is killed by frightened villagers as he tries to present them with a peace offering, a formula for a vaccine that will cure all cancers, and in "The Invaders" we turn out to be the alien invaders who make the mistake of landing on a planet of giants.

Of course, the series does not paint all extraterrestrials as benevolent, peace seeking, or human looking; to do so would have been as badly calculated and simplistic as was the case with the bulk of our SF invasion films. But while The Twilight Zone does craft some narratives that reflect the cultural paranoia of the era, they are typically episodes that turn upon—and hold up for examination—our own human weaknesses and prejudices. "To Serve Man" (Mar. 2, 1962), for example, recounts how humans eagerly sign up to visit the alien planet of the Kanamits, which has been depicted as a paradise—a place of unlimited resources, advanced technology, and peace. But as the first ship of humans prepares to leave for the alien world, a code breaker discovers that a book entitled To Serve Man, misplaced by one of the nine-foot-tall Kanamits, is in fact a cook book, and that those so eager for the good life to be found on Kanamit are simply destined for the aliens' menu. Perhaps the best illustration of the series' revisioning of the alien invasion narrative, though, can be seen in another Serling-scripted episode, "The Monsters are Due on Maple Street." In this episode a mysterious sound, a fleeting image of something in the sky, and a sudden black out of all electrical power disrupt a normal afternoon in a sleepy, middle-class neighborhood and lead the people to fear that aliens have landed nearby. Normally friendly people begin to suspect that their neighbors are, in fact, an invasion vanguard of aliens, and panic ensues with people reaching for weapons and attacking each other. A concluding scene, shot from a hill looking down on the panic on Maple Street, shows that two aliens are indeed manipulating the electricity and looking on with great satisfaction at the chaos they have created, as one notes how these humans, when under pressure, "pick the most dangerous enemy they can find, and it's themselves." That coda precisely sums up the thrust of The Twilight Zone's various versions of alien invasion, as it suggests that we often are our own worst enemies, while also urging us to a higher degree of humanity.

However, the series probably had a greater impact not through its traditional SF concerns with space travel, other worlds, or aliens, but rather with its unsettling narratives in the fantastic register, stories that seem to correspond directly to the voice-over introduction with which Serling began each episode:

> There is a fifth dimension, beyond that which is known to man. . . . It is the middle ground between light and shadow, between science and superstition, and it lies between the pit of man's fears and the summit of his knowledge. This is the dimension of the imagination. It is an area which we call the Twilight Zone.

As we earlier noted, fantastic narratives are precisely those that occupy a "middle ground," as they recount strange events that might emanate from the human mind or that might evidence some inexplicable external power. As examples, we might consider two of the series' best-known episodes, "A World of His Own" (July 1, 1960) and "Nightmare at 20,000 Feet" (Oct. 11, 1963), for each presents us with the sort of unsettling combination that we have previously described as a strangeness that seems to exist "out there" and an equally disturbing strangeness emerging from within the self.

"A World of His Own" tells of a playwright, Gregory West, who believes that he is able to bring to life any character he describes on his dictation machine—and to eliminate that character by cutting and destroying the part of the tape on which he or she is described. The notion seems very much like a writer's conceit, a way of explaining—for himself—how his imagination functions so effectively and why his characters seem so real. The fact that we see him talking to an attractive blonde, who shortly thereafter disappears, or that an elephant suddenly seems to appear in a hallway, gives us pause, but only until his wife announces that he is insane and that she plans on committing him to an insane asylum. When he then produces a tape containing her description and she destroys it to demonstrate that he is delusional, she disappears as well, leaving Gregory not to recreate her, but to describe a new, more compliant wife, the blonde woman with whom we first saw him talking and enjoying a drink. Whether his dictation machine is indeed some mysterious piece of technology that literally allows him to manipulate matter—and such strange devices recur in other Twilight Zone episodes—or if all of these events, including the wish-fulfillment replacement of his wife, are simply the products of a writer's imagination we cannot know with any real certainty. And the episode's conclusion, wherein Gregory silences Rod Serling's usual closing commentary, one in which he terms the narrative's preceding events "nonsense," as he destroys a tape with Serling's name on it, only offers a comic wink to the audience. It is as if the entire tale were an elaborate joke, or as Shakespeare's Macbeth might describe it, "a tale told by an idiot, full of sound and fury, signifying nothing."

The question of insanity figures even more prominently in "Nightmare at 20,000 Feet," an episode describing a just-released mental patient's first flight since his mental breakdown, which had occurred on a plane six months earlier. As the plane flies through a storm, the passenger, Bob Wilson, sees a strange creature, a gremlin as he later describes it, tinkering with one of the plane's engines, but strangely no one else notices it, and when he tries to convince his wife, a stewardess, and other passengers that something is amiss, no one believes him and he is told to calm down, take a sedative, and realize that the gremlin is simply a product of his stressed mind. And indeed, at various times others, at his urging, gaze out his window—while we share their gaze—but see nothing. Driven to a state of panic, Bob steals a deputy's gun, opens the emergency door, and shoots the gremlin—apparently saving the plane from destruction but leading to him being put in a straitjacket when the plane lands and carted off in an ambulance. As he is being taken away, Bob's wife assures him that "it's alright," and his response, "I know, but I'm the only one who does know, right now," underscores his plight. He is seen simply as a lapsed mental case, the gremlin as nothing more than a delusion, although a track back shot, revealing damage to the engine cowling, suggests it might be otherwise and that he might well have saved the plane from gremlins. But his emphasis on the "right now" reminds us, as do most Twilight Zone episodes, that our world

Figure 2.5 *The Twilight Zone*'s "Nightmare at 20,000 Feet": the "uncanny" and the "marvelous" collide

should always be open to reassessment, to learning more about both it and our fellow humans (Figure 2.5).

Appropriately, both "A World of His Own" and "Nightmare at 20,000 Feet" fashion their web of fantastic hesitation through a process of story-telling, as both Gregory West and Bob Wilson describe events and try to convince others of the truth of their experiences. They are, at least in this regard, models of the entire series with its weekly succession of narratives that challenge belief. Moreover, despite their common thrust, these epi-sodes function in very different registers, the former drawing from the play-wright's account and his wife's disbelief a comic resolution, and the latter finding an element of terror in Bob's tale of a gremlin attack. We might pay special attention to that variety of narrative approaches, though, because it is another signpost of *The Twilight Zone*'s narrative range. For in its most seri-ous installments, the show recalls the best work of the various live anthol-ogy dramas of the era, often verging on tragedy, while at other times—and we especially recall the time-travel episode "Once Upon a Time" (Dec. 15, 1961), which starred silent-film comedian Buster Keaton—it took a very different tack, testifying, as Stewart T. Stanyard puts it, "that comical regions of the fifth dimension were present and accounted for" (64) here.

That range must itself have been a bit surprising to those who, in the 1950s, had come to associate televisual SF with the ubiquitous space operas and kids' shows that had followed the successful model of *Captain Video*. However, Rod Serling's wife Carol observes that her husband "never considered himself . . . a great science fiction writer"; rather, he simply found that "this particular genre gave him the chance to say for a time what he wanted to say. . . . He just used this vehicle" (qtd. in Stanyard 135)—a vehicle with which, since it had not often been used for serious purpose on television, he could experiment and say what he wished. Of course, seeing SF as a suitable vehicle for serious story-telling, finding in it equal possibilities for tales of space exploration and alien invasion, for marvelous and fantastic narratives, for ranging across tragic and comic modes was itself a significant accomplishment. It marks *The Twilight Zone* not only as a predictor of the narrative flexibility that our SFTV would increasingly demonstrate, but indeed as a kind of "unconscious" version of television's diverse narrative "flow."

3

CULTURAL ISSUES AND SFTV

While *The Twilight Zone* helped explore many of the narrative models available to a developing SFTV, its greatest legacy may well lie elsewhere. For in the wake of the space operas that dominated SFTV production from 1949 to 1956, with their emphasis on providing mainly masculine heroic models for a largely children's audience, *The Twilight Zone* used its varied and more adult-oriented stories to tune viewer attention to many of the key cultural issues of its day. If, prior to its time, many critics saw media SF as essentially an escapist form, Serling's show demonstrated that SF could also provide an important space for cultural examination and critique—a project that would, in later years, result in the racial and cultural explorations found in the original *Star Trek* series, the ideological and political issues examined in *Babylon 5*, the gender considerations of *Battlestar Galactica* and *Terminator: The Sarah Connor Chronicles*, and the critique of science itself that has surfaced in a host of contemporary shows, including *Eureka*, *Warehouse 13*, and *Dollhouse*. As suggested in Chapter 2, SFTV often asks us to recognize aspects of our own world in its futuristic, other worldly, or simply exaggerated depictions, and then to think about the implications of those resemblances. In this chapter I would like to comment on the range of those comparisons, to consider some of the ways our SFTV has—at times indeed under the guise of "escapist" entertainment—posed some of the most crucial questions about our world and ourselves.

This assertion that SFTV is a fertile ground for cultural critique may initially seem something of a stretch, particularly given the emphasis so often put on the form's reliance upon spectacle and its concern with producing what we have termed a "sense of wonder." Indeed, for many viewers media SF is essentially defined by its use of special effects, since they help us to imagine ourselves elsewhere—in another time, place, or even dimension. That accomplishment is not insignificant and, indeed, is one of the form's major appeals. Yet that effects emphasis is not simply an end in itself, but rather part of the genre's *method*, one term in what Mark Bould allusively describes as media SF's complex relationship "between the conceptual and the spectacular" (*Science Fiction* 7). In fact, the form's "spectacular" dimension directly links us to its "conceptual" concerns by helping to achieve what Darko Suvin famously described as a "cognitive estrangement," or "an imaginative framework alternative" to our "empirical environment" (7). Framed in a context of science and technology, the form asks us to *recognize* elements of our world, even as it renders them unsettlingly *unfamiliar, strange, or spectacular*—thereby producing a rather compelling paradox of the *like yet unlike*. But it is in that paradox that the form manages, so effectively, to do its cultural work on and for us.

In this chapter we explore a few key elements of that "conceptual" work. As Rod Serling rather famously noted, "A Martian can say things that a Republican or Democrat can't" (Javna 16)—a reminder that out of the mouths of aliens, cyborgs, time travelers, or spacemen can come important observations about our world and indeed our humanity, in fact, that these strange figures and the narratives in which they operate are *allowed* to say certain things that other sorts of show might not, particularly in network series that have to appeal to a wide viewership and avoid offending sponsors. Yet the problem for many viewers, as well as for many critics of the genre, is that they do not expect those observations, do not expect to hear anything crucial, and so frequently we simply *do not hear*. But by briefly considering the examinations of racial difference in *Star Trek*, the play with gender expectations in *Dollhouse*, class and cultural concerns as they are developed on an epic scale in *Babylon 5*, and the troubling fascinations of science and technology seen in *Eureka* and *Warehouse 13*, we might better attune our hearing and appreciate some of the cultural commentary and challenges commonly posed by the best in SFTV.

RACE AND RACISM

Given the frequency with which SF narratives, because of their very nature, deal with the alien, the outsider, or an *other* of some sort, we should only expect that they would provide a good platform for displaying our own cultural issues involving race. In fact, as evidence of the extent to which a concern with race and racism was besetting post-World War II United States, even an early children's series like *Captain Video* raised this specter, and in typically conflicted fashion. For in one story arc Dr. Pauli, the Captain's primary nemesis—and chief threat to the galaxy—allies himself with a menacing group of Orientals, although he shows his skepticism about them as he withholds information, tricks them, and sneeringly refers to them as "stupid natives," illustrating what Edward Said terms the "positional superiority" that has typified most Western relations with peoples of the Orient (7). Probably fallout from the ongoing Korean War, this attitude, which underscores Dr. Pauli's malevolent nature, runs quite counter to the sort of moral message that, during narrative breaks, the show often presented to viewers, such as one "Video Ranger Message" focused on our common "job of fighting discrimination." In this special communication to all of the "boy and girl Rangers," the Captain explains that "there's no room for un-American prejudice" and reminds that "those who turn thumbs down on one race or religion one day are just as apt to turn against another race or religion another day, yours perhaps." Appealing to both patriotism and logic, the Captain takes a firm stand in what was, even at this relatively early stage in the Civil Rights Movement of the 1950s and 1960s, already a growing national concern.

While that concern would surface in a number of other SF series in the 1950s and early 1960s—particularly *Rocky Jones* and *The Twilight Zone*—it is in *Star Trek* that race relations and the issue of racism would surface most starkly, and even stylishly. The series is often cited—however, incorrectly—as offering the first instance of an inter-racial kiss on network television, as Captain Kirk (William Shatner) kisses Lt. Uhura (black actress Nichelle Nichols) in the "Plato's Stepchildren" episode (1968), an act he would repeat in "Elaan of Troyius" (1968) with Asian actress France Nuyen. But as visually appealing and headline grabbing as such interpolated and convention-challenging love scenes may have been, they paled in comparison to the more mundane plot point of having a black woman like Uhura hold a major position of authority. It was, very simply, a signal development not just for SFTV but for American television in general in the 1960s, and it was part of a recurring concern with rapidly changing racial attitudes and cultural roles that would be played out over the entire course of the original *Star Trek*'s run.

Of course, by its very design *Star Trek* was rather explicitly opening the door on repressed cultural attitudes towards race and the other. For the crew of the *Enterprise* immediately evoked an unusually multicultural realm, with its inclusion not only of recognizable Earth nationalities—such as a Russian, a Scot, and Americans—but also of various races, including Asian and black, along with the alien Vulcan Mr. Spock. As series creator Gene Roddenberry recalls, network executives from the start resisted this vision, expressing "concern that the viewer might reject the concept of different races, particularly Negro and white, working side by side" (Whitfield and Roddenberry 112). But Henry Jenkins argues that *Star Trek*'s multiracial starship society was a central feature of the show's design and appeal, a visual shorthand for the kind of utopian goal it was projecting for American culture, as well as a call to action. Thus, he suggests that in real life "affirmative action became the vehicle for realizing" the show's "vision of a future without racial prejudice" (Tulloch and Jenkins 191).

However, anchoring itself in the difficult present of the 1960s, *Star Trek* also repeatedly recognized the problematic nature of achieving such racial harmony. The episode "Let That Be Your Last Battlefield" (1969) is the most dramatic—and perhaps an all-too-obvious—case in point (Figure 3.1). In this story the *Enterprise* unwittingly becomes the battleground between representatives of two races from the planet Cheron that have been at odds for 50,000 years. Shortly after picking up Lokai aboard a stolen and damaged shuttlecraft, the *Enterprise* is intercepted and boarded by Commissioner Bele, a policeman from Cheron who has been tracking Lokai and insists that he be placed in his custody and both be returned to Cheron. Each tries to convince Kirk to take sides in their dispute, Lokai describing himself as a "freedom fighter" and explaining how Bele and his kind created "a land of murdering oppressors," and Bele terming his opponent a "terrorist" and his followers "savages." Moreover, each insists on the visible evidence that the other is "of an inferior breed": Lokai is white on the right side of his body and black on the left, while Bele's black-and-white color scheme is the reverse. And when Kirk, Spock, and the others fail to recognize any significance in their coloring, they are met with incredulity, as Bele protests, "Are you blind?" It is to the show's credit that the very absurdity of this situation shifts into the background to allow for a focus on the effects of such, in fact, "blind" hatred: the way in which logic (despite Spock's best efforts) is easily overlooked; the similarly easy dismissal of the rights of those who have been accidentally caught up in this conflict, in this case all of those on board the *Enterprise*; and the immensely destructive potential of such prejudice. In fact, when the *Enterprise*, after being commandeered by Bele, eventually reaches Cheron, it is revealed that the people "have annihilated each other—totally," and that these two are now the last representatives of their race(s). Still, they resume their chase, apparently destined to fight out their illogical hatred for the rest of their lives.

If "Let That Be Your Last Battlefield" today seems a bit heavy handed or too starkly schematic, we might recall that the United States was still struggling

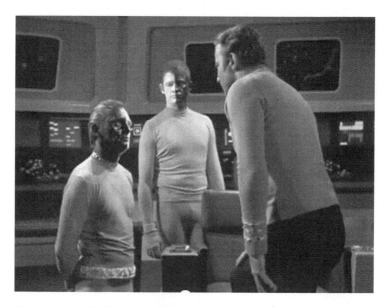

Figure 3.1 *Star Trek* addresses race relations in "Let This Be Your Last Battlefield"

with the implications of Martin Luther King's assassination in 1968, as well as with a rising anti-Vietnam War movement that had found a sympathetic chord in the Civil Rights protests. It was, in short, a time when social concerns seemed to have taken on a stark coloring and sense of urgency. So the episode's final warning, about how an illogical racial hatred might eventuate in self-destruction, should seem well taken and a reminder of the extent to which Roddenberry and his collaborators saw themselves as participating in a quite crucial cultural debate, one that might even decide the fate of the nation.

In one of the more measured assessments of the series, Lincoln Geraghty sees "evidence of a strong desire to visualize difference, both physical and cultural, in ways that challenge the audience" (*American Science Fiction* 45). And here the starkly painted and costumed characters, as well as their seemingly irreconcilable ideologies, well illustrate that "challenge" facing American audiences just off-screen from their SFTV.

Even beyond its initial three-year run, *Star Trek* would continue to address issues of race and ethnicity, continue, as its opening injunction promised, to "go where no man has gone before." Thus in the first continuation of the *Star Trek* franchise, *Star Trek: The Next Generation* (1987–94), a new starship *Enterprise* is again run by a multiethnic crew, featuring the black helmsman and chief engineer Geordi La Forge (played by Emmy-winning actor Levar Burton), although much of the racial focus shifts to the Klingon security chief Lieutenant Worf (played by black actor Michael Dorn). While originally Asian in look and often portrayed as brutish enemies of the Federation, with Worf the Klingons become more complex, in some cases even noble allies of the Federation, but also, thanks to their distinct racial difference from humans, a convenient touchstone for plot developments focusing on bigotry, cultural misunderstanding, and interracial love relationships. The popularity of the character Worf eventually led to his reappearance as a part of the cast in another series spin-off, *Star Trek: Deep Space Nine* (1993–99), a show perhaps more noteworthy for its central character Benjamin Sisko (played by black actor Avery Brooks), commander of the space station *Deep Space Nine*. While Sisko would, at times, provide a point for meditation on earlier human racial attitudes—most notably in the episode "Far Beyond the Stars" (1998) in which he dreams he is a frustrated black SF writer in the 1950s—his simple position of authority and his centrality to the *Deep Space*

Nine narrative speaks more forcefully about the trajectory of race relations envisioned for the show's 24th century setting. Ultimately, as Jan Johnson-Smith observes, all of the "worlds" of the various *Star Trek* series "try to suggest equality by inclusion and collaboration, rather than exclusion and conflict" (82), as they draw their ethnic figures into the central action, construct those figures in complex and usually sympathetic ways, and put them in positions of power and authority. But such simple narrative moves, while often taken for granted, can convey strong messages.

Star Trek's consistent emphasis on and respect for diversity has, however, come in for some challenges. M. Keith Booker, for example, notes that, despite its best intentions, the original series often failed "to transcend" the sort of racial stereotypes that are embedded in Western culture, and he points specifically to the way the Klingons were typically portrayed via "irrationality, violence, and excessive devotion to tradition and ritual" (201). In this same vein, Daniel Bernardi sees the racial and ethnic depictions in the series—as well as that of its cinematic and other offshoots—as essentially imaginative extrapolations of a "white-dominant" culture, reluctant to indict itself; as he notes, it "rarely depicts racism among humans, preferring to project it as a problem within an alien culture or between two alien worlds" (28). Moreover, he sees the future it typically projects as evoking a "superior world of whiteness. This is apparently where we should be going: back to the far past of traditional values and white domination" (122). And indeed, both commentaries remind us of how difficult, perhaps even impossible, it is to project a vision that is not colored by our contemporary cultural context, as well as our shared past. However, as these oppositional voices should also help us see, it now seems almost impossible to produce a series that does not in some way resonate with or pose questions about our common concern for racial justice and harmony. These have become central issues for contemporary culture, and in their repeated visitation and visualization afford an ongoing, cultural signpost of how far we have come in working out the utopian vision of the series.

GENDER ROLES AND RULES

No less central to contemporary SFTV is a reassessment of conventional gender roles and the cultural "rules" under which those depictions have generally functioned. While the space operas of the 1950s often—particularly in their live commercials—directly addressed the "boys and girls" of the audience, the girl "space rangers," "space cadets," or "rocket rangers" were generally faced with a more difficult spectatorial situation, since the shows typically provided them with few gender models to emulate—and those often compromised by costume and circumstance. Figures like Carol Carlisle of *Space Patrol*, Dale Arden of *Flash Gordon*, and Vena Ray of *Rocky Jones, Space Ranger* typically wore short skirts and seldom figured centrally in the action. In fact, Rocky Jones' assertion in that series' first episode, that space is "no place for a girl," seems like a warning that might have been uttered in any of these series. However, these largely male-oriented action shows did make some small effort at stretching gender boundaries. As Rocky would learn, Vena Ray was an expert navigator and trained linguist, in effect, a valuable asset to his future missions. Carol Carlisle was a brilliant scientist, as well as the daughter of the Secretary General of the United Federation of Planets. And the generally male group of cadets in *Tom Corbett* took instruction from Dr. Joan Dale, their professor at the Space Academy. While these female characters were less involved in the physical action of the series, then, they were typically *credentialed*—as skilled personnel involved in the exploration of space. In fact, recalling her experience watching these shows in the 1950s, historian Amy Foster notes that the "message about careers for girls in science, engineering, and technology was unambiguously positive" (72), and she argues that what made such shows "unique from other programs of the era and particularly powerful for girls was that they depicted women participating as equal partners in the fight to defend the Earth (or the United States), not as temporary replacements for male labor as they were during World War II and not as preservers of the home front" (73). In sum, these roles, far more so than those found in situation comedies, Westerns, and the popular detective shows of the era, at least suggested a broadening range of possibilities for women at some point in the future, and that space, in its vastness, did indeed have "place" for them.

However, few of the next wave of SFTV series would expand upon those gender possibilities. While *The Twilight Zone* centered some of its more interesting episodes on women, and in a show like "Beauty is in the Eye of the Beholder" (1960) took on the cultural fixation with female physical beauty, even *Star Trek* in its original version did not provide many primary, much less convention-challenging, roles for women, save as love interests for Captain Kirk. Generally, the women characters, while varied, largely function in traditional female roles—as nurses, counselors, and communication officers—until the advent of *Star Trek: Voyager* (1995–2001), which has Captain Kathryn Janeway commanding the starship *Voyager*. That series' authoritative woman figure might be seen alongside another strong female figure from the same period, Dana Scully of *The X-Files* (1993–2002), who also assumes what we might think of as a traditional male role. Paired with fellow FBI agent Fox Mulder, Scully draws on her background as a doctor and forensic pathologist to remain for much of the series a thoroughly rational and hard-headed skeptic about the various conspiracy theories, paranormal events, UFOs, and monstrous appearances in which her partner so readily wants to believe, and about which he often becomes—in a conventionally feminine way—quite emotional. It is a concerted effort to overturn our usual assumptions about gender attitudes, and one that contributed to the series' appeal which, Lincoln Geraghty suggests, "rested on the fact it attracted an audience who felt in some way estranged from contemporary life and saw something personal and relevant" in its upset of many of our cultural conventions (*American Science Fiction* 101), including those associated with gender.

These series would also open the door for a number of shows over the last decade that have featured strong and even convention-challenging female roles—series like *Firefly* (2002), *Terminator: The Sarah Connor Chronicles* (2008–2009), *Revolution* (2012–present), and especially, as its title might ironically suggest, *Dollhouse* (2009–10). It is on the last of these that we might briefly focus precisely because of the way it foregrounds and challenges so many of our gender expectations, ingrained as they are in the whole tradition of SFTV. Films like *The Stepford Wives* (1975, 2004), wherein the women of the planned community of Stepford are all turned into robots, effectively parody a long line of films and television series in which father—or husband—always knows best, and in which the mother/wife is little more than an obedient helpmate. While that tradition has largely disappeared from contemporary television because of the shift in cultural notions about gender that mark our postmodern society, some of its informing attitudes remain. Joss Whedon's series *Dollhouse* directly interrogates a number of those issues—particularly those involving personal objectification, control over one's body, and what constitutes the self or human identity.

The very premise of the series establishes a concern that has been central to much of gender studies: the extent to which a male-dominated culture tends to objectify the female body, treating it as something to be seen or as a commodity to be bartered. *Dollhouse* tells of an international medical research group, the Rossum Corporation, that has developed a technology for wiping minds clean and implanting new personalities, activities that it experiments with in a series of Dollhouses scattered throughout the world by providing the promise of money or simply the ability to start over to select individuals who will allow their—typically young and attractive—bodies to be used for a five-year term. During that period they are implanted with a variety of personalities and talents, depending on what the Dollhouse's wealthy clients might need or simply desire. And while the "Actives," as these human dolls are termed, are both male and female, the primary focus throughout the series is on the females, particularly the appropriately named Echo, a beautiful young woman who has gotten herself into a "mess," wants to obtain "a clean slate" so that she can "start over," and in the course of being provided to various clients is frequently put into sexually compromising or exploitative situations ("Ghost," 2009). In fact, both the opening episode "Ghost" and the later "A Spy in the House of Love" (2009) offer images of her in sexual bondage situations, with one character referring to her derisively as "S&M Barbie" (Figure 3.2).

After such "engagements," though, the Actives are brought back to the Dollhouse, their minds are wiped clean of all memories of their actions, they are "repaired" of any injuries, and eventually put to sleep in comfortable boxes on the floor of the facility. It is, in effect, a new take on prostitution, with Echo and her fellow Actives turned into customized dolls, commodities for the wealthy. However, the series is clearly indicting this sort of human reduction that, it suggests, is already bound up in society's gender roles, while also pointing to its ultimate consequences. FBI agent Paul Ballard, who is investigating the Dollhouse case, provides an element of that moral voice here. While his supervisors dismiss the investigation as just politically inspired—as indeed some might simply dismiss the notion that society objectifies women—he insists that this reduction of the self is "essentially murder."

Figure 3.2 Gender concerns: Echo is transformed into an "S&M Barbie" in
Dollhouse

Coincident with—and in fact a key part of—that cultural objectification
of women is the tendency to control their bodies. In one of the seminal
essays on the SF film, Vivian Sobchack has suggested that "women pose a
particular threat to science fiction heroes and their engagement with technology" which is often encoded as sexual ("Virginity" 109). So to deal with
that threatening presence, female sexuality typically undergoes, as she says,
"a purposeful—if unconscious—repression" ("Virginity" 103), one figured
here in the Actives' programming to fulfill the sexual desires of some clients,
but also in their reduction to a child-like, asexual state between assignments.
The difficulty of addressing this issue of control via sexual manipulation and
repression is one that series creator Whedon well understood; as he notes,
"when you're dealing with fantasies, particularly sexual ones, you're going
off the reservation. You're not going to be doing things that are perfectly
[that is, politically] correct. It's supposed to be about the sides of us that we
don't want people to see" (Ryan). So here, instead of the social methods of

sexual control and repression, the series emphasizes an actual mechanism: the technology for mind-wiping and programming perfected and wielded by the brilliant scientist Topher Brink. He is a character who is not above imprinting a female Active like Sierra to serve his own needs, and, fittingly, one whose name hints at his repressive role ("top her"), as well as the cultural calamity ("brink") to which his technology eventually leads at the end of the first season ("Epitaph One") when the mind-wiping technology goes out of control.

That use of technology in the service of such human control recalls the argument forwarded by cultural critic Donna Haraway who, in assessing the impact of technology on gender roles, suggests that in contemporary society "technology has determined what counts as our own bodies in crucial ways" (Penley 6). It is a point made vividly in the apocalyptic "Epitaph One" episode (2009) when several survivors of the zombie-like apocalypse that has resulted are killed by Iris, a little girl they have been harboring ("a little bitch," as she disconcertingly describes herself) whose body has simply been appropriated by an adult who is jumping from one body to another. Yet for all of its capacity for such appropriation and control, that technology—and by extension society's own gender mechanisms—is not foolproof. Thus in an earlier episode Topher becomes alarmed when, while using another control technology, the monitors, with which he is voyeuristically watching the Actives shower, he notes that several of them are becoming sexually aroused. That response, he had assumed, was simply not possible in their doll state, when they had been rendered child-like (like Iris) and their sexual urges supposedly fully repressed. However, their unexpected sexual awakening becomes a sign of hope that his, his technology's, and even the subtler sexual repression and gender programming of the culture—referred to alternately as a "fairy tale" and a "curse" in the "Briar Rose" episode (2009)—can indeed be overcome.

That sexual awakening experienced by several of the Actives is also part of a larger gender issue at play in Dollhouse, one involving the very nature of the self. Haraway has suggested that women in postmodern society have become very like "cyborgs," "odd techno-organic, humanoid hybrids," whose identity is partly constructed by their culture and partly their own, and that one of the key tasks they face is to "refigure the kinds of persons we might be" ("Actors" 21). Obviously, the situation of the various Actives, but especially Echo, recalls this troubled hybrid state. While Adelle DeWitt, the head of the Dollhouse, remarks that her Actives are rumored to be little more than "robots, zombies, slaves," she notes that Echo has demonstrated a special "talent for adaptability," for becoming whatever her controllers need her to become ("True Believer," 2009). However, she is also someone who, in the course of the series, manages to awaken from her doll state, to "refigure" herself as something more than just this "techno-organic" construction of a woman, and eventually to lead a resistance against the "wipe" technology and its destruction of society. By the end of the first season she has once again become herself—Caroline—and she follows the advice of fellow doll Sierra (who warns about the need for "someone to lead us back" ["Epitaph One," 2009]). She leaves behind a hard-drive copy of her "self" so that someone can be imprinted with her identity and knowledge, and thus lead others to what is referred to as "Safe Haven," a realm free from such self-destruction. Of course, nothing is sure in the apocalyptic vision that Dollhouse imagines, although by the end of the show's second season, with most of the identity drains reversed, it seems that Caroline's plan—"I hope we find me alive," she offers—might have been realized.

Admittedly, the patterns of objectification, control, and identity construction that we see modeled at every turn in Dollhouse are not restricted to women. In fact, it is one of the series' strengths that it frames these common concerns of most gender criticism as broadly applicable, showing how they open onto the repressions and manipulations that affect a broad spectrum of contemporary life, as we try to convince ourselves that what we "desire" is what we really "need"—a conflation articulated many times in the series. But because women have often been victimized by that equation, rendered as figures of desire, Whedon generalizes from their situation, deriving a powerful vision of a woman's ability (Echo/Caroline) to overcome her cultural programming and to "lead us back" to a better place, a better state of mind. When Adelle DeWitt first discusses enrolling in the Dollhouse, Caroline, clearly feeling a sense of desperation, says, "I don't have a choice, do I?" It seems, at that point, a rhetorical question, indicating her resignation at having no other choice, but it follows Adelle's opening statement— and indeed the first line of the series—that "Nothing is what it appears to be." Read together, these two comments become the propelling (and most compelling) message of *Dollhouse*. For they remind us that, despite all appearances, we do have choices; we can become something more than the roles society has apparently quite rigidly established for us. That message is very much a universal one, but also a reminder of how gender concerns, like those raised in this series, are also ultimately universal in their implications and worth pursuing through the spaces of SFTV.

CLASS AND CULTURE

While much of SF literature and indeed most SFTV has emphasized a heroic individualism as central to its narrative model, the long tradition of utopian thinking and visual projection in SF has also ensured a strong strain of class and cultural consciousness, often seen as running counter to that individualistic emphasis. Within that tradition, exemplified by works like H. G. Wells' novella *The Time Machine* (1895) with its tale of the brutish Morlocks who in the far future feast on the peaceful Eloi, and Fritz Lang's landmark film *Metropolis* (1927), which depicts a privileged, highly technologized society, only made possible by a working class relegated to underground slum life, there is typically a critique of class-structured societies wherein life and prosperity largely depend on the repression and exploitation of a lower class. It is a theme that would surface from time to time in the original *Star Trek* series, as Captain Kirk and his crew would visit a "backwards" planet and, despite their Federation's directive against interference in other cultures' development, would typically use Earth's supposed history of overcoming such primitive social structures to help educate their hosts—and the television viewers. However, seldom do such series do more than sketch the broad outlines of such social/economic issues. As M. Keith Booker observes, they instead have tended to "focus on problems rather than solutions . . . presumably because problems generate drama and lend themselves to more compelling narratives" (65). But the problems themselves have in recent years been consistently presented, if not from a Marxist perspective then from that of a nearly allied tradition of "critical utopian imagining" (Csicsery-Ronay 120) which has focused attention on collective versus individual action, on power and class repression, and on the emergence of a new and potentially subversive form of consciousness or social awareness.

To illustrate how some of these concerns have been worked out in SFTV, we might turn to *Babylon 5*, described by Jan Johnson-Smith as "one of the most innovative and consistently challenging sf television series ever produced" (10). While that is a large claim, the show's epic scope draws on a five-year planned story arc, overseen by J. Michael Straczynski, who had an established reputation in media SF thanks to his writing for various SF shows: the radio program *Alien Worlds*, a revival of *The Twilight Zone* (1985–89), and *Captain Power and the Soldiers of the Future* (1987–88). This designed trajectory allowed the series to develop a complex social—as well as philosophical—vision. Its large story arc explores the pivotal role played by the space station *Babylon 5*, a kind of United Nations in space, in providing a venue where, as the first season's opening narration offers, "humans and aliens could work out their differences peacefully." And with that cross-species and cross-cultural dynamic, most of it played out in the confines of, as we are told, "2,500,000 tons of spinning metal, all alone in the night" of space, the series is able to develop a vision of how groups can work together, how power manifests itself, and how a better society might be formed.

Because of the diplomatic function of the space station, the narrative of *Babylon 5* typically emphasizes the comings and goings of larger-than-life figures—ambassadors, alien royalty, religious leaders, high-ranking officers from Earth Force military, and representatives from the mysterious Psi Corps, a powerful agency of telepaths. And indeed, the show does suggest the importance of such individuals, including their ability quite literally to change history. The most dramatic example is easily Jeffrey Sinclair, first Commander of the *Babylon 5*, who later in the series is revealed to have the soul of a Minbari, is transformed into (or reincarnated as) the great Minbari hero Valen, and takes the *Babylon 5* space station back 1,000 years in time, enabling the Minbari to defeat the Shadows in their earlier war with this ancient race. Yet this sort of "great man" figure is set alongside the larger thrust of the series, which emphasizes how individual responsibility and action must be coordinated with others—other members of a military unit, like Sinclair's original fighter squadron, other members of the ruling council on board *Babylon 5*, and the other great races of beings who must eventually come together to defeat the Shadows and Vorlons, forcing them to leave the galaxy (Figure 3.3). In fact, it is that capacity for putting aside the self's

Figure 3.3 Negotiating a multiethnic society in *Babylon 5*

desires and working for others that, the Minbari teacher Draal recognizes, is one of the most intriguing and attractive qualities of the human race, as well as the Minbari's own Third Principle of Sentient Life ("A Voice in the Wilderness, Part I," 1994).

Along with the constant emphasis on important individuals involved in various sorts of political intrigues, negotiations for resources, and even large-scale thievery, *Babylon 5* also develops a focus on the workaday world, composed not only of Commander Sinclair (succeeded in the second season by Captain John Sheridan) and his team who control the space station, but also of the common workers who make the space station function. The episode "By Any Means Necessary" (1994), for example, highlights the labor conditions of the dockworkers on *Babylon 5*. After one of their number is killed due to unsafe conditions, the dockworkers go on strike, leading the Earth Senate Labor Committee to send a negotiator to the station, but his clumsy efforts, which include a veiled threat of force against the strikers, only result in a riot that Sinclair manages to deal with by shifting unused funds that had been allocated for station defense to meet the strikers' demands. It is a telling illustration of how power might be used badly, for repressive purposes, but also imaginatively, to constructive and humane ends.

This episode's emphasis on the working class also links to another concern that runs through many episodes, that is with what is called Downbelow and its inhabitants. A section of the station that, when construction funds ran out, was left unfinished, Downbelow over time became the home to the unemployed, squatters, the poor, and criminals, as well as a place of disreputable and indeed dangerous business. Here, like inhabitants of present-day slums and ghettos, an underclass, disparagingly termed "Lurkers," lives in poverty and squalor, often turning to crime to survive, as in the case of the young girl Alisa who, in the "Legacies" episode (1994), admits that, after being orphaned at 12, she learned to steal in order to survive. Yet more than just, as M. Keith Booker offers, a "darkly pessimistic reminder that the poor may be with us always" (Science 133), even far out in space, Downbelow provides a structural reminder of the loopholes in our current social system. Thus when chief of security Garibaldi asks for permission to "clean out the Lurkers" because doing so would "wipe out 9/10 of the crime" on the station, Sinclair observes that "Most of them are just people with nowhere to go. They come here looking for a new life, a new job, and when they don't find it, they can't afford transport back" to Earth. It is a recognition that class structure might well be built into the system—and that the social system, like Babylon 5 itself, might also be in need of further "construction" for everyone's good.

A part of that "construction," though, as the series suggests, is that of consciousness itself. For to address such social issues involves the sort of raising of awareness that we glimpse in Sinclair's explanation to Garibaldi, in effect a foregrounding of the people's concerns that, by leading us to see things differently, might question or even alter the status quo. And Babylon 5 can be seen as developing that shift of consciousness in a variety of ways. One of them is this sort of individual encounter with the workers—and low-level criminals—whose situations contrast so starkly with those who in every episode are making decisions that affect not only entire worlds but their forgotten situations as well. When Alisa is discovered to have telepathic abilities and is offered a position in the Psi Corps—a position which, once accepted, one can never just leave—she responds with a note of resignation, "I don't have much of a choice here, do I?" ("Legacies," 1994). It is a response that codifies the sort of closed-off possibilities that many of those in Downbelow see for themselves. Another way that *Babylon 5* effects that shift in consciousness is through the recurring background of revolutions and overthrown governments that become points of reference in numerous episodes and, as the series proceeds along its five-year arc, increasingly crowd into the foreground of the action, prompting the space station, under the new leadership of Captain Sheridan, to declare itself independent from Earth in season three. And in this context we might note the revolt on Earth's Mars Colony, the assassination of the American president, and the terrorist nuclear bombing of San Francisco, among many other such momentous events. All remind us of how people's needs, when long frustrated, can eventually lead to violent action and ultimately to social chaos.

The larger presentation of raised consciousness, though, is that which quite literally occurs in several of the key players in this interstellar drama. We have already noted Sinclair's gradual realization that he has become a host for the spirit of the great Minbari leader Valen. In undergoing a transformation into a Minbari (through the process of "chrysalis") and, in effect, *becoming* Valen, Sinclair rises to a new and more comprehensive consciousness. His successor, John Sheridan, also has to attain a level of higher awareness to become the sort of leader that circumstances demand—in dealing with the increasingly repressive regime on Earth, in forging an alliance of the "young" races to defeat the Shadows, and in leading a new Interstellar Alliance as its first President. But even beyond these characters, *Babylon 5* finds its real thrust in its epic confrontation of those young races with the ancients, as they—the humans, Minbari, Narn, and others—must discover how they have been manipulated by the older ones—the Shadows and Vorlons—and declare their own independence from that influence, even exile them beyond the galaxy. That larger multicultural awakening serves as a reminder that repression and exploitation go on at many levels, and that awareness and resistance too are multidimensional, as well as a continuing challenge.

What *Babylon 5* works out over its complete story is, admittedly, not the currently fashionable Marxist vision of class struggle. As Sherryl Vint notes, for all of its "criticism of the economic consequences of capitalism," the series concludes with an Interstellar Alliance that itself seems to accept a "capitalist social organization" (258). Moreover, instead of a strictly materialist position, the show repeatedly emphasizes the worth of religious belief and may even, as Jan Johnson-Smith suggests, be "the first sf programme to seriously suggest an existence beyond death" (191). However, *Babylon 5* does explore patterns of worker repression and exploitation, of class conflict, and the sort of raised consciousness that are central to what we earlier termed "critical utopian" thinking and that can model for us other and important ways of critiquing and understanding SFTV. The appropriately titled post-apocalyptic series *Revolution* with its vision of warlords conscripting slave labor readily lends itself to similar examination, as does the genre-straddling *The Walking Dead* (2010–13), which concluded its second season with Deputy Sheriff Rick Grimes announcing, "this isn't a democracy anymore," as he assumes absolute control over his group of survivors. Despite the genre's repeated emphasis on technology and spectacle—both of which *Babylon 5* offered viewers aplenty—all of these shows remind us of the human dimension that underlies and makes possible such attractions; all, in fact, challenge us to a new level of *human* awareness and complicity.

SCIENCE AND TECHNOLOGY

In the two-part episode "A Voice in the Wilderness" (Part 1 and Part 2, 1994), the *Babylon 5* space station observes strange seismic activity on the nearby planet Epsilon 3 and, upon investigation, discovers a massive machine housed within the planet, that has become unstable and threatens to explode, taking with it the space station and other ships in the vicinity. Modeled on a similar planet-sized machine in the film *Forbidden Planet* (1956), the "Great Machine," as it is simply termed here, requires a sentient brain to control it and restore its usefulness. That image, with its elements of instability, great power, and necessary humanoid involvement, seems a compelling one to link this chapter's various cultural concerns with what has become the very condition of contemporary culture—as well as a fundament of all SF—the pervasiveness of science and its technological products. To consider this dimension of SFTV's cultural commentary, we might best turn not to a single show, particularly since all of SFTV to some extent depends on this context, but rather to a variety of series that can help us sketch some of the range that our broad cultural concern with science and technology has taken.

That sense of instability and menace, as well as the enormous potential that the Great Machine holds out, has long been a sustaining concern of SFTV. The early space operas, which often seemed to vie for the introduction of the newest, most exciting, and most scientifically sounding technology, are one very obvious measure of the interest that was already attaching to the rise of technological culture in the postwar period. For in addition to their various rockets and jets that were needed to patrol the galaxy and explore the unknown, these series identified much technology, such as *Captain Video*'s "nucleamatic pistol," *Tom Corbett*'s "paraloray," and *Space Patrol*'s "paralyzer ray gun," as part of an armory that was to be used against similarly equipped forces of evil. While I would not go so far as to suggest that much of the anxiety felt by people in the 1950s—and reflected in our films, literature, and television series—"was caused by no reason other than too much technological change in too little time" (Lucanio and Coville 43), that assessment does remind us of the extent to which this period, culminating in the space race, the heated, often frightening rhetoric of mutual deterrence, and the problematic development of nuclear power, was colored by a new scientific and technological consciousness that could be, by turns, both thrilling and disconcerting and that seemed, at any rate, rather unpredictable.

In more recent times we have seen series that have focused on one or another of those implications attached to the products of a highly technological society. For example, both *The Walking Dead* and *Revolution* have sought to envision what life would be like if we were completely stripped of our technology, if, as the former's protagonist Rick Grimes tries to explain to a group of prisoners who have been isolated for nearly a year, "it's all gone" and we are inexplicably left with "no phones, no computers, and as far as we can tell, at least half the population's been wiped out" ("Sick," 2012). That circumstance is even more marked in *Revolution*, a series that begins with a husband trying desperately, yet almost incoherently, to explain to his family that "it's all going to turn off . . . and it will never, ever turn back on" ("Pilot," 2012). Soon after, airplanes begin to fall from the sky, all cars come to a stop, lights and power indeed turn off, and characters are left to ask, "what the hell is going on?" As the opening retrospective narration explains to the audience, "We lived in an electric world. We relied on it for everything. And then the power went out. Everything stopped working. We weren't prepared. Fear and confusion led to panic." And the series then details the results of that panic, how, 15 years after that mysterious event, centralized governments all over the world have dissolved, warlords and militias have taken over, and people just try to eke out a living by farming and bartering in what has become a kind of second Dark Ages.

Both of these narratives essentially reformulate the "sense of wonder" that, as we have seen, is one of the hallmarks of all SF. While *Babylon 5* drew on early yet impressive CGI effects to produce its amazing vision of a planet-sized "Great Machine," as well as the great variety of spaceships and the space station itself, the much more recent *Revolution* and *The Walking Dead* replace that impressive technological vision with something almost mundane. For they simply ask what happens when weeds, vines, and all manner of plant life begin, inexorably, to take over—and take back—the familiar world of concrete and steel, and these series' visual astonishments (likewise achieved through digital effects) are precisely on that order: of a world seen anew, in the midst of a struggle between past and present, between the inevitable workings of nature and that of human culture, as our world recedes from view. This vision, mirrored in the very violent struggles for survival of the various groups depicted, provides the primary sense of "cognitive estrangement" on which both of these series depend, as they similarly ask us to imagine our world and our lives without much of what we usually think of as constituting that world and those lives.

This strategy of cognition by subtraction can be an effective way of refocusing our attention, although it has, in the past, proven difficult to pull off. Certainly there have been other post-apocalyptic shows, such as *Jericho* (2006–08) with its tale of a mysterious series of atomic attacks on various American cities and the aftermath of those attacks; *Falling Skies* (2011–present), which details an alien invasion that wipes out 90 percent of the Earth's population and neutralizes all the planet's technology; and *Jeremiah* (2002–04), which looks at the aftermath of a plague that has killed most of the world's population and created its own Dark Age. Typically, such shows have had relatively short runs, and their thrusts have been similar. Whether disease, atomic devastation, or alien invasion, the calamitous events that propel their narratives serve to separate humanity from the science and technology on which it has become so dependent that we have begun to see science and technology not just as part of the environment we inhabit but, effectively, as part of ourselves, the way we interface with reality. Through this bracketing off, these shows force us to consider how we might function without all of modern life's supporting systems and ultimately to examine what does make us human. Thus when the protagonist of *Revolution*, Charlotte "Charlie" Matheson, goes to her uncle Miles for help in finding her kidnapped brother, he asks why he should jeopardize his own comfortable situation and help her, and she reminds him of something very fundamental, "Because we're family" ("Pilot," 2012). That reminder resonates beyond the immediate bond of relatives to the larger human family, as this series and others ask us, often in disturbing ways that might help explain their generally short lifespans—and the frequent bloodbaths that punctuate episodes of *The Walking Dead* point up this disturbing dimension—to consider those larger family ties.

Rather than emphasizing the sudden absence of science and technology, other recent series have moved the question of their place in our lives directly into the foreground. Shows such as *Eureka* (2006–12) and *Warehouse 13* (2009–present) focus precisely on the uncanny appeal of various technologies, artifacts, or gadgets—as well as their unpredictability and potential danger. In fact, both shows are simultaneously about the wondrous nature of a particular gadget or creation, and about keeping it secret or sequestered somewhere relatively "safe." *Eureka* is centered on the small town of Eureka, Oregon, a place populated largely by scientists who have themselves been sequestered, brought together by the U.S. Department of Defense and the research corporation Global Dynamics to work on new projects like a paranoia beam ("Alienated," 2006), a constantly expanding force field ("Try, Try Again," 2007), and an artificial sun ("Here Come the Suns," 2008), while also keeping those projects, as well as their often equally strange creators, away from the general public, lest they—like the artificial sun that threatens to go supernova—produce some calamitous situation. *Warehouse 13* focuses on the work of several Secret Service agents who locate and return various strange devices or artifacts to a remote warehouse in South Dakota where they too can be safely kept, and kept away from the general population. Among the many devices that have often fallen into "the wrong hands" and had to be retrieved are an electrical stun gun created by Nikola Tesla

("Pilot," 2009), Beatrix Potter's teaset, which produces paranoid hallucinations ("Don't Hate the Player," 2011), and Ignaty Gryniewietsky's Tattoo Box, which turns the tattoo bearer into a walking firebomb ("The Ones You Love," 2012). That very range of devices and their often strange effects—effects that leave one stunned character to remark, "Something 'warehousey' just happened, didn't it?"—help explain the mixed tones of both series, as they repeatedly veer between the comic and the melodramatic.

As the catalogue above should already suggest, a large part of the attraction of both *Eureka* and *Warehouse 13* lies in the very outrageousness of the various devices and artifacts that they regularly put on display. For through those strange gadgets—many simply mentioned in passing and left for us to imagine—these series suggest a world in which our science and technology, both contemporary and ancient, seem able to real-ize anything we might conceive of. Moreover, they allow our SFTV to demonstrate its own capacities, particularly its ability to use the latest regime of digital special effects to do precisely the work of the various scientists and geniuses of these stories: to visualize what has been imagined and thus to produce an immediate version of that science fictional sense of wonder. Just as the characters of *Eureka* stand around and marvel at the holes in solid matter produced by an out-of-control tachyon accelerator ("Pilot," 2006), or those of *Warehouse 13* try to combat a lightning storm that has inexplicably broken out *inside* the warehouse ("The New Guy," 2011), so too can the audience not help but share in the sense of wonder that these shows so convincingly materialize.

In light of that reflexive dimension, we might note another way in which these series, like a number of others today, try to generate and interrogate a sense of a fully technologized culture. Both *Eureka* and *Warehouse 13* are produced by the Syfy Channel and are part of that network's strategy of fashioning a shared fictional universe, a narrative approach previously employed to link *Star Trek: The Next Generation* with *Star Trek: Deep Space Nine*. This strategy typically involves characters and events from one series showing up from time to time in the other series' world, and in the case of *Eureka* and *Warehouse 13* (as well as another Syfy series *Alphas* [2011–12]), that has led to Claudia, the Warehouse's electronics expert, visiting the Global Dynamics facility in Eureka, Oregon, and a character from *Eureka* coming to the Warehouse to update its computer system. But more than just an opportunity to tout the network's other shows or to let viewers take some delight in recognizing that episode's "visitors" and knowing their backstories, this crossover strategy projects the notion that this world is all of a piece, that it quite possibly intersects with our own world, and that the environment of science and technology that they project is indeed pervasive, in effect, the air that today we all breathe.

That notion, that we inhabit a world defined by the constant presence of and interaction with science and technology, is hardly a challenging one. But making us aware of the climate, priming us to interrogate its nature and its impact, is part of the important work of SFTV, as well as part of the larger cultural picture that the form consistently sketches for us—a picture that also incorporates other key components, such as the racial, gender, and class issues briefly discussed here. For more than just catering to our desire for that experience of wonder—by extrapolating a vision of the future, by visualizing various technological breakthroughs, or even by speculating how we might interact with other, non-human beings—SFTV helps us to frame important questions about our science-and-technology-inflected culture and where it is headed. As they are being rushed out to investigate another strange case, of people literally "rusting" away, *Warehouse* 13 agents Pete and Myka pause and one asks, "Do we even know the risks of doing this before we try any wacky plans?" ("Second Chances," 2012). It is a good and, in fact, symptomatic question, one that speaks to a broad cultural sense that the latest science and technology can often seem, at first glance, a bit "wacky," but also one that reminds us about the need for pausing, for considering "risks," and for deciding whether we are indeed pursuing the best direction for all that is human culture.

It is on that note of pausing and questioning that we might conclude this discussion. For it reminds us that viewing—or reading—our SF texts can constitute an important moment of intervention in the larger and ongoing process of acculturation. Series like those discussed in this chapter do for the most part operate within a system of what Catherine Johnson has termed "regulated innovation" (68). That is, as the products of a competitive, profit-driven industry, they do not want to make their audiences, networks, or advertisers feel too uncomfortable, so even as they introduce novel concepts and employ unusual visuals, they also try to contain any "narrative disruptions" within their "action-adventure format," and to ensure that "normality" is restored by the end of most episodes (92). However, because of their fantasy dimension, these series do open the door of "innovation" in a fundamental cultural context, for they make it "safe" to ask questions, to think innovatively. From within that dynamic, we can not only relish what our world might *look* like, but also consider what we might *be* like in our near and far futures, and thus also consider how we might employ our science and technology to help construct that often almost invisible of elements, our human culture.

KEY SERIES: *BATTLESTAR GALACTICA*: A NEW *WAGON TRAIN* AND ITS BAGGAGE

In introducing the rebooted version of *Battlestar Galactica*, Lincoln Geraghty immediately notes one of its most important and appealing characteristics, its effort at directly tackling some of the "more pressing problems in American culture such as the threat posed by international terrorism, the nation's position as a global police force, religious fundamentalism and the loss of Earth's natural resources" (*American Science Fiction* 18). While an impressive catalogue of the series' very serious concerns, including those efforts at examining the nature and causes of terrorism, against which America and its allies were waging a war, it in some ways actually understates the show's scope, for *Battlestar Galactica* readily opens onto the broad spectrum of contemporary cultural debate, including a wide array of racial, gender, and class issues. And yet, it probably could not have done otherwise given the series' storyline. In recounting the near destruction of human society by the robotic Cylons and the survivors' efforts to locate and settle on a lost human colony named "Earth," all the while struggling with the ongoing problems of human society, it simply could not avoid that broad cultural thrust. The result is what we might term a foundational story for Earth culture—albeit a culture that is given a distinctly American face—and thus one that naturally touches on much that would be implicated in that culture's difficult, and ongoing, historical development.

Of course, that scope also owes a great deal to the show's narrative model. We might here recall the legend surrounding the creation of another and certainly influential series involving space exploration, the original *Star Trek*. As Chapter 1 noted, producer/author Gene Roddenberry reportedly sold his show to the NBC network by telling executives it would be a "*Wagon Train* in space"; that is, it would resemble the popular Western series of 1957–65 about a motley group of settlers, traveling in their covered wagons across the American prairies, searching for a place to start a new life. In the course of its weekly stories about the journey west, *Wagon Train* easily drew on its core situation, of having many different elements of nineteenth century American society thrown together in a common adventure, so it might better—and quite appropriately—explore a variety of topical cultural issues. It is a model that *Battlestar Galactica* has adapted and that serves it just as appropriately, since its chronicle of a limited number of survivors, trekking across the frontier of space, carrying with them all the baggage of human history, provides plenty of opportunities for the series to unpack and offer its commentary "from the past" on much of that cultural baggage that we continue to carry with us as we look, hopefully, to the future. These include our fixations on racial difference, our gender prejudices, our nationalist leanings, and especially our most violent species tendencies, allowing the series' storyline to question precisely what it is that makes us human.

While the original *Battlestar Galactica* series all too easily drew lines of distinction between its gleaming metal race of Cylons and their human victims, when the reimagined show appeared as a miniseries in 2003 and then as a weekly show in 2004–09, it presented viewers with a more difficult and challenging proposition. Besides updating the look of the metal Centurion fighters, it also introduced a new breed of Cylons who are indistinguishable from humans, who practice a monotheistic religion, and who believe that, given past enmities, their efforts to exterminate the human race are quite justified. As many viewers readily recognized, the Cylons' surprise assault on humanity was a metaphoric replay of the events of 9/11, but their justifications—based on a long history of animosities and reciprocal violence— their repeated demonstration of human-like concerns, including a love of life itself, and even the obvious *attractiveness* of the human-looking ones (with Cylon Number Six, played by Tricia Helfer, often demonstrating her obvious physical appeal) complicate our responses. And later episodes, in which the human survivors act in ways that recall Iraqi insurgents or resort to their own terrorist tactics to combat Cylon repression, result in a troubling mirror effect, suggesting that, when viewed through those cultural resonances, they and we look—and act—much the same.

The point that the series seems repeatedly to underscore is that these cultural debates do not admit to any easy resolutions, and certainly not the sort that had been found in many earlier space operas. Even given the familiar and often exaggerated ideological landscape of our SF narratives—a landscape wherein determining a moral center is usually a simple matter, since aliens are typically invaders, technology often wears a threatening face, and scientists repeatedly pursue their research in dangerous directions—things are complicated, much as they usually are in real life. And *Battlestar Galactica*, for all of its forthright confrontation of pressing cultural concerns, seldom settles into what Geraghty terms "the predictive nature" of the genre (*American Science Fiction* 114), even in the form's most "progressive" moments. Thus, while the series in a variety of ways challenges traditional gender roles, it also problematizes the alternatives. As it presents us with new racial—even species—relationships, it acknowledges the challenges built into those same relationships. Even when modeling political decisions that enable human survival, it illustrates how much those decisions are embedded in a *realpolitik* that repeatedly spurs compromises and misrepresentations. But this sort of recognition—of the difficulties that attend all of our cultural debates—finally may be one of the series' key accomplishments.

As an example, we might consider the show's treatment of gender concerns through its many central women characters. We have already noted how Number Six is presented. The first of the new, human-seeming Cylons to be introduced, she easily recalls the seductive robot Maria from the seminal SF film *Metropolis* (1927), as well as a host of cinema's more recent dangerous feminine androids or cyborgs, such as those of *Blade Runner* (1982), *Steel and Lace* (1990), and *Eve of Destruction* (1991). When she first appears, accompanied by two of the gleaming metal Cylon Centurions, Number Six in stark contrast wears a form-fitting, low-cut red dress and long brown suede boots, as she approaches a human military official and begins kissing him as the Cylon attack gets under way. As Susan George has noted, here, as she administers a quite literal "kiss of death" and in much of the series,

All of her military service is thus tinged by a sense of guilt and loss, even as she also struggles with a basic part of her feminine character. Wounded in guerilla operations against the Cylons on the planet Caprica, she awakes to find herself in what looks like a human hospital but is actually a Cylon "farm," a facility where they have gathered various human females, to conduct experiments on women's sexual organs, as the Cylons try to learn how they might reproduce biologically. When told by a Cylon, pretending to be a human doctor, that she must "keep that reproductive system in great shape. It's your most valuable asset these days," Starbuck is troubled, for she understands the apparent logic in what he says—that humans desperately need to reproduce if they are to survive as a species—but she also knows how equally valuable a skilled pilot like her is to the fleet's and humanity's protection from the Cylons. When she finally learns this "doctor" is a Cylon and that she too is being "farmed" for reproductive experimentation, she frees herself and, with the aid of human resistance fighters, helps to destroy the facility, including the other women being held there. While her resistance and escape are presented as heroic actions, this episode, as Patrick Sharp observes, could also be seen as a kind of "visceral rejection of motherhood," as if she were little more than "a man in a woman's body" (66). But that "rejection" also represents her resistance to any sort of conventional gender role, while also preparing us for her eventual development as a figure of salvation—as she seems to return from the dead and, through a vision of her father, finds a route to a habitable planet where humanity might start afresh. In effect, the show suggests that the sort of complex revisioning of gender roles that she demonstrates might be one of the keys to a more hopeful future.

Like Starbuck, Sharon "Boomer" Valerii—who, because she is a Cylon, also has other incarnations, such as Number Eight and Sharon "Athena" Agathon—is a woman warrior and highly skilled Viper pilot, as well as someone whose potential maternal role becomes crucial to the narrative. But as a Cylon, secretly implanted among the humans and programmed with false human memories, Boomer also becomes a key touchstone for the series' ethnic concerns. She is someone who "passes" for human, and even after she learns of her true nature, she is willing to do anything to avoid being "outed," including compromising her boyfriend Chief Tyrol.

In a later incarnation as Athena, a known Cylon, but one who is trusted by Admiral Adama, she must endure the sort of suspicions that attach to that "racial" difference and is constantly being forced to prove her allegiance to the human cause. In fact, at one point she shoots and kills her earlier version, Boomer; in another instance she helps the human fleet destroy an attacking flight of Cylon ships; and she later allows herself to be "killed" so that she might be resurrected at the Cylon base, thereby enabling her to rescue her own human–Cylon hybrid child Hera. Over the course of the series she thus repeatedly demonstrates her chosen commitment to aid the humans, in effect, rising above simple racial considerations, in order to help build a new relationship between humans and Cylons, one in which, following the successful birth of Hera, the two species manage to breed a new and stronger humanoid type, a hybrid race that, as the series' conclusion suggests, will effectively inherit the earth and might eventually overcome the destructive "racial" attitudes of their forebears.

Moreover, since Number Eight/Boomer/Athena is played by the Korean actress Grace Park, she also gives Battlestar Galactica's racial/ethnic explorations a more immediately recognizable context, that of Asian–Western relations. In their discussions of the series, both Leilani Nishime and Eve Bennett examine how this dynamic works in concert with the character's Cylon nature in order to foreground traditional racial stereotypes and attitudes. In Nishime's analysis, Park's character, particularly in the Athena identity, evokes two very familiar contemporary depictions of Asian–American interracial connections: that of the adopted Asian child and the marriage of the Asian woman to a Caucasian man. Both subjects are reimagined here through the mixed-race (or doubly mixed-race) child Hera and the relationship between Athena and the colonial officer Helo by whom she has become pregnant. But beyond simply offering fairly familiar versions of "the alien Other as a stand in for racial and ethnic difference" (453), the mixed-race child and marital relationship, Nishime offers, serve a distinct ideological purpose, and one that she suggests might undermine the series' otherwise complex presentation of racial issues. For in mobilizing these two familiar tropes and bringing them to a satisfying end, she argues, Battlestar Galactica actually tends to normalize rather than work through the difficulties of such human circumstances, as it narrates a "colonial, paternalistic story of abandoned and rejected children who need to be guided and cared for," as well as one about "the liberal, global, adult female who can and does choose the U.S. over all others" (461–62). In this crucial instance, Nishime suggests, the series does accept too easily an answer for the complex cultural concerns that it foregrounds.

In the latter discussion, Eve Bennett comes to a similar conclusion, as she examines the two principle versions of Eight—Boomer and Athena—in terms of two enduring Western myths of Asian femininity: that of the seductive and treacherous *femme fatale*, and that of the long-suffering and tragic Madame Butterfly figure. Of course, both are largely traditional cultural constructions, or as Bennett offers, "ways in which imperial powers represent the people of the countries they wish to colonise or otherwise exert authority over" (24). Here those stereotypes are writ large, with Boomer repeatedly seducing human men and, because of her Cylon programming, trying to assassinate Adama who has always trusted her; and with Athena, who also seduces Helo, but ultimately proves faithful to him, and who even fights against her own "race" to save her hybrid child Hera. However, we should note that Athena has been programmed to act in these ways—that programming effectively foregrounding how all cultures unconsciously sway, or program, the actions of their members. Despite Athena's ability to break free from her programming and to choose a fate for herself, to play an "active, productive" role (41) in determining the future, Bennett still sees her ultimate assimilation into human culture as troubling, something less than a subversion of traditional Western "orientalist" attitudes, although she is unable to suggest what might have been a more satisfying alternative.

Perhaps more revealing is the series' gradual shift in emphasis from the Number Eights to the interracial child Hera, and the accompanying focus on Athena's and Helo's attachment to their child. Giving birth in these troubled circumstances, as we have noted, is itself a difficult thing, and as the narrative emphasizes, no other efforts at human–Cylon breeding have succeeded. In fact, the series suggests, through both the extreme efforts required of Athena and Helo to rescue their child and Athena's ability to comfort the child when she becomes ill—and when no other Number Eight can—that a special bond of love binds together this new family, a love that might well be the only solution to traditional, culturally programmed racial attitudes.

Moreover, Athena's giving birth to what the series figures as the mother of all future humanity, a Mitochondrial Eve, as she is described, adds a further dimension to this interracial narrative. For in Hera, in that child who is finally *Battlestar Galactica*'s best trope for racial unity, Athena—named, after all, for the Greek goddess of wisdom, courage, and *civilization*—presents us with at least a possibility for a world (or civilization) beyond racial division.

In keeping with both its gender and racial explorations, *Battlestar Galactica* also offers a vision that, as is the case with most of modern American culture, is unavoidably political in nature. In fact, through its drastically reduced, small-scale version of human society, the show is, from the first episodes, able to let us see behind the scenes of society's workings. It reminds us that no culture-affecting decisions are simply made or "natural," but rather that all are negotiated, sometimes with allies, as in the expedient inauguration of Laura Roslin as President, sometimes with opposing parties, as when President Roslin at several points makes deals with the political activist and later an opposing candidate for the Presidency, Tom Zarek, and sometimes with the apparent enemy, as in the case of the alliance between the humans and a group of rebel Cylons who eventually join in the colonization of a new Earth. Moreover, those negotiations, as the series several times points up, often proceed not on the basis of what is seemingly "right" or moral, but, as Laura Roslin points out in one of the show's final episodes, on the basis of what is "smart" and necessary.

The result of this repeated emphasis on political machinations is a complex portrait of human acculturation. As Dylan Pank and John Caro observe, *Battlestar Galactica* offers a number of examples of "morally ambiguous decisions taken by ostensibly sympathetic protagonists. This permits the characters to be rather complex and to even exhibit self-contradictory behavior" (202)—as real humans so often do. A pre-eminent example is the situation we have already noted, when in "The Farm" episode (2005) Starbuck frees herself from the Cylons' baby-making machinery and then helps destroy the facility—and with it, the other women who are attached to the machinery there. Yet even more telling is the pattern of action we see in President Roslin. Far more than the hack political appointee many initially see her as, she repeatedly demonstrates her earnestness and even care for "her people," as she terms the survivors. But as we have noted, she is also not above lying or taking politically expedient stands to achieve her ends. Thus, in "Downloaded" (2006) in an effort at covering up the successful birth of the Cylon–human child Hera, she spirits away the newborn and lies about her survival, saying that the child died right after birth because of defective lungs. In the two-part "Lay Down Your Burdens" (2006), Roslin conspires to rig the Presidential election in her favor when she suspects that her main opposition, Gaius Baltar, is working with the Cylons and thus cannot be trusted to rule. And in the episode "Dirty Hands" (2007), she tries to confiscate and burn the manuscript of Baltar's book on class consciousness, which is leading to labor problems in the fleet, and to do so she lies to him, indicating that the copy he attempted to smuggle out of jail has been intercepted. However, these and other, similar decisions are, almost without exception, ones made in desperate circumstances, apparently with the fate of humanity depending on them. They serve to remind us *not* that politics and politicians are corrupt, but that real-world circumstances prompt difficult decisions, often made hastily or without full knowledge, and that such decisions must often be revisited and altered, as when Roslin eventually cedes the Presidential election to Baltar. But *Battlestar Galactica*'s ability to illustrate such complex situations—and to suggest their consequences—demonstrates its unusual commitment to cultural commentary, as well as the potential for SFTV to engage viewers in an exploration of issues central to the very life of their culture.

4

SFTV AUDIENCES

While our previous chapters have emphasized the content of SFTV, this one will center on something that might seem all too self-evident, the *appeal* of SFTV, specifically by focusing on the form's audience and on how that audience has changed in recent years. This discussion follows from the frequent contention that the audience for SF has typically been rather different from that for most mainstream literature, film, and television. Commentators, particularly in the 1920s and 1930s when SF was first establishing its popular identity, often claimed that, more so than the audience for any other genre, the SF reader/viewer is interested in ideas, in speculation (thus the alternative, and indeed appropriate, term often used for much SF writing today, that of "*speculative* fiction"), in how our science and technology function *and* in the implications of that functioning, for individual life and for society as a whole. Yet as the proliferation of SF series in recent years suggests, the genre has become very much mainstream, aimed not at the children's audience of early space operas like *Captain Video* and *Tom Corbett, Space Cadet*, but at a broad cross-section of American viewers.

Moreover, that audience has demonstrated a powerful passion for its shows, as has been evidenced at various points in television history, such as with the famous audience mobilization against NBC to save Gene Roddenberry's milestone series *Star Trek* and a similar but ultimately unsuccessful effort by *Firefly* fans to rescue that show. Both the difference and the power of that audience seem worth examining, and we shall later trace out that audience heritage in a later beneficiary of the same sort of enthusiasm, *Far-scape*, a series that *TV Guide* has ranked number four among the top cult series of all time (Figure 4.1).

In his discussion of the development and growth of SF fandom throughout the various media, Edward James observes that this development "owes a great deal to the permeation of our culture by science-fictional ideas" (*Science Fiction* 149). This too seems an almost obvious point, particularly given the extent to which, as we noted in Chapter 2, even a number of cable channels that advertise their dedication to science, nature, and factual presentation—The Science Channel, National Geographic Channel, The History Channel—are now framing entire series around what can easily be described as science fictional concepts, such as UFO research (*UFO Hunters*), alien visitation (*Ancient Aliens*), and simply weird or scientifically unexplained phenomena (*Dark Matter: Twisted but True*). But James' point is worth underscoring because the "permeation" he notes points us towards three key components in the evolution of the special relationship between SF and its

Figure 4.1 *Space Patrol*'s direct address to a children's audience

fans, and thus the particularly keen fan involvement with SFTV: 1) a general cultural turn towards science and technology issues; 2) the existence of a widespread and generally like-minded viewership for science fictional concerns and themes, that is, the recognition by audiences that, to use an almost trite phrase drawn from the SF lexicon, "we are not alone"; and 3) the increasing media effort at accommodating both, that is, at reflecting common cultural concerns and addressing what has become something much more than a niche audience. To better frame this discussion of SF audiences and television, we might briefly consider each of these components.

THE CULTURAL TURN

The cultural turn should hardly be surprising, since some of the signal events of recent human history have been bound up in the achievements—for good or ill—of our science and technology. And here we might simply note a few such world-changing moments: the explosion of the atomic bomb that effectively marked the end of World War II and brought with it the potential for world-ending destruction; the Apollo moon landing in the midst of the Cold War, that galvanized public attention around the world, making all of humanity feel bound up in a signal scientific achievement; and the advent of the personal computer, which placed artificial intelligence in the hands of hundreds of millions of people and in the process essentially changed how we go about our daily lives. These and numerous other world-involving developments are clearly hard to overlook, their reverberations have been felt in all areas of our culture, and they have been subsumed in all of the SF we consume today and in all of the media in which we encounter SF, framing, for better or for worse, the human potential for world destruction, for exploring other realms, and for creating other forms of intelligence.

However, the sort of cultural turn that has contributed to the development of our interest in both science and technology issues, and of course in SF itself, goes back much farther, has been changing our lives for longer than just the period since World War II, and has left us an important legacy for thinking about—and working through—such changes. For Western culture has been "turning" in this way for hundreds (if not thousands) of years, and has long been refining what we think of as science and technology, while inserting them more and more obviously into the work of daily life—and into our entertainment. It has even, at the very least since the turn of the nineteenth century, been providing us with a special lens for seeing and speculating about science and technology that, after some time, we came to label SF. And it has helped us develop new technologies to assist in that seeing and speculating—technologies such as radio, film, television, and the internet. That turn thus might let us think of SF itself, and especially, for our purposes here, SFTV, as itself a technology and an important part of that larger cultural development, of our "permeation" by science and technology.

Keeping that cultural turn in mind is especially important for thinking about the evolution of the SF audience or fandom—both broadly considered *and* for a medium like television. For the constant presence and influence of science and technology have become very much our common climate, a kind of air that we all breathe. In fact, noted SF historian Brooks Landon has suggested that "the felt experience of science and technology has so permeated contemporary life as to render our culture itself science fictional" (xiii). As such, contemporary culture unconsciously encourages—and facilitates—certain *technological behaviors*, ranging from the widespread fascination with rockets and space exploration that we saw during the period of the space race of the 1960s; to an addiction to on-line shopping, as the internet has taken on a pronounced commercial character since the late 1990s; to today's absorption with "tweeting" the most casual of observations, thanks to the combination of pervasive smartphones and the Twitter application. We might even include the fairly frequent cult-like dedication to various television series—but especially to SFTV series like *Star Trek*, *Farscape*, *Firefly*, or *Lost*—that have managed to touch a meaningful portion of viewers' lives. These and many other behaviors are both culturally symptomatic and culturally binding, as they fundamentally draw people together into shared activities, reflect shared concerns, affirm shared values, all of them associated with that "science fictional world" that Landon notes.

But that point also reminds us how much the contemporary world does indeed seem like science fictional work, how much it seems constantly new and imaginational—as well as *challenging*. As such, we are constantly confronted with situations or possibilities that reflect what we encounter in the world of SFTV, as when a zipline accident leaves a woman being consumed by flesh-eating bacteria, a double-amputee runs in the 2012 Olympics using carbon-fiber prostheses, or, against all odds, human curiosity lands the Curiosity rover on the surface of Mars. And these situations can not only bring us up short, causing us to see our own world and beliefs a bit differently, but also challenge us to *evaluate* that world differently, even question its status quo. It is for this reason that SF has often been described as an implicitly *subversive* genre, or to draw on the famous definition of the form offered by Darko Suvin, a form "whose necessary and sufficient conditions are the presence and interaction of estrangement and cognition" (7). What Suvin suggests is that in allowing us to recognize elements of our world, while also shifting them somewhat, estranging us from that world's constructs, SF opens a door on questioning that world and possibly on suggesting alternatives or even solutions to its more pressing problems. So the genre, while mirroring the scientific and technological turn of contemporary culture, becomes a significant and, more important, a *useful* technology, one that allows us, either through the proxy of series' characters or through the inspiration the programs personally provide, to participate in the reworking or remaking of our world.

THE AUDIENCE

As the second dimension cited above suggests, the "we" who are thus invited to participate in the activity of SFTV often tend not to be (or not to see themselves as) quite the same as those who read other genres or view other sorts of television programs. However, as the sheer number of new series suggest, they are an increasingly large audience, and one that finds many opportunities for what we might term community formation. It has long been suggested that SF fans who comprise this community, whether their interests are in literature, film, or television, tend to think of themselves as, in various ways, *different* from other popular audiences—as better educated, as having more interest in scientific and technological issues, as being more concerned about the future. As John Tulloch and Henry Jenkins argue, that audience has "its origins in a reforming, professional middle class" (57), one that was originally characterized by an optimistic tendency and that embraced a kind of technological utopianism. However, in more recent times—and influenced by a variety of contemporary concerns, such as environmental problems, technological failures, economic collapse, and authoritarian politics—that optimism has been tempered, and the SF audience has become somewhat more pessimistic, as the recent appearance of numerous post-apocalyptic and dystopian series (among them, *Firefly, Jericho, The Walking Dead,* and *Revolution*) might readily suggest.

To better frame this shift, we might briefly consider the early formation of that rather distinctive audience. As Edward James reminds us, "sf fans existed before sf itself was named" (*Science Fiction* 52) as a genre. While in its developing days SF was known by an array of terms—scientification, scientific romance, scientific fiction, invention stories, and so forth—all of them essentially denoted a genre that was perceived to be "not merely entertainment: it had a mission" (53), and one that involved its audience.[1] It seemed to speak directly to those who understood the crucial importance of science and technology for the modern world, those who were adherents of the emerging gospel of scientific progress, or more broadly, those who saw themselves as part of the future, which was an especially attractive premise for those who, after 1929, were living through a world-wide depression and then a variety of wars, both large and small. Thus it was hardly a coincidence that one of the *earliest*—although it was probably not the first—of World Science Fiction Conventions took place in conjunction with the 1939 New York World's Fair, the theme of which was "Building The World of Tomorrow."[2] In effect, SF aficionados of this era, those who read such pulp magazines as *Amazing Stories* and *Astounding Stories,* saw movie serials like *Flash Gordon* (1936) and *Buck Rogers* (1939), listened to radio adaptations of *The Time Machine* and *War of the Worlds,* and dreamt of television, were people who, unlike most of the populace, "got it," people who understood the importance of preparing their minds and their world for a very different and more positive "Tomorrow."

Moreover, in constructing those visions, SF also spoke for those adherents, giving them a voice—and in a way that other popular genres did not seem to do—in helping advance the cause of modern science and furthering the development of life- and world-changing technologies. The editors of those early SF journals, *Amazing, Astounding, Wonder Stories,* and others quickly found that the letters columns, or what some referred to as the "backyard" section of the magazines, were a major component of their popularity, allowing enthusiasts to debate the quality of the stories being published, to discuss the scientific premises for those stories, and, more generally, to exchange ideas with like thinkers, including the editors and the story authors themselves. Powered by what John Cheng describes as an underlying "vision of a progressive and democratic science" (249), those exchanges resulted, especially in the interwar period (that is, from approximately 1926 when *Astounding* was first published to America's entry into World War II in 1941), in the formation of the first fan clubs, the publication of fan-produced fiction magazines, the development of specialized science and technology organizations (such as the International Scientific Association, the American Interplanetary Society, and the German Verein fur Raumschiffahrt), even political action groups (like the Committee for the Political Advancement of Science Fiction). Such developments prompted the editor of one fanzine of the period to remark, "The average Science Fiction fan is also a scientist in the making" (qtd. in Cheng 289). Another, and especially visible, effect of these exchanges is that they would give birth to what has become one of the most distinctive markers of SF fandom, the fan convention or "Con."

These fan events, with which most of us are now quite familiar, go by a variety of names, such as Worldcon (the World Science Fiction Convention, its history tracing back to the 1939 New York Con), PulpFest, Star Wars Celebration, SciFi Expo, DragonCon, ConQuest, Dimension Jump, and literally dozens of others. They occur fairly regularly, both within the United States and in various other countries; are organized by fan groups and by professional, profit-making companies; and all typically involve a wide variety of informative, entertaining, and celebratory activities, including panel discussions, special speakers, author readings, autograph sessions, costume shows and contests, game-playing venues, art shows, a marketplace, cocktail parties, and a ball (or dance). And while they have come to accommodate a great diversity of fan types—those interested in literature, film, television, gaming, comics, animation, puppetry—it is noteworthy that SFTV has both bulked increasingly large in most of these gatherings and has itself spawned a number of specialized Cons, including ones dedicated to such popular series as *Babylon 5*, *Farscape*, *Firefly*, *Doctor Who*, *Stargate SG-1* (with the aptly named Timegate combining fans of the time and dimensional-traveling *Doctor Who* with those of the *Stargate* franchise), as well as multiple annual Cons dedicated to the expanded world of the various *Star Trek* series and films (Figure 4.2). This diversity of formal conventions and their generally festive nature certainly suggest that the SF audience has undergone some changes from the earlier serious advocacy of science and technology's transformative potential that had fueled the first such meetings in the late 1930s; in fact, they represent a more broadly focused enthusiasm for the speculative and the fantastic.

Those changes reflect a variety of causes, a few of which we might note here because of the way they reflect on—and have been reflected in—SFTV. As Robin Anne Reid sums up the contemporary situation, SF fandom has gone through "a period of intense and continuing growth and diversification because of changes in technology, media, demographics, and fan activities" (206). Television especially has expanded the scope of the SF audience and, thanks to the famous rescuing of *Star Trek* from cancellation through a letter-writing campaign, given viewers a new sense of power

Figure 4.2 Posters advertise multiple *Doctor Who* fan conventions

and participation in the "life" of their favorite series. The advent of cable and satellite broadcasting, along with the internet and the marketing of shows for individual consumption, has also provided new venues—and an increased demand—for SF product, including opportunities for syndicating old shows, and new ways of encountering both current and older SF texts. Today we simply have new ways of encountering and consuming media SF, with many fans purchasing or digitally accessing complete seasons of a series, watching its episodes in close succession, and in effect approaching it not as discrete, commercially interrupted episodes, but as a kind of long-form narrative.

And these same developments have given fans new opportunities for responding to those texts, as in the case of on-line fan continuations/ expansions of popular SFTV series, such as *Star Trek*, *Blake's 7*, and *Stargate SG-1*. The aging of the Baby Boomer audience, brought up on SFTV in the form of the early 1950s space operas, *The Twilight Zone*, and *Star Trek*, has also resulted in a mature and relatively stable viewership, possessed of the sort of economic clout that sponsors readily take note of. Perhaps more important, that matured audience has generated expectations for more—and more *ambitious*—SFTV. But perhaps the most significant of those changes follows from the simple fact that SF, and more generally speculative fiction, has itself become so mainstream (again, part of that air we breathe). As Donna Haraway has suggested, today it seems like any "boundary between science fiction and social reality is an optical illusion" (*Simians* 149). Consequently, SF's concerns naturally tend to mirror and work through the broader concerns of the culture, reaching an audience that is far more conventional, and one that is, in some cases, even skeptical of the very science and technology that were formerly at the core of the genre's appeal and utopian promise.

For some this growth and broadening of the SF audience also represents an inevitable and troubling fragmentation as well, one that sees some segments of the SFTV audience embracing shows that might previously have been linked to another genre such as horror—as in the case of series like *Grimm*, *The Walking Dead*, and especially *Buffy the Vampire Slayer*—even as more conventionally science and technology-oriented series, like *Eureka* and *Fringe*, remain popular. Also, there has been an increased effort to target more specialized audiences, resulting in, for example, variations on the teen melodrama with such series as *Smallville*, *Roswell*, and *Misfits*; more animated SF aimed at different segments of the audience—children (*Adventure Time*, *Jimmy Neutron: Boy Genius*, and *Planet Sheen*), teens (*Star Wars: The Clone Wars*, the knock-off from George Lucas's *Star Wars* films), and a hip older audience (*Futurama*, *Mary Shelley's Frankenhole*, and *Tron: Uprising*); and an increased effort to tailor SF for a growing female audience, as we shall discuss below. This sort of fragmentation of SF fandom could simply be, as Edward James suggests, a broad cultural symptom; that is, it might be "related to the fragmentation of culture at large, the replacement of widespread values and loyalties by smaller subcultures, which some see as the most typical feature of postmodern or postmodernist culture" (*Science Fiction* 166). Yet it is also noteworthy for the way it is producing new and culturally important variations on what we might think of as traditional SF subjects and themes.

Drawing on the work of various cultural studies scholars, John Tulloch and Henry Jenkins have suggested that the different "streams" of fans or audience segments that we are noting might also be explained by the "different reading positions" that have resulted from the emergence of competing ideologies, changing subject positions, and shifting cultural attitudes (54). To place these "positions" in a less abstract context, we might note how all of them are interwoven in the emergence of an increasingly strong female audience for SFTV. It has often been suggested that the "grand narrative of science" has been largely male dominated, thereby implicating a male "subject position" from which most of the history of scientific and technological development has been presented, read, and valued (Tulloch and Jenkins 45). Taking its lead from that cultural "grand narrative," SF, consequently, has been seen by some as sharing in purported capitalist, sexist, and bourgeois attitudes—attitudes that have found some of their strongest challenges and interrogation in recent feminist criticism (such as that of Haraway, cited above) and that have been foregrounded in a recent wave of more gender-conscious SFTV. And in this context we might especially point to series like *Terminator: The Sarah Connor Chronicles*, a spin-off from the *Terminator* film series; *Dollhouse*, produced by and starring Eliza Dushku, one of the stars of the highly popular *Buffy the Vampire Slayer*; and *Battlestar Galactica*. These series, partly due to the involvement of women in their production, direction, and writing, have offered up a variety of strong female characters:

an action hero-type in *The Sarah Connor Chronicles*, a woman coming to self-awareness and realizing how she has been used in *Dollhouse*, and a female President in *Battlestar Galactica*. Through such characters, these and similar series are providing useful templates for rethinking gender roles, both within and outside of the SF genre.

In fact, those "different . . . positions" are prompting audiences to "read" series like the ones noted above in rather different ways than in the past and have prompted different responses to them. In both *The Sarah Connor Chronicles* and *Battlestar Galactica*, for example, viewers encounter a dramatically revised vision of the cyborg—a figure that feminist scholar Donna Haraway has identified as a potent image for thinking about our culture's ongoing "reinvention" of the feminine, and indeed of human nature (*Simians* 3). Far removed from images of the sexless, tin-clad robot that recurred across the media landscape from the 1930s through the 1950s and that were often rather simplistic technological menaces, these figures, whether the highly sexualized and seductive Number Six (played by Tricia Helfer) of *Battlestar Galactica* or the seemingly more demure and vulnerable teenaged persona of Cameron (Summer Glau), the Terminator in *The Sarah Connor Chronicles*, are never quite what they seem, and consequently they trouble any easy response (Figure 4.3). And that same problematic response attaches to the actions of both Cameron and the programmed "Active" Echo (Eliza Dushku) of *Dollhouse*—not a cyborg but a figure whose mind has been "wiped" so that she can be used, robot-like, for various exploitative purposes—both of whom represent a fundamentally different cultural representation of female heroism for SFTV. Lorrie Palmer argues that they signal a "recuperation of femininity" (94), in combination with a send-up of traditional tropes of the genre, such as that of the helpless and imperiled female, previously cast as an assistant to or love interest for the male scientist or hero. In these—and many other cases, Palmer observes—we see "slightly built, unapologetically feminine women taking over the job of butt kicking from the hypermuscular and excessively gendered stars of 1980s and 1990s cinema" (84), all reflecting not only the new gender images that are emerging in our culture, but also a steadily growing female audience for SFTV that indeed expects more contemporary gender representations.

And yet it might be worth recalling an observation made earlier—one that still suggests an important unifying point for our thinking about SF fandom

Figure 4.3 Marketing to female fans: the woman as Terminator in *Terminator: The Sarah Connor Chronicles*

and the SFTV audience. For even amid this sense of fragmentation, of different reading positions, and of a growing female fandom, there still seems to persist among SF fans as a group—as those many Cons might suggest—a tendency to see themselves as a bit different from the audiences for other genres and, in many ways, sharing a common concern. If no longer fans with a simple technocratic social purpose or utopian agenda, if no longer united by a kind of scientifically based optimism, they remain linked by a fascination with the visionary power of the imagination, by what we might term the lure, and indeed the pleasure, of *speculation*. For the genre presents them with examples of, and thus the possibility for what Brooks Landon has described as "science fiction thinking" (xiii), that is, for considering the prospect of change or progress, even envisioning what such change might look like. And the spread of SF across the whole range of media, to where, as Landon notes, it "has become a universally recognized category of film, television, music, music videos, electronic games, theme parks, military thinking, and advertising" (xv), only further validates the significance of that "thinking." It reminds the SFTV fan, for example, that he or she "is not alone," that there are others out there who are eager for those messages, attentive to them, and willing to engage in some of the serious work of culture, whether that involves building the future or guarding against some of our seemingly inevitable technological follies.

THE MEDIA AND FANDOM

As the above comments about efforts to address a growing female fandom should remind us, the media also play an active role in constructing and appealing to the SFTV audience. In fact, all of our media are today well aware that there is an audience hungry for SF out there—in fact, what might seem like *various* niche or fragment audiences—and the networks, cable companies, and media producers have made increasing efforts to address that SF fandom through programming that operates according to certain fundamental principles. SF historian Gary Westfahl notes that, even as pulp SF was first appearing early in the twentieth century, one of the form's founding fathers and most active publishers, Hugo Gernsback, was already observing that there were three things that fans seemed to be looking for from SF media: they wanted it to "provide entertainment," to "furnish . . . education," and to "offer inspiration" (Westfahl, *Hugo Gernsback* 20). And today, we can find these same concerns—with entertainment, education, and, after a broad cultural fashion, even inspiration—still marking the primary ways in which SFTV interfaces with, appeals to, and even helps build its audience.

The appeal of *entertainment* seems almost self-evident. From its widespread introduction into American culture in the post-World War II era, television was anticipated as a visual replacement for what had become the ubiquitous domestic entertainment medium, radio. As Jeffrey Sconce offers, it was presented as a device that could "alternately transport viewers into another world and transport other worlds into the home" (127), functioning like a kind of electronic theater, while also endowing viewers with their own sort of electronic presence, that is, a place within those imaginary worlds. And in that doubly transportive effect, television has always assumed something of a science fictional quality, suggesting a technological ability to transcend the limits of space and time—like the TARDIS of *Doctor Who*—to take us anywhere.[3] It seems only appropriate, then, that a number of early SFTV shows would foreground television itself, underscoring its entertainment function, as in the case of *Captain Video*'s presenting episodes of old serials on its "Special Remote Carrier Beam," *Johnny Jupiter*'s television that could capture signals (actually puppet shows) from the planet Jupiter, or even *The Outer Limits* with its opening self-conscious injunction to viewers: "For the next hour, sit quietly and we will control all that you see and hear. You are about to participate in a great adventure. You are about to experience the awe and mystery which reaches [sic] from the inner mind to . . . the Outer Limits."

But it was always assumed that this entertainment experience was related to the audience's own special fascination with what they might encounter at those "Outer Limits," that is, to the pleasures fans found in SF itself. For SF has always been up to something more than simply depicting the possibilities of science and technology; as Edward James explains, it has also been intent on "providing a particular kind of emotional fulfillment" (*Science Fiction* 103) through those depictions, for generating what has often been described as a *sense of wonder*. And with its constantly expanding technical capacities—for producing cinematic-style digital effects, for transmitting high definition 3-D images, for providing multi-track surround sound, all while employing wider and larger screens—SFTV has entered into a new era of depicting and presenting that which once might have seemed to stand beyond those "Limits," that is, to be unavailable in a medium like television. But *Farscape* has introduced audiences to a sentient, living spaceship (*Moya*); *Stargate SG-1* (and its sequels) has visualized a wormhole technology capable of transporting viewers (much like television itself) practically anywhere in the universe; *Fringe* has depicted a parallel universe that mixes various similarities and alternatives to our own, and it often has characters interacting with their parallel selves (and thus their own, slightly altered images). All, in their distinct ways—through the use of puppets and models, through digital imagery, and through compositing techniques—display television's increasing capacities for visualizing the wondrous, while also catering to the SF audience's delight in and special appreciation for that sense of wonder.

The assumption that the SFTV audience, at least in part, craves an element of *education* is also a long-standing one, hearkening back to the early description of SF as a "tale of science" (*Science Fiction* 13), as well as to some of the overheated rhetoric that greeted television's introduction, such as one critic's prediction that it would prove "the greatest force for world enlightenment . . . that history has ever known" (qtd. in Corn and Horrigan 25). Consonant with those notions, we might note (and as a footnote to our discussion of SFTV history in Chapter 1), that accompanying the first great wave of SF programming, those space operas of 1949–56, there were various highly popular science education programs, such as *The Johns Hopkins Science Review* created by public relations man Lynn Poole, the *Bell System Science Series* overseen by famed film director Frank Capra (known for his "Capracorn" brand of feel-good comedy), and the *Disneyland* series' "Man in Space" shows, featuring German rocket designer Wernher von Braun, as well as some of Disney's best animation. These were all, as Patrick Lucanio and Gary Coville point out, successful efforts at delivering "science for the masses," for an audience clearly interested in the impact of science and technology on their lives, as well as an audience that could "make things happen" (*Smokin' Rockets* 151), as the popular support for the soon-to-be-initiated and highly expensive space program of the late 1950s and 1960s would demonstrate.

Yet we also need to underscore that such programs were never meant to be simply informational or dryly instructional. Rather, as Poole himself describes, these shows all aimed for a new sort of combination, as they mixed speculation, humor, animation, even stunts. The result was one that, much like SF itself, could "entertain, delight, and hold audience attention while giving out worthwhile information" (LaFollette 219). And that strategy— an approach that Walt Disney would evocatively label "edutainment"—has resurfaced powerfully in more recent times, as television executives, recognizing the broad appeal of what we have come to know as "reality television," have looked for new ways of presenting the "real," including the combination of SF and documentary-style programming in the form of shows like *Chasing UFOs* (2012), *Ancient Aliens* (2009–13), *Ghost Hunters* (2004–present), and *Sci-Fi Science: Physics of the Impossible* (2009–present). While hardly all of a kind, these shows typically mix some hard science with an element of sensationalism, thereby capitalizing on a dynamic always implicit in SF, that between the unknown or mysterious and the explanatory power of science. Moreover, they commonly build in an emotional pay-off through re-enactments, effective, quick-cut editing, and various subjective techniques (especially the case in the short-lived *Chasing UFOs*) that together create a sense of immediacy and audience involvement. And like more traditional SF programming, they are usually organized around what Catherine Johnson terms "a perpetuated hermeneutic, in that the questions upon which they are premised are never fully resolved" (3).

Of course, both entertainment and education are closely implicated in that third category of media impact that Gernsback noted, audience *inspiration*. For the pleasures and satisfactions that SFTV can produce effectively allow viewers to engage with its ideas, reassuring them that it is okay to think "outside of the box" of contemporary culture—and science. A number of early SFTV figures have acknowledged that this sort of engagement was precisely their aim, even as they crafted series that, at first glance, seemed like little more than generic entertainments. When Rod Serling proposed doing a SF/mystery series to be known as *The Twilight Zone*, it was widely perceived as something of a retreat to formulaic story-telling for someone who was well known for his controversial teleplays, but as Rodney Hill chronicles, Serling and his collaborators well understood how SF and the relatively new medium of television might together function as "a tool for creating important, socially critical drama in a form that would not incur the wrath of network executives, advertising agencies, corporate sponsors, or congressional committees" ("Mapping" 124), in short that they could thus inspire audiences without getting in trouble. And while Gene Roddenberry, for example, often repeated the story about selling *Star Trek* to NBC executives by explaining that it was simply "*Wagon Train* to the stars," that is, a popular Western dressed in new trappings, his aim, as he has said, was always to present "subject matter and situations on *Star Trek* that would challenge and stimulate the thinking of the viewer" (Whitfield and Roddenberry 112). Of course, both series are remembered today largely *because of* their uncommon ability to inspire viewers, taking them into other, perhaps unsuspected realms, or as Serling's prologue for *The Twilight Zone* evocatively put it, into "a fifth dimension, beyond that which is known to man . . . the dimension of the imagination."

And that same desire for the inspirational continues to drive contemporary SFTV audiences, as several particularly noteworthy developments demonstrate. One is the cult-like following that a number of shows have attracted—a development that has led industry executives to target specific audiences and to be more mindful about their marketing and licensing practices. Of course, the best known of these fervent fan groups is the Trekkers (often disparagingly referred to as Trekkies) of *Star Trek*, fans so taken by the extended *Star Trek* series' mythos—one involving world peace and unity, a respect for and curiosity about diversity, and a version of technological utopianism—that they create and wear Star Fleet uniforms, exchange Vulcan greetings, learn elements of the Klingon language, and freely quote lines from many episodes. Moreover, they have provided a pattern for a number of subsequent fan groups. In his study of such fan activities, *Textual Poachers*, Henry Jenkins cites similar activities that have clustered around a variety of other series, both within and outside of the SF world, including *Beauty and the Beast*, *Starman*, *Cagney and Lacey*, *Twin Peaks*, and the British series *Blake's 7*. More recently the abruptly cancelled series *Firefly* (with only 11 episodes broadcast at the time of cancellation) inspired a highly active fan community that adopted the name Browncoats, after a rebel group in the series. Their activity led to several specialized conventions, raised money for a number of charities, prompted Universal Studios to produce a feature version of the series, *Serenity* (2005), and has resulted in a fan-made documentary *Done the Impossible* (2006), a fan-made sequel *Browncoats: Redemption* (2010), and a comic book series. On the basis of that strong audience response, *Entertainment Weekly* has ranked the series 11th in its recent poll of the top 25 cult television shows.

Another of those developments, already implicit in some of the cult-like activity just described, is the audience appropriation of favorite SF texts, or what Jenkins terms "poaching." As the rebellious fan activity noted above should begin to suggest, the audience for SFTV is generally not, as they were early on perceived by the television industry, simply passive recipients of sponsored products. They might more often—and more accurately—be described as active participants who have been in some way inspired by their encounter with particular shows and, as a result, have found themselves to be part of a new sort of community, one that has allowed them to "transform the experience of watching television into a rich and complex participatory culture" (*Textual* 23). That poaching can take a variety of forms, including the writing of fan novels and stories, the creation of video sequels and extensions of SFTV series, the composing and singing of fan songs and other music (termed *filking*), the production of art that appropriates—and that allows fans to effectively reinterpret—elements of favorite shows, and the creation and distribution of toys, clothing, and other products that adapt and sometimes put into unexpected contexts (including unconventional sexual relationships) the characters and situations of SFTV. As a result, the fans—little concerned with traditional copyright issues—have actually become active text producers, "participants in the construction and circulation of textual meanings" (Jenkins 24), and in effect artists in their own rights.

A third—and perhaps the most compelling—piece of evidence that the audience continues to find inspiration in the industry's SF efforts can be seen in the appearance of a specialized outlet dedicated to that fervent fan base, the Syfy (originally Sci-Fi) Channel. Launched September 24, 1992 as a joint venture of the USA Network, Paramount Pictures, and Universal Studios, the Sci-Fi Channel was designed both to appeal to a fast-growing niche audience, that of SF fans (who had begun to spread across the whole media spectrum), and to provide an outlet for various movies and series—including the original *Star Trek* and Rod Serling's follow-up to *The Twilight Zone*, *Night Gallery* (1970–73)—that these studios controlled. Since being acquired by NBC-Universal, the Channel has offered a programming mix of older, syndicated television series, new, original SF and fantasy series (such as *Taken*, aka *Steven Spielberg Presents: Taken*, and *Battlestar Galactica*), reality shows (such as *Monster Man*), made-for-television movies, and, as an indication of its obviously mixed audience, wrestling shows. And the Channel's rebranding as Syfy in 2009 reflected not only the parent company's desire, as Syfy President Dave Howe offers, to establish "a unique and distinct brand name that we can own for the future, that works in the multiplatform, on-demand world" of contemporary broadcasting (qtd. in Leopold), but also a recognition that its audience has grown beyond traditional conceptions of SF, beyond what was becoming simply a catch-all term, and certainly beyond the stereotype of "geeky teenaged boys" that Howe almost dismissively cites.

That move, while it puzzled many of the Channel's long-time viewers and even opened up new possibilities for confusion over its primary programming focus, also suggests that the Channel has attained a certain level of maturity. Indeed, the naming of Bonnie Hammer as Executive Vice-President and General Manager of the Channel in 1998, signaled a new mindfulness of the audience in cable broadcasting, a sense that a channel like Sci-Fi was not limited to a small niche of SF fans; as Hammer offers, "we wanted to know how we could open up the channel to make people see how it relates to them" (Anderson). Increasingly, as shows like *Battlestar Galactica*, *Painkiller Jane*, and *Lost Girl* suggest, the Channel has courted the female audience. In doing so it seems to have recognized that, like science itself, SF is not just for guys, while it has also sought to build an array of different show types—conventional dramas, dramedies (that is, a mixture of comedy and drama, as in the case of *Eureka* and *Warehouse* 13), reality shows, game shows, movies—all clustered around the notion of the speculative, whether that speculation is connected to science and technology, the supernatural, the mythic, or even the world of entertainment itself. Of course, this description could well apply to many other channels or networks today, since it is hardly only Syfy that has sought to cast its audience net more broadly or that has deployed a variety of show vehicles to tap into current fashion. But Syfy foregrounds an emerging situation, that across the television spectrum there simply seems an increased awareness that our world is indeed more science fictional in character and that an SF inflection—or at least a speculative one—may be one of the more effective ways of connecting with a wide range of contemporary viewers.

Given this context, it should be somewhat clearer why the title of this chapter referred to "audiences," rather than simply "the audience" for SFTV. For what we have been noting in a variety of ways is the very plurality of that genre audience—one that has changed over time, one that in many ways seems more fragmented today (by genre distinctions, by gender, by activity, etc.), and one that is subject to a variety of different industry appeals. Yet these audiences still have much in common. They continue to seem among the most passionate of audiences in support of their favorite shows, as the various Cons with fans involved in parades, filking contests, and cosplay suggest[4]; they are still interested in what lies beyond the conventionally established "outer limits"—of conventional science or conventional thinking; and they remain intrigued by and invested in our media, and especially by SFTV's ability to *real-ize*—that is, to present or visualize as seemingly real— all that we speculate about. More to the point, SFTV has simply established itself as one of our most effective technologies for delivering all that those audiences most want from their public media.

KEY SERIES: *FARSCAPE*: CHARACTER AND AUDIENCE

In her effort at introducing viewers to the US–Australian co-production *Farscape*, Jan Johnson-Smith rather breezily describes it as a "marvelous and whacky 'lost in space' story," and notes its "remarkably mixed" array of characters—characters who, on the one hand, hint of "a youngish audience" for the series, but who, on the other, are frequently engaged in some obviously not so "youngish" antics (161). For the "cast" of the series is made up partly of animatronic puppets, created by Co-Producer Brian Henson and the Jim Henson Creature Shop, their lineage tracing back to the Muppets of *Sesame Street*, *The Muppet Show*, and a variety of other youth-directed shows and films. But it also includes a wide array of humanoid characters who come in various sizes and shapes, act violently, wear revealing costumes, and demonstrate "frequent and blatant sexuality," including what Johnson-Smith accurately labels as "a tendency to bondage/torture" (161). That combination of seeming escapees from children's programming with other figures who, as Rygel, one of the Muppet creations, observes, seem to "enjoy their freedoms far too much" ("Look at the Princess, Part I"), certainly makes for a difficult estimation, much less analysis, of the series' intended audience.

However, *Farscape*'s audience, and especially the show's tendency to figure that audience within the text, is a dimension of the series worth exploring, particularly since *TV Guide*, with an eye to the series' fervent following, ranked it as one of the "top cult shows ever". As Johnson-Smith's comments suggest, the series seems to have directed its appeal across a curiously wide viewership, even as a number of its elements at times appear to target specific segments of that audience at the expense of some others. In fact, Jes Battis prefaces his study of the show with a nod precisely in this direction, as he notes how he had over time watched a few scenes, all of which he initially thought "confusing and irredeemably silly" (21), as if aimed directly at a much younger viewership. However, that first, and not very positive impression dissipated, as he came to realize that what previously put him off about the show might actually have been part of *Farscape*'s rather "innovative" approach to both televisual and SF narrative—its emphasis on multiple characters, including multiple *types* of characters, and multiple points of view, resulting in lines of action and dialogue that reach across many episodes and story arcs to gradually unfold in significance as viewers encounter additional characters, learn about other races/species, and begin to recognize and appreciate the complex relationships that, despite their often strange appearances and behaviors, all share—and in many ways share with us.

Admittedly, the series' action does center largely on one rather conventional character, the "lost" astronaut John Crichton who, while testing out a new theory for space travel, is accidentally sucked through a wormhole and deposited in a distant part of the universe. He is the only human in the show's strangely "mixed" range of "species," and thus the figure who most effectively represents the audience in the narrative—or at least the figure with whom audiences might most readily identify. And yet Crichton's point of view, while dominant, is often challenged, and his sense of what is right or wrong never stands—for long—as the only measure of things. Rather, he, like the very varied fandom we have noted, is repeatedly surprised by new information, such as the fact that the "biomechanoid" ship on which he suddenly finds himself, *Moya*, is itself a living entity with a mind of its own, as well as a Pilot who is bonded to *Moya* for life and who typically speaks for her. And the other occupants of *Moya*—a group that would undergo some changes over the course of the series' four-year run—is largely made up of escaped prisoners, all of whom initially regard him as some kind of lower life form. In fact, when in the first episode one of them says, "Let's eat," Crichton, because of his very consciousness of difference, at first fears he might be on the menu. Surrounded by a variety of strange-looking characters and relegated to the distinctly uncomfortable (and unusual for series television) role of "the alien" here, he can only marvel to himself—and to the audience—in the sort of media-conscious commentary that would become one of the show's hallmarks: "Boy, was Spielberg ever wrong. *Close Encounters* my ass" ("Premiere").

Accidentally transformed into another world's E.T., Crichton thus finds that his own perspective is constantly being qualified by others, as the larger narrative of *Farscape* unfolds, and as he begins to help us, as Matt Hills has described such figures who direct our perspectives, "perform" our own role as audience (16). His comment to the rest of *Moya's* crew in the opening episode, "What is *wrong* with you people?" ("Premiere"), quickly forecasts a key thematic point for the show, namely, his need to reorient himself and reassess how he sees, and *understands*, things. And in the process, Crichton's comment tells us a bit about what is "wrong" with him—and perhaps with us as well: that he is too troubled by difference, too quick to form judgments about situations in these "Uncharted Territories" of outer space, too ready to see things only from a conventional, Earth- and human-centric vantage, a vantage that will invariably be challenged as episode builds upon episode to unveil a complex universe, and in the process to remind viewers, by way of analogy, of the complex world that they too inhabit.

We can see one dimension of that complexity in the show's history, which itself reminds us that there are other perspectives out there, at least others beyond those found in the boardrooms of traditional television networks where decisions about a series' future are made. For when in fall 2002 the Syfy Channel (or Sci-Fi, as it was then named) announced the cancellation of *Farscape*, just as the series' fourth season was about to air, it initiated a storm of response from that broad if hard-to-measure array of fans that Battis would eventually join, not just in the form of letters and telephone calls to the network, after the fashion that had helped save *Star Trek* from premature oblivion decades before, but also in the form of an internet and e-mail campaign that very quickly demonstrated the new power of computer technology—the power to draw people together on short notice, to mobilize them in common cause, and to produce a landslide of electronic messages in support of a clearly much-loved if also—from the Syfy Channel's perspective—too-expensive-to-produce show. As one of the initiators of this digitally driven campaign, CNN correspondent Renay San Miguel would announce, "Who knew that fans of the science fiction series . . . would use the Web to educate me and Headline News about just how powerful technology can be in spreading an idea" (San Miguel).

But spreading ideas, as we have already suggested, is very much at the core of the *Farscape* experience, and one of the reasons for that devoted cult following. Its many and diverse characters obviously convey different ideas—about themselves and about others—and in the process constantly challenge any sense of normalcy, including the notion that the Syfy Channel was dealing with a conventional SF show. Among that accidental and far-from-normal "crew," we might especially note: the blue priestess Zhaan, who is actually of a plant species, and one with strange sexual habits; the Luxan warrior Ka D'Argo who resembles a lion, has a frog-like tongue that injects venom, and often reacts to troubling situations by going into a violent state known as hyper-rage that can be dangerous even to friends and loved ones; and the ironically titled "Peacekeeper" soldier Aeryn Sun, who acknowledges that she is "a product of my upbringing," as she refuses Crichton's offer of friendship, views the other aliens onboard *Moya* as her enemies, and, when urged to feel some "compassion" for them, at first disavows knowledge of the term before allowing, "Oh yes, I know that feeling. I hate it." Through these and other characters' often puzzling but intriguing challenges to the norm—as measured out in Crichton—*Farscape* continually shows us that, as Battis observes, "Alien mores and ethics are as complex as human ones, and they often don't look anything like ours" (111). It is in this context of surprising differences that we need to see the series' attitude towards its audience, and its efforts at constructing that audience's own point of view through the manipulation—or "performance"—of its central human character's perspective.

Like many other television series, *Farscape* begins each episode with a montage of characteristic images—shots of Crichton as he is being sucked through the wormhole, close-ups of all of the central characters, brief images of them interacting and of *Moya* traveling through space, all accompanied by

Crichton's angst-laden voice-over in a kind of S.O.S. message, as he explains his situation to anyone who might be listening, even pleading: "Is there anybody out there who can hear me?" That opening, which would undergo some changes during the series' run, accomplishes many things. Besides (re)introducing the show's major characters, situating events in the far reaches of space, and even anticipating the nature of some relationships—as when we see Crichton and Aeryn in embrace—it sets a tone for the narrative that follows with its dark, jarring images and fast-paced editing. Working much like the recap introductions of old movie serials, all of these effects serve to open the door to new viewers, while also winking at the established fans who might pleasurably recognize these images lifted from previous episodes.

More than an invitation, though, that epigraphic matter communicates something important about this narrative. Through Crichton's anxious direct address to the audience, we learn about *Farscape*'s larger trajectory, not only that he "got shot through a wormhole" and is now "lost in some distant part of the universe," but also that he "is being hunted" by a Peacekeeper commander, is in need of "help," even as he continues "just looking for a way home." With no idea where in the vast reaches of the universe he is, audiences can assume that Crichton's picaresque wanderings might take him—and them—almost anywhere; however, his only hope for ever reaching "home" is through the help of others, of "anyone out there." This message, this reaching out to others, then, implicates them/us in the narrative and establishes a central thematic thrust for the entire series—an emphasis on the importance and ultimately the *need* of others, the need for connection and understanding.

This opening matter also forecasts an important narrative device for the series. We might recall how some of the earliest television space operas, particularly *Captain Video* and *Space Patrol*, would often break down the fourth wall between action and audience by having, in the former, Captain Video or the Video Ranger, and in the latter Commander Buzz Corry or Cadet Happy directly address the viewers (in costume and *in character*), whether to introduce the serial actions of the Captain's "special agents," to hawk sponsors' products, or to give moral directives to their young viewers. That unconventional strategy, accompanied by offered memberships in fan/support groups like the Video Rangers or Space Rangers, wove a web of intimate involvement with the series' characters and actions—a strategy to which *Farscape* in its own innovative way would return. For throughout the show's run, Crichton resorts to various versions of such outward-directed dialogue, including at various times: seemingly talking—aloud—to himself; carrying on a conversation with an imaginary character, such as his frequent antagonist Scorpius, who has implanted in Crichton's brain a neural chip version of himself; and interacting with other characters who, for different reasons, show up in his conscious or unconscious mind, waking or dreaming states. All of these situations manipulate point of view to blur the boundaries of the narrative world and in the process to provide the audience with another, often unexpected, level of address and involvement in that world.

The first of these strategies, that in which Crichton simply talks to himself, usually in response to some surprise or astonishing event, is common and occurs in practically every episode. It is, of course, partly a sign of Crichton's outsider/alien status, a reminder that, at least in the early seasons, he feels he has no one—apart from himself and the audience—with whom he can share his reactions, or who might actually understand them. Thus the comment earlier noted, "Boy, was Spielberg ever wrong," not only acknowledges how out of place he feels in these "Uncharted Territories," but also invites the viewers, undoubtedly familiar with Steven Spielberg's rather whimsical view of aliens offered in films like *Close Encounters of the Third Kind* (1977) and *E.T. the Extra-Terrestrial* (1982), to share his sense of amazement—an amazement that mirrors and gives voice to our own response to many of the strange (Muppet or prosthetic-produced) species we repeatedly encounter here. It is the type of response repeated in "Look at the Princess, Part 1" when Crichton, faced with a forced marriage to a local Princess and an array of outlandish robes he must wear for the ceremony, can only, in a note of submission, mutter to himself, "Welcome to Barbie World." The audience readily understands, and in a way that no characters in the narrative could, that he sees himself reduced to the role of a doll, a Ken to the Princess's Barbie, and that he has resigned himself to his fate (since doing so will ensure the safety of his shipmates). But that sense of having no control over his situation, as if he were a life-size plaything to forces he cannot really comprehend, is a recurrent one here, as we see in another of Crichton's passing comments in "Out of Their Minds." When the various crew members find that, as a result of an attack by an energy weapon, their minds and bodies have been switched, Crichton-in-Aeryn's body slugs Rygel-in-Crichton's body and storms off, noting, "It's the three freaking stooges and I'm hitting myself." It is a remark that allows Crichton/ Aeryn to vent his/her frustrations at this strange turn of events, but more importantly, it signals to the audience that there is an absurd dimension to this predicament, and one that they are quite justified in recognizing—and enjoying. While the others do not understand such remarks and often act as if they do not even hear him, we certainly do, and we recognize that he is actually addressing us, drawing the audience into this strange world, making them a part of his experiences there, while also providing a suitable model for their response to the "experience of wonder" that is this SF text.

Another version of this boundary-breaking style of address occurs in the episodes that develop the antagonist Scorpius' efforts at getting inside of Crichton's brain in order to retrieve his knowledge of wormholes. Introduced late in the series' first season ("The Hidden Memory"), this plot line begins when Scorpius captures Crichton and implants a neural chip in his mind that produces an imaginary version of Scorpius, one that Crichton, in another of his many Earth-centric, media-oriented wise-cracks, nicknames Harvey, after the imaginary six-foot rabbit that Jimmy Stewart envisions in the 1950 film Harvey. As in that film, only Crichton can see this strange, incorporeal presence—or what Scorpius describes as "something to remember me by"—and as a kind of defense mechanism against its intrusions, he begins to have conversations with the invisible character. But since none of the other characters can see Scorpius, those conversations only extend that pattern wherein Crichton seems to be talking to himself (in fact, he quite literally is). At the same time, these situations add another level of action to the narrative and involve the audience as "in" on the situation in a way that none of the other characters can be, as we too begin to see Harvey, while the others simply assume that Crichton is once again acting in his own peculiarly "human way."

The second-season episode "Beware of Dog" nicely demonstrates these effects. Early in the show Aeryn sees Crichton alone, playing a game of chess and, as is often the case, talking to himself. It prompts her to wonder if he is breaking down, developing a case of what she terms "transit madness," which occurs when one spends too much time traveling in space. But what becomes clear to the audience—as we briefly glimpse Harvey—is that Crichton is trying to find ways of coping with those neural eruptions which, as he notes aloud, give him the impression that Scorpius is present and "talking to me." In this instance, Crichton's various moves on the chessboard correspond to his efforts to avoid what the imagined Scorpius tells him is a "trap" he has set, and one that, he assures Crichton, "You'll never see . . . coming."

However, all of these "moves" seemingly have little to do with the central plot of "Beware of Dog," which focuses on parasites that have accidentally been brought onto *Moya* and threaten to destroy the ship's stores as well as its crew. We eventually see the extent of that threat when Rygel is silently seized and replaced by a plant-like replication that, in turn, begins stalking the others. In those moments here when Crichton glimpses Scorpius, talks to him, or plays chess with him, we—as audience—assume a privileged place in the narrative, not only joining our point of view to Crichton's, but also gaining a special sense of the interrelationship of all these actions. Crichton, we recognize, has himself been *parasited*, albeit in a different manner, and the quite strategic way he and the others cope with that parasite on board *Moya* helps model his own attempt to "checkmate" the parasitic Scorpius and keep him too from possibly hurting others. In this shared vision, that momentary predicament facing the crew—what some might describe as a "monster of the week episode"—merges with the series' larger narrative trajectory to again remind us how intertwined all things, and all fates, are in these territories and in our own world.

As another example of this involving technique, we might turn to a season three episode, "Revenging Angel," a show that also involves two levels of audience involvement, as it operates by turns in both near-tragic and highly comic registers, even suggesting how closely allied the two modes are here. When D'Argo believes that Crichton has accidentally interfered with the controls of a ship he has discovered, he goes into hyper-rage, accidentally putting Crichton into a coma and, in the process, starting a self-destruct sequence on the ship. With Crichton apparently dying, and with *Moya* and the crew also seemingly doomed by this self-destruct mechanism, the imaginary Scorpius reappears, taunting his host with the notion that "Your mind is no longer strong enough to control my comings and goings." Challenged by this vision that only he—and the audience—can see, Crichton, even as he lays dying, rises to the occasion, envisioning Scorpius, the still angry D'Argo, Aeryn, and himself all as cartoon characters, actually inhabiting the Looney Tunes world of Warner Bros. animation. When again taunted, he transforms Scorpius into a Daffy Duck-like character and drops an animated 1,000-ton weight on his head. When D'Argo begins chasing him, Crichton envisions the chase as a Road Runner and Wile E. Coyote encounter, one in which D'Argo suffers the same sort of falls from great heights, malfunctioning of his various Ozme (instead of Acme) gadgets, and collisions with barriers—such as a painted image of a wormhole through which Crichton manages to fly—as so often does the Warner Bros. Coyote. When Aeryn appears to question his feelings for her, he grabs a pencil and redraws her in the exaggerated proportions of Jessica Rabbit from *Who Framed Roger Rabbit* (1989) (Figure 4.4). And when challenged to take revenge on D'Argo, Crichton instead imagines a series of cartoonish, but ultimately harmless

Figure 4.4 *Farscape* takes us inside Crichton's mind as he envisions Aeryn as Jessica Rabbit

obstacles—a rake on which D'Argo steps, an oversized banana peel, a bucket into which he strides—all capped by a Bugs Bunny-like query, "Eh, what's up, D'Argo?" The result is that he demonstrates the power of the imagination, even in such extreme conditions, to deal with both friend and foe, to turn a tragic mood into a comic one, even to bring life out of death.

More to the point, this strange hybrid of animated and live action involves the audience, much as do those other instances we have seen of direct address, while also telling us much about that intended audience. Here again, Crichton's imagined dialogue with these figures gives us a privileged access to his unconscious mind, letting us glimpse the sort of internal drama that is going on and that none of the other characters in the narrative can see. And the shape he gives to that drama, one drawn, as Crichton notes, from the work of "Dr. Chuck Jones" who "wrote the book on these situations," is itself pertinent, for with this homage to the artistry of Warner Bros.' most famous animator/cartoon director, the episode underscores *Farscape*'s highly media-conscious sensibility—a sensibility that is part of its special audience appeal. In effect, with its animated scenes, along with the episode's various references to William Shatner, Priceline, Marilyn Monroe, *The Wizard of Oz*, and Madonna, as well as Crichton's comment, "God, I love science fiction," the show weaves a web of cultural referentiality that speaks most directly to an audience already situated in and saturated by such material, offering them an unusual perspective on the series' events. In these and other such situations it is as if we had suddenly stumbled onto an unexpected dimension of the scene, one intended specifically for *us* to inhabit.

What we see in these various reflexive moments in the narrative, as well as in Crichton's persistently reflexive manner of speech, is an interesting commentary on the nature of communication here and on Crichton himself. Of course, in the world of *Farscape* the *act* of communication is usually not itself a problem, thanks to the presence of "translator microbes" that effectively explain how different species can all seem to speak the same language, and that recall similar efforts at explaining such narrative turns in other series, most famously in *Doctor Who*'s reliance on the TARDIS' translator function. But as Crichton repeatedly demonstrates, that communication is often at odds—full of slips, confusion, and only partial understandings—thus

Zhaan's remark to Crichton, "Most of the time I have no idea what you're saying" ("Dream a Little Dream"). In such a context his comments, imagined dialogue, and visual transformations take on added resonance, as they are aimed both at himself and also *at us*—that is, at an audience that is specifically constructed not simply as passive consumers of an SF fantasy, but as active viewers: culturally "knowledgeable" (Hills 37), media savvy, and even—following Crichton's comment noted above—as loving SF.

Those varied sorts of communication repeatedly give the impression that we are accidentally overhearing, and thus *sharing*, someone's thoughts, or that we have by chance tuned into a kind of message being sent out into the ether that only we can understand. As such, they resonate with Crichton's introductory commentary wherein he wonders if there is "anybody out there who can hear me?" But in hearing Crichton, understanding him in ways that no one else in his strange environment can—knowing, for example, that when he imagines himself and Scorpius preparing to fight the Scarrons as the Crash Test Dummies from television safety ads, he sees almost no hope for survival—we become more than a typical television narrative's audience. We are effectively invited to share his complex situation, as he resolves to struggle even in the face of apparently impossible odds. His immersion in, yet ironic detachment from this strange universe, in fact, becomes evocative of, even *performs*, our own cultural situation. This accidental recognition that others *do* speak the same language as we do, that even across cultures we share certain touchstones, common feelings, and interpretations, thus becomes part of the cultural glue that binds audiences to this series and helps explain its lasting appeal.

NOTES

1 For a discussion of the variety of names for SF that have been advanced over the years, see Edward James' history of the term in his *Science Fiction in the Twentieth Century*, pp. 7–10, and Brooks Landon's commentary in *Science Fiction After 1900*, p. xv.

2 There are a number of claimants to being the first organized SF convention in the United States. Small gatherings of fans devoted primarily to the literature of SF—as well as the popularizing of scientific discourse—had previously occurred in 1936 at Philadelphia (the "First Science Fiction Convention"), in 1937 at

New York (the "Second Eastern Science Fiction Convention"), and in 1938 at Newark (the "First National Science Fiction Convention"). See Cheng's account of these gatherings, p. 235.

3 For background on early conceptions of television and its relation to SF, see my "Lost in Space: Television as Science Fiction Icon."

4 Cosplay is a term that designates the creating and wearing of costumes based on media figures, especially those from SFTV. More broadly, it suggests the playfulness of these fan efforts at inhabiting the identities and worlds of such figures, and at creating a community of other such players.

5

BOUNDARY CROSSINGS: SFTV IN A HYBRID MODE

Throughout the preceding chapters, we have often brought into the discussion series that some might not see as truly—or purely—science fictional. *The Twilight Zone*, for example, thanks to its combination of an anthology approach with a broadly construed fantasy agenda, often, although hardly to anyone's surprise, ventured into a variety of related realms: SF, horror, the supernatural, even the comic. *Lost*, while repeatedly revealing mysterious technologies and offering fleeting glimpses of monsters, also drew some of its formula, as well as its look, from reality shows like *Survivor*. And despite its efforts at giving its zombie apocalypse a scientific foundation, *The Walking Dead*, especially in its bloody, zombie-killing and human-munching scenes, frequently seems a closer kin to gross-out horror than to SF. Indeed, we can find many other such instances of what we might term *generic hybridization* throughout the catalogue of SFTV. This chapter explores that fairly familiar tendency to violate the familiar, to step across generic borders, in part because it has become such a common element of our television viewing experience, but also because it speaks especially to the rather protean, flexible, perhaps even evolving nature of our SFTV.

In his discussion of genre, Steve Neale notes how important various genre definitions and characterizations have been in the area of film studies, typically serving as what he calls an "instrument for the regulation of difference" (119). Simply put, setting up definitions and establishing rules for inclusion and exclusion within a genre has provided us with convenient ways of making critical, industrial, and even personal judgments about what we see—or like. Those judgments allow us to group narratives and to draw lines around those groups so that we can think about them more easily, lending order to our world and our aesthetic experience. But in practice, we might note, that "regulation of difference" has never proven to be very strict, and efforts at offering audiences something different, which often involves deliberate efforts at formula-busting, are easily found throughout both television and film history. It seems that *conventions*—that is, the customary ways of doing and saying things—always give rise to *inventions*, as formulas are refashioned to fit new times and new cultural needs.

Throughout its history, the SF film especially has been marked by this practice of boundary-crossing, genre-straddling, and reinvention. Georges Melies in a variety of his early *feerie* films, as he termed them, commonly mixed horrific and comic effects, as in the case of *The Terrible Turkish Executioner* (1904) wherein heads, recently separated from their bodies, roll about, stack and unstack themselves, and come back to torment their executioner. Another, quite obvious instance can be seen in the various versions of the *Frankenstein* story, many of them, but especially James Whale's 1931 adaptation, closely balancing the charnel-house horror trappings of Mary Shelley's novel with an emphasis on the scientific creation of life and on a medical science gone wrong. In 1930 *Just Imagine*'s tale of a utopian society and rocket travel to Mars would be interspersed with elaborate musical numbers, resulting in the first SF musical. A few years later *Murder by Television* (1935) would frame its futuristic story about the deadly use of television signals as a murder mystery, while also taking on something of a horrific atmosphere by starring Bela Lugosi, primarily known for his horror roles. And *The Phantom Empire* (1935) would have the singing cowboy Gene Autry discover the futuristic underground realm of Murania and then battle against its rockets, robots, and heat rays in order to save his Radio Ranch. More recently that same generic melding has resurfaced numerous times, but most obviously in the tellingly titled film *Cowboys & Aliens* (2011) with its narrative about various figures banding together to thwart alien abductions in the old West. But admittedly, these works tend to stand out and seem strange in description precisely because they do so clearly violate our common expectations, which have been built on a long experience of generic conventions and the film industry's tendency to expand that set of conventions, to build what we might term the *supertext* of a particular genre, usually in a logical or slow, progressive, and barely noticeable manner.

Television programming, however, has often been seen as demonstrating far less generic coherence than film—and moving far more quickly to adopt change. Observing how "the property of 'flow' blends one program unit into another, and programs are regularly 'interrupted' by ads and promos," Jane Feuer has speculated that with television we might look for more narrative "coherence . . . at a larger level than the program and different from the genre" (131)—for example, in an entire evening's programming on the Syfy Channel. However, such programmatic coherence is not very common, and Feuer's observation that television genres "appear to have a greater tendency to recombine *across* genre lines" than do film genres (131) seems to beg the question of why they would more frequently—and freely—engage in such hybridization. It is a point noted as well by Catherine Johnson in her study of television fantasy texts, wherein she suggests that not *all* television programs, but just certain kindred "telefantasy" works seem to draw upon "a range of generic expectations," as if they were able to "participate in different genres," rather than adhere to a single, discrete form, resulting in somewhat permeable and ultimately indistinct borders (6). Since that explanation still sidesteps the issue of why there is this tendency to "generic participation," as Johnson terms it, we might extend that explanation, consider it as *symptomatic*, and as possibly telling us something important about SFTV. In fact, all of these observations suggest that we might also think about SFTV not simply as a form that, because it does "participate" in various genres, lacks singularity, but rather as one that, by its very nature, plays at and with boundaries, more readily blending with other forms.

In this chapter we focus precisely on that playfulness, on SFTV's varied but also symptomatic ability to plug in other formulaic elements, to combine with other generic components, in part to offer audiences something "new"—which is no small feat in the increasingly competitive world of television programming—but also in part to address contemporary cultural concerns and thus meet contemporaneous audience needs. To do so, we focus briefly on only three of those hybrid formations, the SF Western, as exemplified by Firefly (2002–03), a SF version of the teen melodrama, as represented by Roswell (1999–2002), and the SF mystery, probably best embodied in The X-Files (1993–2002). By considering these hybrid series, we might come to a better understanding of why SFTV has been so accommodating to other forms, and perhaps as well a better sense of why SF—in the broadest sense of the genre—has proven to be one of the dominant program types on contemporary television.

THE SF WESTERN

We might recall that Gene Roddenberry pitched the original Star Trek series to NBC by linking it to the Western, describing the proposed show as "Wagon Train in space." Taken together with the show's opening injunction about "space—the final frontier," that conception should underscore the extent to which this most influential series was from the start seen as sharing some of the Western genre's identity, and SFTV as possibly representing a kind of evolutionary development of that form. This kinship would be especially underscored in the episode "Spectre of the Gun" (1968), wherein Kirk, Spock, Dr. McCoy, Mr. Scott, and Chekov are captured by the Melkotian civilization and transported to a setting that resembles the town of Tombstone, Arizona—a site that the Melkotians have cobbled together in bits and pieces from reading Kirk's imaginings. There the crew members are apparently fated to play out the famous gunfight at the O.K. Corral, thrust into the roles of those who were shot by Wyatt Earp, his brothers, and Doc Holliday. However, they recognize that these events might only be illusory and speculate that the situation is a test by the Melkotians to determine if these representatives of the Federation still bear any of the violent inclinations embodied in this near-mythic event from the Wild West. In passing that test by refusing to fight, Kirk and the others not only convince the Melkotians of their peaceful intentions, but also suggest, even in this futuristic realm, the continuing resonance of that Western mythos and its usefulness as a measure of human civilization in its dealings with this new "frontier."

Other SF series have also sought to mine this generic connection, among them Space Rangers (1993), a short-lived series about life on a frontier planet protected by a motley group recalling the Texas Rangers; *The Adventures of Brisco County, Jr.* (1993–94) with its steampunk approach to advanced technology in the American West of 1893; a similar and unsuccessful effort from 1995, *Legend*; and the anime series *Cowboy Bebop* (1998–99) with its team of bounty hunters wandering the frontiers of space, and its central figure Spike often evoking Clint Eastwood's "Man with No Name" Western hero. And following *Star Trek*'s pattern, other series, particularly those involving time travel, have included episodes set in the American West, among them *Doctor Who, The Time Tunnel*, and *Red Dwarf*. Certainly, most of these cases are to some extent mining an element of nostalgia, drawing on the typical dress, speech patterns, independent spirit, and heroic characters of the Western as valued cultural touchstones. But we should remember that, in its purest form, the Western has not had a major presence on American television since the 1960s, and the typical SFTV audience of today has actually had little contact with that genre which might produce much in the way of nostalgic feelings. Probably more important are the iconic characters and situations that have entered into American—and indeed world—culture: the laconic and independent hero, the desolate and harsh frontier, iconic elements such as the horse and six-gun, and the emphasis on a conflict between civilization and savagery. In deploying these elements the Western has accommodated important social and psychological functions for American culture, and in lending some or all of these elements to genres like SF, it has provided that form with an additional richness, a mythic component that has resounded even for audiences with little real knowledge of the Western itself.

As a focus for this discussion we might turn to the SFTV series that has in recent years most prominently deployed the Western's key elements, Joss Whedon's *Firefly*. In fact, it is a series whose Western components became a point of contention, with some claiming that those elements are central to the series' appeal—an appeal, as we have earlier noted, that has resulted in a strong cult following—and others arguing that the show's Western trappings were actually one of its failings, a reason for its precipitous cancellation after only 11 episodes had aired. Noting the series' resemblance to John Ford's classic film about the post-Civil War frontier, *Stagecoach* (1939), Fred Erisman describes *Firefly* as "a testament to the continuing vitality of the Western" (257). However, Jane Espenson, one of the show's writers, admits that its invocation of that "post-Civil War American West had never held much allure" for her, and that "stories set there were invariably dusty, very male and rarely whimsical" (2). And in her commentary on the series, Ginjer Buchanan underscores that reaction, marveling that series creator Whedon had not "noticed that the western was . . . totally moribund," and that "there wasn't any television western audience around to reach" (53).

Of course, the continuing audience that *Firefly* has found in syndication, the popularity of its movie adaptation *Serenity* (2005), its comic book continuations, and its specialized fan cons (populated by fans who call themselves "browncoats" after the Western-style duster worn by some of the characters) have suggested that the series did indeed reach an audience—and perhaps that there is something more than a simple generic conflict at the series' core (Figure 5.1). Rather, these indicators might mean that the very *combination* of generic elements has resounded with an audience and that, as Espenson admits, although she "didn't get it" initially, Whedon was onto something with his "space western" (2). Certainly, it seems that the linen duster, suspenders, boots, and nineteenth century six-shooter are all essential to the make-up of the central figure Malcolm (or Mal) Reynolds. He is, very simply, an individualist with a decidedly old-fashioned attitude (which

Figure 5.1 *Firefly*: an Old West shoot-out in outer space

those elements of dress underscore), someone who appreciates the measure of freedom to be found on the "outer planets," and who is willing to fight to maintain that freedom. Those ever-dusty, frontier-like worlds with their rough-hewn towns furnish an appropriate backdrop for the efforts of the crew of the Serenity as they struggle to eke out a living, pointedly away from the centers of human civilization and with few resources apart from their own determination and mutual support. And the backwash of an epic conflict between the Alliance and the Independents, fought over the issue of "unification," not only resonates with the American Civil War, but also echoes much of that war's sense of loss. Here the nature and values of that victorious "civilization" are called into question and, as in the very best Westerns, juxtaposed with the values that might be forged in the crucible of a new frontier.

While the sort of strong and adventurous type who recalls the figures of the early space operas, such as Rocky Jones, Flash Gordon, and Buck Rogers, Mal is also, like many Western heroes, someone who reflects the often hazy morality that characterizes the frontier. Although he prides himself on what he terms his "moral compass," but he is not reluctant to shoot first when necessary, and he has a number of moral blind spots, such as the "proper" behavior of women. Thus, while he accepts "Companion" Inara as a regular on his ship, he frowns on her occupation as a courtesan, even though in the world of the Alliance it is a respected profession and one that, as several episodes illustrate, involves far more than simple sexual activity. But as Joy Davidson has offered, Inara puts Mal, as well as many viewers, on "a collision course with the cultural artifacts of Earth's checkered past," and especially the sexual role of women, as she becomes "liberalism's enterprising dream-girl, radical-feminism's oppressed victim, the conservative right's sinful temptress," effectively straddling "the juiciest memes of ancient history, the present day and an alarmingly possible future" (114). And the implicit contradictions here are played out in the dynamic relationship between Inara and Mal, as he both repeatedly denies her respect by referring to her as a "whore," yet in the "Shindig" episode (2002) fights a duel to defend her honor, although only after she bridles at his own disrespect to her, noting, "You have no call to try to make me ashamed of my job. What I do is legal . . . and how is that smuggling coming?" But "legality" and morality have obviously become muddled in this new space frontier and in the backwash of the recent civil war, just as they often seem to be in our own time, and Joss Whedon tellingly uses this historically outcast type, the stereotypical prostitute with a heart of gold (specifically recalling the girl Dallas from *Stagecoach*), to help Mal and the others sort things out, as one of the series' final episodes, the appropriately titled "Heart of Gold" (2003), emphasizes, when Inara convinces them to defend a brothel against the actions of another recurring Western type, the vicious landowner—who acts like he also owns the people—Rance Burgess.

Of course, the land itself also situates this series between genres, for the outer planets and moons on which Mal and his crew so often do their questionable "business" have little more development, hospitality, or law and order than was the case on the post-Civil War frontier. While the Alliance is ostensibly in control, the very distance between these worlds— echoing the enormous distances that mark "outer space"—renders that control impractical and leaves them, in effect, run by characters like Rance Burgess: Patience, the de facto ruler of the moon Whitefall, who would prefer to shoot those she does business with—as she once did Mal—than to pay them ("Serenity," 2002); and the Magistrate Higgins of Higgins' Moon, who is also a slave-owner ("Jaynestown," 2002). And the lands over which these figures exercise such questionable control are invariably bleak, places where humans struggle to scratch out an existence in whatever way they can—as with the "mud farmers" or "mudders" of the "Jaynestown" episode, the miners of "The Train Job" (2002), who suffer a degenerative disease because of their job, or the prostitutes of "Heart of Gold" (2003)—and where shacks, bars, and crude general stores mark their tentative presence. Appropriately, the Firefly-class freighter *Serenity*, both home and workplace to Mal and his group of outcasts, is of a piece with these locales, thanks to its generally dingy and always-in-repair state. But as both these struggling outerworld communities and the *Serenity*'s crew suggest, these very crude and oppressive conditions also help to bring people together, to form a human community, as the downtrodden mudders of "Jaynestown" especially illustrate.

Perhaps the key effect of these intersections between *Firefly*'s Western elements and its space opera circumstances lies in its ability to frame together some of the main concerns involved in both genres. Both the nature of civilization and what has often been seen as one of its major signposts, the advance of technology, are equally held up for examination here, and equally called into question. The Alliance, we might note, is presented as both the center and guarantor of civilization in these new worlds. Its few buildings that we see, such as the gleaming hospital in "Ariel" (2002), and its massive space cruisers, like the one that captures *Serenity* in "Bushwhacked" (2002), speak of a futuristic and powerful technology, if one that ultimately has little impact on the everyday lives of the people, and a progress that affects only a privileged few. As a result, civilization itself becomes marked by the small groups that gather together to make society work, as when the mudders gather around their statue of Jayne, the "hero of Canton," who had accidentally dumped a box of money he had just stolen on the poor people; when the *Serenity*'s crew joins the whores in "Heart of Gold" to fight for their rights; and even when that same crew assist at the funeral of a one-time comrade-in-arms in "The Message" (2003).

Through its hybrid elements, what *Firefly* envisions is no technological utopia awaiting us in a new galaxy, but a frontier-like *starting over*, with all of the uncertainties and contingencies that attend such pioneer-like beginnings. Still, it is a vision of hope and possibility, ultimately bound up—as is so often the case in Westerns like *Stagecoach*—in the human community as it learns to adapt to strange new worlds, to use what technology it has at hand to the best of its abilities, and also to cope with the possible impingements or problems of that technology, as is especially underscored when, in "Out of Gas" (2002), *Serenity* suffers one of its frequent breakdowns, leaving the crew with no life support, adrift in space, and forced to make hard choices about who might be able to escape this situation. That they all do survive this adverse situation, that both a technological dependence and a hostile environment can be overcome, speaks to the courage and mutual concern of these new-style pioneers. But in the process it also points up the appeal of this series, and perhaps as well the ability of SFTV to plug into other forms, to find in the six-guns, horses, saloons, and imperiled frontier towns of the old West evocative emblems of the new frontier that our SFTV and its audience are more accustomed to exploring.

SF TEEN MELODRAMA

Far from any sort of nostalgic or historic genre appeal is the SF teen melodrama. But as Sharon Ross and Louisa Stein observe, what is often referred to as "Teen TV" is really more an "idea" than a genre in itself, since there is such "a wide variety of programs that could be considered 'teen' because of content, audience address, programing context, or demographics of reception" (4). As a result, in looking at this television "idea," one almost necessarily winds up "exploring surrounding meta-texts" (4), including the relationship of such "idea" shows to other, more established genre forms. In short, teen television almost naturally presents us with material that typically invites hybrid consideration. In television's early days, probably because it was perceived as a domestic or family-oriented medium, efforts at young adult programming usually avoided the serious concerns that had only recently begun to surface in such film melodramas as *Rebel without a Cause* (1955), *Blackboard Jungle* (1955), and *Crime in the Streets* (1956), with their focus on the postwar era's emerging social problems: juvenile delinquency, school violence, integration, parent–child alienation. Instead, they resulted in situation comedies like *The Many Loves of Dobie Gillis* (1959–63), *The Patty Duke Show* (1963–66), and *Gidget* (1965–66). But as teenagers increasingly became a key audience demographic, the teen "idea" would become linked to a variety of other genre formulas: romance (*Dawson's Creek* [1998–2003]) horror/fantasy (*Buffy the Vampire Slayer* [1997–2003]), adventure (*The Young Indiana Jones Chronicles* [1992–93]), mystery/detective (*Veronica Mars* [2004–07]), and especially SF, as evidence such series as *The Powers of Matthew Star* (1982–83), the animated *Galaxy High* (1986), *Superboy* (1988–92), *The Secret World of Alex Mack* (1994–98), *Phil of the Future* (2004–06), *Smallville* (2001–11), and *Roswell* (1999–2002).

Despite these very different genre associations, there are common elements that cut across the various forms and provide for an element of hybrid identification and consideration. Broadly considered, teen television, as Ross and Stein emphasize, is a form that has become identified "as much with its assumed audience (of teens) as with its content" (4–5), and thus with certain "culturally specific ideas about adolescence and what it means to 'be' teen" (6): problems of identity and self-image, social/class consciousness, experimentation with sex, alcohol or drugs, and conflicts with adults or authority figures—all usually situated in a high-school setting and frequently punctuated by popular songs on the soundtrack. Most of these concerns are bound up in a larger narrative trajectory about coming of age, since the typical teen series, according to Ross and Stein, "purposely contains and attempts to fix the experience of crossing from one identity (childhood) into the next (adulthood)" (7), thereby emphasizing its essentially liminal character. That is, the form addresses a human boundary situation (adolescence as a liminal state), and, for that very reason, produces interesting resonances when it becomes linked to other forms, and particularly SF which, as we have previously noted, is typically involved in exploring its own liminal arena, that between what might or might not be.

As an example of this sort of hybrid narrative, we might briefly consider *Roswell* (aka *Roswell High*), a series that emphasized its borderline character by capitalizing on a basic characteristic of much teenage life, a sense of personal alienation. As Neil Badmington observes, it takes the familiar theme of teen alienation quite literally, offering its audience "human teenagers [who] are (almost) as alien(ated) as the aliens they befriend" (169). Those aliens—initially three, although many others and even their clones would appear over the series' three-year run—are students at Roswell High School who are mysteriously connected to the famous Roswell UFO crash and supposed cover-up of 1947, and who find that the only humans they can trust are a handful of their *normally* alienated classmates at the school. Based on a popular series of books for young adults written by Melinda Metz, the show was pointedly designed to attract a teenaged audience, with the UPN network, which broadcast *Roswell* for its final season, scheduling it immediately following *Buffy the Vampire Slayer*, a series with a similar audience demographic. Moreover, as Miranda J. Banks has pointed out, while most teen melodramas have targeted a largely female audience, *Roswell*, much like the superhero-oriented *Smallville*, used its SF trappings and what she sees as more of a male emphasis (in fact, Banks describes it as a "teen male melodrama" [18]) to "widen the male audience for what would otherwise be a more female-oriented teen melodrama" (20). Yet as the series increased its quotient of action and emphasis on SF issues—introducing various alien races, dimensional portals, shape-shifters, clone alter egos, and government conspiracies—it also lost much of its viewership, suggesting that its initial ability to effectively straddle or balance the teen melodrama with SF was actually one of the keys to its short-lived success.

The terms of that balancing act are quickly set up in the series' opening episode as high schooler Liz Parker writes an entry in her diary: "I'm Liz Parker and five days ago I died. After that, things got really weird" ("Pilot," 1999). Of course, for a high school student "weirdness" can be a relative measure, perhaps even itself the norm, but the notion that she has, in some manner, returned from the dead is arresting, and the combined effect of these matter-of-fact observations establishes the challenging tone of the show. The following flashback to "five days ago" then fleshes out this strange combination, as we see Liz and her best friend Maria working in a UFO-themed diner, wearing themed waitress costumes—including antennae—that they see as both weird and mortifying and about which they exchange ironic quips. When two customers suddenly begin a violent argument, several shots are fired, one apparently hitting Liz and sending her slumping into a corner, lifeless. At that point her classmate Max Evans, who had been stealing longing glances at her, hurries over, lays a hand on her wound, and heals her. Again the quick shift in tone, from the bizarrely comic to the violent and deadly, is striking, but the scene also establishes the basic situation here, as it introduces a world that, for all of its normal appearances, is indeed strange and unpredictable, and places its characters in circumstances that will require them to question all that they have learned (and *are* learning in school, as the episode's classroom scenes underscore), and to react quickly and seriously to unexpected—and definitely weird—events.

This complex introductory scene and the rest of the "Pilot" episode also set up the blossoming romantic relationship between Liz and Max, an alien who, when confronted by Liz, jokingly admits to his status, that he is "not from around here," and that relationship gives further resonance to Liz's diary entry that bookends the episode: "Five days ago I died. But then the really amazing thing happened. I came to life." That notion of coming "to life" is meant to be more than literal, more than the bringing her back from the dead that Max has managed. It is, of course, a common trope in romantic stories, including those dealing with adolescents' coming-of-age. And here that phrase bears extra weight, reminding us of the hybrid nature of this narrative. Strange, potentially deadly, and clearly science fictional things have occurred, but amidst these alien and alienating events, in this sudden coming together of the human and the "not-of-this-earth," as Max also describes himself, a love relationship has bloomed, and both Liz and Max have begun to see not just their world, but also each other, in a new light (Figure 5.2). It is a comforting conclusion to this episode, if also one that poses a challenge for the rest of the series to balance these potentials for youthful romance and SF surprises in a similarly effective way.

Indeed, many of the subsequent episodes would rather directly address this difficult narrative situation, in part because it resonates so neatly with the typical adolescent condition, but also because it would obviously become the "trick" constantly facing the series' creators. One of the key ways it surfaces is with a recurrent play upon a notion that is foregrounded in practically every teen melodrama, that of normalcy—or more precisely, what constitutes normalcy in the strange and stressed world of the typical teenager. Of course, after learning the truth about her truly alien high school classmates—Max, his sister Isabel, and his best friend Michael Guerin—and

Figure 5.2 The alien–human romance of *Roswell* sparks fireworks

feeling compelled to protect them by keeping their secret, Liz can never feel normal again. As she notes in another diary entry, "Even I, Liz Parker, the smallest of small-town girls with the simplest of lives, even I have something to hide" ("The Morning After," 1999). And before the series ends, this honor student has lost interest in school, lied to the local Sheriff and the FBI, and even been involved in a convenience-store robbery. Meanwhile, Max, Michael, Isabel, and Tess—a new classmate who is also an alien—all of whom know almost nothing about their own backgrounds, simply want to go about their everyday "human" existence, hiding their special powers and trying to blend in as regular high school kids. Almost every episode during the show's initial season finds some way to restate this desire, as Max does in the season's finale when he confesses to Liz, "I wish I could go back . . . back to when things were normal" ("Destiny," 2000).

But "normal," as the show keeps reminding both its characters and the audience, is a most difficult, and perhaps also just a relative measure. Troubled by Liz's strange behavior, Maria, in another of those tone-shifting comments, reminds her friend, "You were on your way to being, like, a world-renowned scientist and I was going to be your wacky friend, okay? I can't be a wacky friend to someone who's already wacky" ("Pilot"). And in the second season the aliens confront another sort of challenge to normalcy when duplicate versions of Michael, Isabel, and Tess suddenly show up in Roswell ("Meet the Dupes," 2000)—duplicates who grew up on the streets of New York, look like punks, live outside the law, and have already killed their leader, the clone version of Max. Their dress and behavior, quickly remarked on by several of the characters who mistake them for the Roswell aliens, underscore the various things that condition our perception of the normal, while also vividly reminding us of the extent to which normalcy is a tenuous or superficial cultural construct—as Max suggests when he tells the others to "Go back to school and act [my emphasis] normal" ("Pilot").

However, acting normal is as difficult—and perhaps as impossible—for aliens and alienated youth, as is maintaining a consistent balance between the different terms of such a generic hybrid. In another diary-entry coda to the episode "Leaving Normal," Liz remarks on how her (literally) star-crossed love for Max has changed everything: "The difficult part is when you follow your heart, you leave normal; you go into the unknown. And once you do, you can never go back" (1999). The episode is aptly titled and a fitting comment on the entire series, which always seems in the process of "leaving normal"—and leaving its audience unsure how to gauge what is normal here. With Max, Michael, and Isabel stoically watching a comic re-enactment of the 1947 Roswell crash that culminates in a spectacle of burning alien dummies (perhaps suggesting their parents' fate), with their clone alter-egos suggesting another, darker potential for their lives, with the discovery of another alien race living nearby, the "Skins," whose bodies are simply husks that hide their true selves and whose leader is a U.S. Congress-woman—with these and many other challenges to how we see and interpret this world, the series seems to be constantly testing and recasting our sense of normalcy, perhaps as a way of indicating to its core teen viewership a level on which it shares their own sense of alienation. In any case, borders are finally not for *Roswell*, and that may be why it seems most fitting that the series culminates with the graduation ceremony from Roswell High, a ceremony that suggests its characters—and audience as well—have finally moved beyond the boundaries of the teen melodrama.

SF MYSTERY/DETECTION

Precisely because it does straddle borders by speculating on what might be, SF has proven fertile ground for another form that deals with the liminal, resulting in a number of mystery or detective hybrids. We have already noted one early effort in this vein, the evocatively titled *Murder by Television* (1935), an SF-flavored murder mystery from a period, that of the Machine Age, when crime thrillers and tales of detection were highly popular (in fact, mystery and detective volumes outnumbered SF in the pulps of that era). Among this group of early hybrids, we might note *Dr. X* (1932), *Trapped by Television* (1936), *Non-Stop New York* (1937), and various serials with SF elements, such as the original *Dick Tracy* (1937) and *The Phantom Creeps* (1939). While most of these works are set in a present-day context, they typically involve mysteries that implicate an unusually advanced science and technology, such as synthetic skin, robots, death rays, and futuristic aircraft. More recent film efforts, notably *Coma* (1978), *Blade Runner* (1982), *The Hidden* (1987), *Robocop* (1987), *Timecop* (1994), *Twelve Monkeys* (1996), and

Dark City (1999), while also working in a mystery vein, have frequently lodged their mysteries and investigations in the future, thereby permitting the detective-like protagonists of these stories to make their way through a world whose very look—frequently adapted from the dark vision of the film noir—appears to the audience as strange or incomprehensible, and in effect plays upon—and with—that central characteristic of the SF narrative Darko Suvin noted when he defined the genre as the "literature of cognitive estrangement" (4).

In fact, Carl Freedman has offered an elaboration on this definition that might be useful in considering this particular hybrid type. He suggests that we might consider all of SF as if it were engaged in a "dialectic between estrangement and cognition" (16)—a formulation that closely allies the audience's experience of SF with their experience of the mystery or detective thriller by emphasizing a constant interplay between the unknown and a desire to understand, an impulse to make things known. In this regard Freedman's terms also echo John Cawelti's account of the typical detective or mystery narrative, as he describes how it depends on the dual impulses of "ratiocination and mystification" and notes how they "stand in a tense and difficult relationship to each other," at least until—or even if—the narrative's mystery is solved (107). That dialectic can help us understand why in different periods, particularly those when cultural circumstances themselves seem so resistant to our understanding, as was the case during the Depression, SF has drawn so tellingly on this generic kinship, as audiences sought answers to, or at least a measure of reassurance about, the puzzle that life had become.

SFTV has been more of a latecomer in exploring and exploiting this relationship, although in recent years the SF/mystery hybrid has become one of its more successful formulations. While a pioneering series in this vein like Kolchak: The Night Stalker (1974–75) was initially not very popular, its pattern of a world-weary reporter who investigates cases involving science fictional or supernatural elements—cases that the police would prefer simply to dismiss—has inspired a cult following, resulting in several novels, a comic book series, a number of graphic novels, and a fiction anthology based on the original Kolchak character, as well as a short-lived reboot of the series in 2005. Perhaps more significantly, it would pave the way for a number of more recent works in this vein, ranging from *Project UFO* (1978–79), *Knight Rider* (1982–86), *Millennium* (1996–99), *The Sentinel* (1996–99), *Life on Mars* (2006–07 [UK], 2008–09 [US]), *Ashes to Ashes* (2008–10), *Grimm* (2011–present), and *Fringe* (2008–13). However, its most important imitator, and indeed one of the more important and longest-lived of American SFTV series, is *The X-Files* (1993–2002), a show that readily acknowledged its indebtedness by offering numerous homages to *Kolchak*, including the use of Darren McGavin, star of the earlier series, as retired FBI agent Arthur Dales ("Travelers," 1998, and "Agua Mala," 1999), described by one character as "the father of the x-files." With its own elaborate vision of intersecting paranormal, extraterrestrial, and simply weird events, *The X-Files* has also built a strong cult following of fans who term themselves "X-Philes," and that following quickly developed a strong internet presence, producing additional information about the series, extended analysis, and fan-written stories based on its characters.

Fittingly described by Lincoln Geraghty as a "mix of detective thriller and science fiction horror, with a dash of postmodern pastiche added for fun" (*American Science Fiction* 98), *The X-Files* has always been recognized as a boundary-straddling series, an appealing "mix" of various generic elements, including the murder mystery, all anchored in an SF premise that recalls alien invasion and conspiracy narratives dating back to the 1950s. That sense of mixed elements, moreover, carries beyond plot lines and iconic images to the level of main characters, as the show centers its investigative activities on seemingly opposite central figures. As we noted in Chapter 1, the narrative is built around two FBI agents, Fox "Spooky" Mulder and Dana Scully. The former, as his nickname implies, is right at home in stories involving "little green men" ("Little Green Men," 1994), a deadly circus freak ("Humbug," 1995), killer cockroaches ("Coprophages," 1996), and sewer monsters ("Agua Mala," 1999); these are the sort of things he readily takes seriously. In contrast, the latter is a trained forensic scientist and a model of the sort of no-nonsense scientific investigator who would become a staple of the various *CSI: Crime Scene Investigation* series. This pairing would result not only in a new take on the familiar "buddy–cop" relationship, but also in a central thematic dynamic that closely mirrors *The X-Files*' larger hybrid structure.

While these two main characters serve to embody the two sides in the public debate about UFOs and other unexplained phenomena, they also underscore the series' ongoing development of a central question about knowledge and "belief"—effectively translating the usual mystery story's concern with truth into a philosophical/theological register. Having witnessed what he firmly believes was the alien abduction of his sister, Mulder readily accepts the existence of extraterrestrial life, while also fearing its malevolent designs on humans. Moreover, his office wall bears a UFO poster with the legend "I Want to Believe," a phrase that recurs in the title for the second film adaptation made from the series, *The X-Files: I Want to Believe* (2008). Furnishing a counterweight to that stated desire, Scully, an MD and surgeon, typically tempers Mulder's ready embrace of the strange and seemingly inexplicable with her own natural scientific skepticism. However, she also repeatedly demonstrates her own, and different, version of that same desire. While Mulder is not religious—somehow feeling that to be so would disqualify his material belief in aliens and in an alien/government conspiracy—Scully comes from a strong Catholic background, once worked in a Catholic hospital, and does on several occasions pose her own version of the sort of big questions that concern her partner. The "Biogenesis" episode (1999), for example, opens with Scully musing in voice-over about the origins and purpose of human life:

> For all of our knowledge, what no one can say for certain is what or who ignited that original spark. Is there a plan, a purpose, or a reason to our existence? . . . will the mystery be revealed through a sign, a symbol, a revelation? . . . Whose idea was this? Who had the audacity for such invention? And the reason? Were we part of the plan ten billion years ago? Are we born only to die? To be fruitful and multiply and replenish the earth before giving way to our generations? If there is a beginning, must there be an end?

As we see, she is herself a questioner, someone who, for all of her skepticism on some counts, just as eagerly as her partner looks for answers, "a sign, a symbol, a revelation" that will match up with those questions about human origins, purpose, and destiny that have always been at the core of humanity's various theological systems. And while she does not use the term, her repeated references to "who" simply skirt around the question of a divine power.

The series also sets up a correlative to that questioning, one articulated in its key tagline (seen in the opening credits and uttered by Mulder on multiple occasions) that "the truth is out there." That phrase becomes the central, and indeed most appropriate, premise/promise for the show—as well as a promise that is oft-broken. As *The X-Files* shifts between multiple-episode story arcs devoted to the larger alien conspiracy plot that drives much of the series, to the individual episodes that investigate what has often been termed the "monster of the week," it at times seems to take us towards that "truth," to promise answers, only to then swerve off or pull back, leaving the truth still somewhere "out there." That seemingly deliberate openness is more than a bit disconcerting, rather like a murder left unsolved, and a challenge to the conventional television experience, wherein plotlines are usually resolved, narratives closed, and beliefs affirmed. As Lavery, Hague, and Cartwright describe this effect, "for many viewers, their weekly encounter with the show is an unsettling, sometimes frightening experience that powerfully interrogates a consensus reality that excludes the paranormal" (12).

But more than just producing a weekly shock, that unsettling effect seems central to the show's theme or purpose, while also tied into its hybrid nature. Like its paired detectives, *The X-Files*' audience is allowed to sift through the various clues that surface in almost every episode, to try to piece together the larger conspiracy mythology, to glimpse hints of the truth about an alien/government alliance to take over the Earth—only then to be sidetracked by smaller if somewhat frustrating truths in the case of those weekly monsters, while a final resolution remains consistently postponed or simply anticipated by additional intriguing clues, as when a UFO is discovered buried on a beach in the Ivory Coast ("Biogenesis," 1999), or when Scully has a baby and it suddenly demonstrates psychokinetic abilities ("Nothing Important Happened Today," 2001). Constantly shifting between such "estrangements" and the possibility of "cognition"—or between Cawelti's formula of "mystification" and "ratiocination"—*The X-Files* simply does a postmodern dance with "truth," as that desire to believe, even the insistence that there is something that needs to be known, either individually or collectively, comes up against its constant frustration, or what Rodney Hill in his commentary on the series diagnoses as "the impossibility of knowing" ("I Want to Believe" 115), a realization that may be far more unsettling

Figure 5.3 The skeptic and the believer investigate mysteries in *The X-Files*

than any single "monster of the week", such as the discovery of a feral cannibal ("The Jersey Devil," 1993), a werewolf ("Shapes," 1994), or zombies ("Fresh Bones," 1995) (Figure 5.3).

And yet that constant dance with knowing was apparently satisfying— or tantalizing—enough to keep the series going for nine seasons and to generate two feature-length film versions, neither of which would quite satisfactorily wrap up the show's mysteries. *The X-Files*' science fictional take on mystery and detection, and its repeated demonstration that even a world thoroughly imbued by science and technology can remain elusively mysterious, or "estranged," managed to strike a cultural nerve—one for which the central notion of an alien/government conspiracy was simply a trope, although a trope that still draws our attention, as evidence the more recent wave of "reality" shows that have adopted some or all of its premises: *UFO Files* (2004–07), *UFO Hunters* (2008–11), *Ancient Aliens* (2010–13), and *Chasing UFOs* (2012). The series reminds us that, even to those trained in the methods of scientific analysis, our world yields few of the answers to those ultimate questions that, each after their own fashion, both Mulder and Scully keep asking. But it also suggests the need for that continual asking, as if it were the detective-like—and Sisyphus-like—fate of humanity to ask, to look for the truths that keep receding from view, but that we almost have to believe are still "out there."

The X-Files' ability to tap into the core activities of the mystery/detective genre— as well as the dark visual "look" of the closely allied film noir—certainly opened the door of possibility for its elaborate vision, providing audiences a special, almost detective-like pleasure in its creation of what Suvin describes as a different or alternative "framework" to what we know (7), or rather, multiple such frameworks that might be true and might help to explain the mystery that is our world—or, as Hill suggests, might not. But as we have noted, it is just one of many such series that have crossed traditional borders, challenged conventional genre formulae, and found a new level of narrative richness in the process. The cultural critic Michel de Certeau once noted that one result of the postmodern condition is that our world seems to be "haunted by narratives" of various sorts and that, as we live our lives, we often seem to be walking "through a forest of narrativities" (152) that are interminably being recited—by advertising, by tabloids, but especially by television, and all of which poach on each other, drawing together bits and pieces from that "forest." Hybrid narratives like The X-Files, Roswell, and Firefly might simply be the natural result of that constant recitation that is the industrial practice of television, points at which several elements of the forest have grown together, and effectively so. In that case we should expect to encounter more such generic hybrids in the future and be prepared to recognize, read, and understand their blendings of character types, visual icons, and plot conventions.

But we should also acknowledge the very specific role of SFTV in generating such narrative blends. As we noted at the start of this chapter, SF seems particularly accommodating to hybrid development, and was so even in its early cinematic forms. That accommodation should hardly be surprising, though, given SF's abiding concern with the work of science and technology, for these are some of the fundamental elements of modern culture; they make up the climate we inhabit, the air that we breathe. Moreover, that concern allows SF to play at and with boundaries, as it speculates at what might be, on what we might discover and construct, and on how we are ourselves constructed. SFTV's ability to draw in other genres—or to lend some of its own trappings and concerns to others, as in the case of a series like Lost—simply attests to the sort of role it plays in contemporary culture, as a key tool for explaining that climate and, as the very title of a show like the highly popular Fringe (2008–13) might suggest, for looking beyond.

KEY SERIES:
FRINGE: NARRATIVE AT THE BORDERS

Like several other commentators, Jason Mittell has noted the extent to which contemporary television programming has become "dependent on intertextuality" ("Cultural" 6), as different types of texts, different types of audiences, and different industrial practices increasingly inflect our narratives and result in various sorts of hybrid programming. In response to the resultant "shifting and fluid" nature that has become a mark of much television programming, he suggests that, to make best sense of the typical television series, we should approach it not as a discrete genre, but rather as it groups different "discursive practices" ("Cultural" 8). We have already glimpsed one dimension of this hybrid tendency, with different texts coming together to produce SF Westerns, SF teen melodramas, and SF mysteries, and their varied formulaic elements generating multiple narrative possibilities and resonances for their narratives. For a more detailed look at this hybrid character, we might consider another series that draws much of its richness from this combinatory character, the SF police procedural series *Fringe* (2008–13). While its persistent foregrounding of the processes of investigation and detection at times seem to push its more pointedly SF elements to the narrative's borders—or "fringe"—that very impulse also foregrounds the key role that SF itself is playing in this new world of hybrid story-telling and consumption.

In choosing to combine its more familiar SF generic trappings with borrowings from the crime drama or police procedural story, *Fringe* was mining a rich but also allied vein of popular narrative. As they address crimes like murder, larceny, and other sorts of violations found in the everyday world, our criminal or investigative narratives are always staking out some of the same territory as SF. For both story types play at the fringes of our sense of the norm, and in the process often seem to be crossing and recrossing narrative borders to which audiences have, at least in recent years, become accustomed. In the specific case of *Fringe* that strategy—and suggested kinship—is even more fitting, since the series' very subject is something that already stands at the border: what is commonly described as "fringe science," a term that refers to concepts that are highly speculative and even challenge scientific orthodoxy, such as dark matter, telepathy, psychokinesis, and precognition. In keeping with that subject, the show's central characters, Olivia Dunham, Peter Bishop, his father Dr. Walter Bishop, and Astrid Farnsworth, all work in the FBI's newly established "Fringe Division," tasked with investigating various strange occurrences that seem to defy conventional scientific explanation—and normal forensic inquiry. Perhaps more significantly, several of these characters are themselves what we might term fringe figures, people whose very lives—as we gradually learn over the course of the show's narrative trajectory—echo the narrative's hybrid nature, and whose stories further develop its possibilities.

Of course, the very fringe-y character—of both narrative and figures—that we are noting should only have been expected, since the series was created by J. J. Abrams, the writer/producer/director responsible for such shows as *Alias* (2001–06), *Lost* (2004–10), *Person of Interest* (2011–present), and *Almost Human* (2013–14). All of these programs mix easily recognizable SF elements with the components of another popular genre, in the process suggesting how Abrams tends to see much of the contemporary cultural landscape: on the one hand as fundamentally SF-inflected, and on the other as defying easy or neat categorization. Moreover, these series too—as titles like *Alias* and *Almost Human* should readily remind us—focus specifically on characters who live at the borders of conventional life and culture (especially consider what it might mean to be *almost* human), and who thus embody the sort of hybrid situation that has become such a familiar feature of the contemporary world.

That kinship should also warn us that *Fringe* is staking out narrative territory that other SFTV series have also profitably explored. Given its strange plot twists, its gradual disclosure of a parallel universe and alternate time scheme, and its development of characters with fragile mental conditions—particularly the central figure of Walter Bishop—we might locate one key influence in *The Twilight Zone*, especially since *Fringe* quite literally pursues that earlier series' efforts to, as Rod Serling's introductory commentary always offered, take us "travelling through another dimension." However, it also offers a number of *Lost*-like resonances, particularly with the various mysterious glyphs that punctuate the commercial breaks in each episode—images such as a shot of a frog, inexplicably bearing a Greek "phi" on its skin, a sliced apple with human fetuses inside, a butterfly, or a deeply lined handprint. These glyphs or symbolic images serve to comment on specific narrative events, while also fostering the impression of a world that has been mysteriously encoded and that invites—and as is so often the case with mystery narratives, just as often frustrates—a ready deciphering, much like the mysterious island and all of its contents that so intrigued the viewers of *Lost* from 2004 to 2010.

Perhaps the most obvious model, though, is *The X-Files* with its fantasy variation on the police procedural narrative, its similarly mysterious background for several of its characters, and its persistent emphasis on a large-scale conspiracy that, as in *Fringe*, involves the FBI. When *Fringe* debuted, reviewer Misha Davenport quickly noted this resemblance, describing it as "an update of 'The X-Files' with the addition of terrorism and the office of Homeland Security" (Davenport). But it is much more than an imitation of that successful series. Those strange glyphs and its ongoing investigation into what the show's characters refer to as "the pattern" (of linked strange and typically deadly occurrences) do seem to suggest that, as in *The X-Files*, there is a "truth . . . out there," waiting to be uncovered. However, in its best moments *Fringe* appeals less because of those "truths," which become even stranger as the series progresses, than because of the ways in which it tries to approach them. Especially in its first seasons, the show is solidly rooted in the police procedural tradition, a narrative pattern at the heart of a variety of highly popular but also decidedly non-SF shows, such as *Law and Order* (1990–2010), *CSI* (2000–present), *NCIS* (2003–present), and *Hawaii Five-O* (1968–80, 2010–present).

In that "discursive practice" of the police procedural, process often seems just as important—and in some ways more narratively compelling for the audience—as is the outcome. Thus, while Jason Mittell rightly suggests that some of the key appeals for the usual procedural narrative reside in its dual "discourses of authenticity and truth" (*Genre* 127), I would suggest that their placement within a process, one that allows the audience to follow and even forecast a trajectory for events, is also crucial. There is simply a great pleasure in that process of discovery, in the quite logical and at times even surprising explication of a mystery, combined with an anticipation of a satisfactory resolution for things. And by locating these elements of authenticity, truth, and process within the larger framework of speculative fiction, of narratives that, as is commonly the case for SF, constantly challenge our normal perceptions of the world by trafficking in the unusual—or what Darko Suvin more properly describes as "cognitive estrangement" (7)—*Fringe* has been especially effective at joining its hybrid elements and providing viewers with a complex and apparently quite satisfying SFTV experience.

Early in its run, the series tended to emphasize a science-based mystery or monster of the week approach, thereby firmly anchoring the world of *Fringe* to SF, or more broadly to the realm of fantasy. Thus the first two seasons saw the Fringe unit investigating cases involving a murderer who removes pituitary glands ("The Same Old Story"), a vampire who sucks spinal fluid ("Midnight"), normal people who, under the influence of a designer virus, can transform into beasts ("The Transformation"), and others whose bodies, when exposed to an electrical impulse, can harden and suddenly explode ("Fracture"). And in this early development, the series recalls the pattern Mittell observes in most procedural dramas, wherein viewers "rarely encounter any story developments outside the realms of the specific case" (*Genre* 126). However, over the course of its five-year run, the series gradually develops far more complex narrative arcs that expand this approach and build a more pervasive SF context. The unit discloses the workings of an international group of rogue scientists known as ZFT, discovers a parallel dimension, encounters alternate versions of the central characters—thus, the eccentric but brilliant scientist Walter Bishop has a double in that parallel world, dubbed Walternate (i.e., alternate Walter), while agent Olivia Dunham discovers a counterpart referred to as Fauxlivia—learns that human–machine hybrids have been created in the parallel realm, and finds that the parallel universes are threatening to destroy one another.

This sort of sprawling, fantastic narrative of multiple identities, multiple realms, and potentially multiple outcomes for the future, including a doomsday scenario, could easily overwhelm viewers with its complex and potentially confusing trajectory—even parallel trajectories. In fact, series creator J. J. Abrams, perhaps influenced by similar criticisms of *Lost*, acknowledged as much, noting that audiences needed to feel that the show "exists completely in the real world" that they know (Huddleston). So it only gradually spins out this larger mythology through clues discovered in the course of those seemingly stand-alone episodes, allowing viewers—along with the central characters—to slowly connect the narrative dots. At the same time, it also grounds those fantastic elements in understandable, or at least seemingly logical processes, even emphasizing them after the fashion of shows like CSI and its various procedural offshoots, as the various steps in investigation form an essential part of every episode or narrative arc.

Demonstrating one key element in this process, both the 90-minute "Pilot" episode and the first regular season show, "The Same Old Story" (2008), emphasize the terms under which the eccentric Walter Bishop has been made a part of the Fringe unit. We are repeatedly reminded that the FBI has arranged for his release from a mental asylum, that while his former lab at Harvard had been shut down, the FBI has arranged for it to be reopened, and that he has even been assigned a junior agent, Astrid Farnsworth, as a kind of lab assistant and all-purpose "go-fer." When Walter suddenly decides that, to support his scientific side of the fringe investigations, he needs a cow, a rat, or even a cyclotron for an experiment, he simply asks Astrid to acquire it and, with hardly a raised eyebrow and never a question, she tries to accommodate him (Figure 5.4). Such bizarre turns help infuse the show with a whimsical element that insulates it from some of the grim potential of its larger narrative trajectory—and some of the gruesome images it at times offers up, such as a corpse's exposed and twisted spinal column that, Walter remarks, reminds him of "shrimp cocktail."

Within that lab, which is prominently featured in most episodes, Walter not only indulges his own interests in fringe science—which was one of the reasons he was originally committed to a mental institution—but also helps solve the various bizarre and seemingly unsolvable crimes, like those noted above. Thus when in "The Same Old Story" Olivia asks Walter for help with a series of horrific murders with few clues, he recalls a theory he was once pursuing about visual imprinting, and suggests that the last images a recent victim saw might be stored in her body as a series of electrical impulses. He sends Olivia to the Massive Dynamic Corporation to borrow a special laser-optic device, an Electronic Pulse Camera,

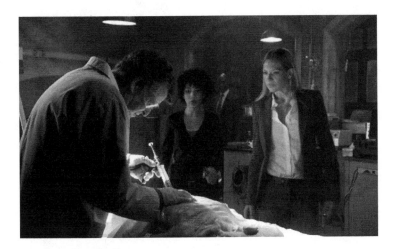

Figure 5.4 *Fringe*: forensic work in the scientist's lab

and we watch as he sets up the device, carefully removes one of the victim's eyes, attaches it to the camera, and then links all to a power source and monitor, allowing him to retrieve grainy images of a well-known bridge. By then obtaining satellite images of the area, the team matches the dead woman's apparent point of view to a section of the city and a warehouse overlooking the bay. Further research yields a specific address, leading the team to the crime scene just in time to save another potential murder victim. Of course, the nature of the murders and their SF-oriented nature—women are being killed so their pituitary glands can be harvested to keep the male murderer young—are themselves intriguing, but since the murderer remains largely a cipher, the narrative's real focus becomes the investigative process, one that demonstrates just how valuable to such investigations a "crazy" character like Walter can be.

Another early episode, "The Ghost Network" (2008), multiplies its "fringe" concerns, but also eventually elevates the act of investigation over the exploration of its wondrous SF conceptions. As it opens, two events converge: the character of Roy McComb is having another in a series of psychic visions about terror attacks and wondering if his visions are in some way *causing* the terrible incidents; and a man boards a public bus on which he releases a gas that soon solidifies into an amber-like substance, trapping and suffocating all those on board. The bus incident, we quickly realize from sketches Roy has made, is another of those attacks he has visualized, and both—Roy's precognitions and the rather spectacular amber attack—because of their unusual dimensions and possible connections are referred to the Fringe team for investigation. While those investigations initially proceed in a straightforward, police procedural manner—with the creation of a secure perimeter to study the bus and its contents, officials briefing Olivia and Peter on details, outlining the apparent time sequence of events, and noting similarities to other recent "terrorist" events involving gas attacks—it quickly becomes clear that the real focus of the inquiry rests in Walter's idiosyncratic involvement. When asked by Peter if he has any idea about "what's happening," Walter smiles and replies in a way that not only seems to promise much, but also points to a key dimension of the show's appeal: "I have no idea, but I'm extremely interested in finding out."

Of course, that element of curiosity is precisely what the series hopes to develop in its audience and capitalize on. And in this episode that interest in "finding out" becomes the driving force, with Walter's at times arcane efforts at understanding both Roy's precognitions and the strange chemical used in the attack displacing more traditional detective work. In fact, the more spectacular of the two events produces the more mundane investigation, as the bodies-encased-in-amber situation—just the sort of thing that constitutes a rather stark SF "novum"[1]—results in a parallel-edited scene between a warehouse where the victims' bodies have been extracted, laid out on the floor, details are being photographed, measurements are being taken, and Walter's lab, where he examines the chemical properties of the amber and looks through a microscope, enabling him to determine that certain proprietary chemicals used in the attack probably came from the multinational corporation Massive Dynamic, the company that repeatedly seems involved in these "pattern" events. Turning to Roy, Walter once again hypothesizes "a theory": "a spectrum of waves lying outside of the range of those already discovered" which "could be used to communicate information." He then designs several experiments to test his hypothesis. Using a CT-scan, a self-constructed "magnetic neural stimulator," and "a bit of brain surgery," he gains direct access to Roy's brain waves and concludes that his bloodstream has been infected with "an iridium-based compound" that "has turned him into some kind of receiver," allowing him to pick up the thoughts and comments of others, thereby explaining his visions. However, neither the precise reason behind the bus attack nor the role of Massive Dynamic in either the attack or Roy's visions is ever clarified. In fact, when Olivia—as she often does throughout the series—interviews the company's head, Nina Sharp, she is told that "Massive Dynamic is, well, so *massive*, that just about everything in the world of science and technology has a tie back to us."

It is a point that underscores the narrative problem facing the show, as well as another part of its appeal, for that connection suggests not only the sort of scientific/technological landscape on which all of these fringe events play out, but also the complex ways in which everything seems inevitably interwoven here, with purposes difficult to sort out and technology applied in ways that seem to have no conventional purpose. Armed with a new understanding of what is causing Roy's disturbing visions and the possibility that the Fringe group too might be able to listen in on any further terrorist plans, both problems are marked—at least temporarily—as resolved. And yet, while the investigation never results in catching the terrorists, linking them to the disturbingly pervasive Massive Dynamic ("one of the ten largest economic entities in the world", as Nina Sharp offers), or even explaining the purpose of that strange amber-forming gas, there is a certain amount of reassurance—and even fun—inherent in the pattern of inquiry, which obviously forms one of the chief satisfactions—or *extreme interests*—of the show in its first seasons.

However, those tantalizing bits of fringe science, the repeated intersections with Massive Dynamic, encounters with the terrorist group ZFT, and a host of mysterious characters—including Olivia's dead partner whom she glimpses in various places and who sends her mysterious communications, Nina Sharp who repeatedly tries to recruit Olivia for Massive Dynamic, David Robert Jones, a biochemist and criminal mastermind behind many of the strange events of "the pattern," and the Observers (time travelers from the future)—are always pointing to other, and far larger, possibilities for investigation. In fact, given the gradually unfolding sense of connectedness here, they eventually force the team (and show) to expand its focus, follow the clues that keep sifting out from their various investigations into strange phenomena, in order to deal with much greater mysteries involving fringe scientific developments. Thus the later seasons find the team accounting for and investigating the existence of that parallel universe, an alternate timeline, other versions of many of the characters we encounter, the intentions of those Observers, and especially their own mysterious pasts, particularly those of Walter, Peter, and Olivia.

As I have explored elsewhere, the crime or mystery narrative, driven by its detective or police protagonist(s), always seems to be more than an investigation into a specific crime. Quite often it becomes as well a story about "the internal, psychic world of the detective . . . and a deeper level of unreason which actually prods his efforts at demystification" (4).[2] In the case of *Fringe*, it seems only natural, then, that the many procedural elements—those various archival investigations, medical experiments, surveillance efforts, and the piecing together of clues—ultimately feed into investigations and revelations about the central characters themselves. We thus learn that Olivia was herself the subject of childhood experiments conducted by Walter and his colleague William Bell— founder of Massive Dynamic—that enhanced certain psychic and physical abilities, including her ability to see objects from the alternate universe and even to cross over into that other dimension. Peter Bishop is himself from that alternate universe, brought into our world by Walter who wanted him to replace his own son who had died from a genetic disease. And Walter, in opening a wormhole into the other universe and taking Walternate's son as a replacement for his own Peter, has upset the natural order, setting the two worlds at odds and creating the potential for mutual destruction. While both intensely personal and important to the whole future of humanity, these individual stories can only come to light through those many fringe investigations that allow them to "connect the dots"—and the universes.

In order to advance that sense of connection—and to push our sense of the narrative beyond that of a mystery-of-the-week experience—the series from the start develops a motif that especially resonates for the process of investigation. It repeatedly shows all of the central characters as afflicted with significant memory lapses or gaps, and frequently prodded by others to "remember." Peter, perhaps to suppress the trauma of having been taken from the alternate universe, has few memories of his childhood and, through much of the first season, demonstrates an inexplicable hostility to his father Walter. Olivia too has forgotten her role in those irresponsible childhood drug experiments and the special abilities she manifested then, while finding in the present that her own memories are confused and frequently invaded by those of her former partner and lover John Scott. And Walter, in keeping with his "absent-minded professor" status, is constantly forgetting—and then remembering—all sorts of things, major and minor. At one point early in the series he suddenly pauses in the midst of an autopsy to note that he now remembers where he parked his car seventeen years ago, although later, when urged to recall where he hid a very important piece of equipment, Walter cannot remember, noting, "I understand how important it is, and I'm very disappointed with myself" ("Midnight"). Such amnesiac episodes, occurring in almost every show, only remind us—and on some level the characters themselves—of that other, internal level of investigation that needs to be pursued here, particularly since all of their individual backstories are linked to a larger cultural story about science and technology that have become so "Massive" and "Dynamic," so linked to every aspect of our lives yet uncontrolled that they threaten our very existence. Moreover, that connection is consistently underscored whenever one of those sudden personal recollections, including Walter's car, which happens to contain key files about his past scientific research, open a door onto the larger "pattern" in which these figures find themselves, and indeed their world, enmeshed.

That memory linkage also helps constitute one of *Fringe*'s main attractions. For it not only sets in parallel two sorts of investigation—the common police procedures involved in solving a specific criminal event, and the efforts at wrestling with the cataclysmic problems of time and dimensionality that are unfolding—but also shows how individual and cultural concerns merge, and how SF might address both. Here we see a narrative playing at the fringes of several popular genres, with its science fictional aspect essentially generating—and justifying—its procedural element, and combining to speak about the need to investigate both the world and the self, in fact, asking us to remember both the world and the self as we head into an increasingly technologized future. Of course, hybrid series like Fringe generally tend to attract audiences because of this very ability to cross borders, to open up new territory, to ally the familiar conventions or trappings of SF with other elements. The hope is that by teasing out some of the implications of those hybrid components, as in the case of shows such as Fringe, Lost, and The X-Files, we might better understand both the appeal of these series and even the manifest attractions of SFTV itself.

NOTES

1 A "novum," as Darko Suvin offers, is a "novelty, innovation"—or metaphoric signpost—that marks a distinct shift in the typical SF narrative away from the familiar world to the "what if . . ." or speculative realm of the genre (63).
2 For a discussion of this aspect of the crime/mystery narrative, see my "The Detective as Dreamer: The Case of The Lady in the Lake."

CONCLUSION: NEW DIRECTIONS FOR SFTV

An appropriate way of concluding our overview of SFTV might be to consider a few of the ways in which it has, in effect, transcended the medium and demonstrated a pervasive cultural influence, including an impact on how many people think about or with SF today. That influence can be at least partially gauged through some new types of programming that have appeared, through new ways audiences are experiencing the SF text, and through the increased production of—and what we might think of as the genre's hospitality to—what are termed transmedia texts. As a result of these varied developments, the very ways in which we think of SFTV today are undergoing significant change. Increasingly, the SF narrative seems like an extended, even participatory event, one that promises to have a major impact on television itself, and to open a door onto what might best be described as a science fictional future: a world of interactive narrative adventure, transpiring in a space beyond that of the traditional television experience.

In the course of the preceding chapters we have at several points noted how a new, reality-style programming has emerged, something that is not quite SF itself, but that owes much of its existence, as well as the attraction of its audience, to more conventional media SF. We might trace the appearance of this reality SFTV back to Walt Disney's Disneyland show of the 1950s. For that program's group of "Man in Space" episodes (arch 9, 1955; December, 25 1955; December 4, 1957), and others in a science fictional mode, mixed documentary and other realistic material on rocketry, astronomy, and the American space program with animated and fictional footage. This mixture lent both dramatic and comic tones to the programs' documentary-like account of our future efforts at putting humans into space and in orbit around the moon, and then speculations about what might lie on "Mars and Beyond" (as the third program in this group was evocatively titled). In the process the "Man in Space" programs also established a pattern, what Disney termed "edutainment," that has been revisited in recent years in a wide variety of "reality" shows, among them, *Ancient Aliens* (2010–present), *Chasing UFOs* (2012), *Dark Matters: Twisted But True* (2011–present), and *UFO Hunters* (2008–09). These programs focus on strange phenomena, accounts of alien visitation, UFO sightings, and similar events that have commonly formed the subject matter of our SFTV series, but they usually frame their presentations as "scientific investigations," even as they often present dramatic re-enactments of those events. Moreover, they ultimately leave the evaluation of their subjects in the hands—or imaginations—of the audience, who must determine if their depictions represent a reality that has been suppressed by the government, religion, or the media, or if it is simply some sensational-istic form of SF.

We should emphasize, though, that while such shows do not present themselves as SF, they clearly draw their identity—and probably a substantial part of their audience—from media SF. Through grainy footage of possible flying saucers, the amazed looks recorded on the faces of re-enactors, and in the case of *Dark Matters* the use of actor John Noble, star of the long-running SFTV series *Fringe*, as on-screen host and narrator, they deploy a recognizable genre iconography that situates their audience in what we might think of as bordering territory, where they can then, in the best tradition of SF, *speculate* on what might actually be. It is an impulse that we find practically literalized in another, kindred, and highly popular series, *Face Off* (2011–present). Presented as weekly special-effects competitions, judged by film and television professionals, it shows erstwhile effects technicians using make-up and prosthetics to design various alien or monstrous fig-ures, effectively constructing the "other" imagined by so many of our SF narratives. While framed as a kind of game show—with the season-ending winner receiving a bounty of prizes—*Face Off* finds its ultimate appeal in that meeting of the real and the imagined, as represented by the working effects artists and their fantastic conceptions, that is, in the SF-like real-ization of our strangest speculations about the other (Figure C.1).

Another sign of SFTV's new directions can be seen in the ways in which we are increasingly consuming such shows. Because of the technology involved, our viewing of SFTV has changed in a number of ways: DVRs encourage both time-shifting and repeat viewings; networks or specific channels (such as Syfy or the Discovery Channel) regularly make recent episodes available for download and streaming viewing on computers, iPads, and even cell phones, thereby encouraging fans to watch in a variety of situations; podcasts by series' creators, producers, and writers offer additional commentary and promote online discussion; and the regular release of entire seasons of a show to DVD both encourage new viewing habits—for example, seeing a full season in just a few days—and also generate ancillary texts—that is, the usual DVD extras, such as "Making of . . . " documentaries, commentary tracks by actors and writers, and additional footage. To be sure, many of these developments are, as Henry Jenkins, Sam Ford, and Joshua Green observe, just part of the larger "television industry's gradual evolution from an appointment-based model to an engagement-based one"

Figure C.1 Real-izing an alien in the reality show *Face Off*

(152)—an engagement scheduled at the viewer's discretion. But even as these changes make for more convenient, more contextualized, and a more self-determined watching, they are also affecting how we approach—and think of—the typical SFTV narrative.

While Lincoln Geraghty suggests that having recorded, online, or purchased access to an entire series essentially "fragments" how we see it, in part by that attendant liberation of the viewers from the broadcast industry's schedule (*American Science Fiction* 124), several other consequences seem to have far more significance for today's SFTV viewing experience. Much more than the common monster/mystery/voyage of the week, and more than a periodic indulging of the imagination—both of them indeed fragmentary viewing events—the SFTV narrative today is typically enjoyed as both a *textured* and a *connected* experience. It draws a sense of *texture* from the wide array of extras that surround and support the central SF text: the various add-ons that accompany every DVD issued; the many ancillary materials, including extra narrative footage and actors' observations on their roles, that increasingly appear online or through podcasts; and fans' blogs or commentaries that engage others in critiquing shows and guessing at how plots or characters might develop. Webisodes (or "phonisodes," if intended for distribution directly through smartphones) also contribute a dimension to this textured experience. These short narrative pieces—most often a brief sequence—have been offered by networks or channels for many of their regularly broadcast series, among them *Battlestar Galactica*, *Sanctuary*, *Lost*, and *Eureka*. They typically unfold other or parallel narrative arcs that complement the main series' storyline, while also helping to build viewer interest and investment in the larger (that is, extra-televisual) "world" of the series.

Such ancillary narrative elements might also begin to suggest ways in which our SFTV narratives are increasingly experienced as *connected* events. Even beyond television theory's notion of "flow," described in the Introduction, today we almost of necessity see series in the context of other shows or segments of shows, and thus as part of a much larger story arc that is composed of multiple text types, of a full season's stories, or even an entire series' narrative design. And here we might recall that shows such as *Babylon 5*, *Battlestar Galactica*, and *Lost* were all originally conceived with approximately five-year story arcs, a conception that gave an almost epic scope to their narratives, while encouraging audiences to think of the individual episodes not as discrete experiences or narrative fragments, but rather as linked, unfolding, and indeed involving tales. Moreover, the custom of seeing multiple episodes in one marathon session—a practice encouraged by some broadcasters, such as Syfy Channel which has run 24-hour festivals of series such as *The Twilight Zone, Star Trek: The Next Generation,* and *Battlestar Galactica*—or of watching a full season's offerings in a short period tends to result in a new regime of televisual knowledge: one in which we experience, expect, or in some cases *impute* a pattern of narrative linkage. In fact, I would suggest that this new watching regime is probably largely responsible for the increased emphasis on *seriality* over the more conventional *series* impulse in SFTV programming; we simply assume—and demand—that episodes and experiences are in some way linked.

These effects also involve, as we are already noting, the creation of new categories of texts, in effect new sorts of SFTV. Those webisodes cited above are one version of what we earlier referred to as *transmedia texts.* Combining SFTV characters and plots with a specialized internet distribution, usually through a network or channel's website, they constitute an instance of what Jenkins, Ford, and Green have termed "spreadable media," that is, a combination of textual materials and communication technologies that allow—even encourage—material to be "shared across and among cultures in far more participatory ways" than was heretofore the case for our popular media (1). That spreadability factor not only accounts for the many sorts of ways that we are accessing texts—that is, via television, the internet, the smartphone, the smart tablet, and so forth—but also how our texts are affected by such multiple access points, including fans' newfound ability to become involved with a show's life, to make its materials at least partly their own. Thus we find our SFTV series taking on a thick character, as they are increasingly propagating other sorts of offspring: fan fiction, documentaries, film adaptations, video games, vlogs that incorporate show clips (and here too we might note that some broadcasters are implicitly encouraging these activities, particularly by making clips available on their websites for those wishing to incorporate them into their own creations—or broadcasts). This great variety of progeny points not only to the thickening of our SFTV experience—as parts of stories are embellished by other contributors (and especially fans), as story arcs multiply and complicate across platforms, and as background material becomes a central part of our involvement with many shows— but also to the way that series material is being *designed* for life on those multiple platforms, created with spreadability in mind.

Of course, fan fiction and fan involvement have long been strong components of SF culture. Fanzines of the 1930s and 1940s published both original stories written by fans and imitations, extensions, or continuations of the work—and worlds—of more established writers. That practice has taken on an especially elaborate life today with the creation of both authorized and unauthorized novelizations of SFTV series (especially *Star Trek*, *Babylon 5*, and *Stargate SG-1*), the online publication of fan fiction focused on specific characters in various series (including speculations about their sex lives, commonly referred to as "slash fiction"), and the production of movies and games based on SFTV. We might particularly note the many games that are now being designed to accompany the release of an SFTV show or, after the fact, to capitalize on its success, such as the games based on *Battlestar Galactica*, *Buffy the Vampire Slayer*, *Doctor Who*, *Farscape*, *Lost*, *SeaQuest DSV*, *Star Trek*, *Star Wars: The Clone Wars*, and *The X-Files*. These games, either produced for specific game platforms or offered as online gaming sites, pointedly provide fans with a different sort of access to the originary SF text: a sense that they are capable of interacting with that world and its characters, entering into it and effectively creating their own version of a favorite SFTV text with each new playing experience.

A more elaborate and potentially trailblazing version of this transmedia experience is fundamental to the way the recent Syfy Channel series *Defiance* (2013–present) presents itself. Developed by SFTV veteran Rockne S. O'Bannon, whose work on such series as *Alien Nation*, *SeaQuest DSV*, and *Farscape* certainly helped his new series concept find backing, *Defiance* recalls many popular video games in its focus on both world building and post-apocalyptic combat. Set in the wake of an alien invasion of Earth that produced a calamitous war and accidental terraforming effects, the series depicts a shattered human civilization and introduces various sorts of mutant plants and creatures, as well as multiple alien species. As a consequence, the Earth as depicted looks very much like an alien world, and its human survivors every bit as much like aliens as do the alien and mutant remnants of this warfare. The dual activities of trying to fight off other and ongoing threats, while attempting to build alliances between different constituencies within the rag-tag community of Defiance, are played out narratively through the often violent actions of Joshua Nolan, the local sheriff (or "Lawkeeper," as he is known), and his adopted alien daughter (and deputy) Irisa. Seen simply from the vantage of this narrative description, *Defiance* easily recalls a number of other post-apocalyptic series of the past decade, shows like *Falling Skies* (2011–present), *Jeremiah* (2002–04), *Jericho* (2006–08), *Revolution* (2013–present), and *The Walking Dead* (2010–present). In fact, it might remind us of how popular that particular story type has become and even prompt us to consider why, as a culture, we have become so absorbed with such post-apocalyptic imaginings.

However, *Defiance* differentiates itself from these other popular entries by a particularly innovative transmedia turn. For it parallels or shadows these familiar actions with another, interactive text, that of the massive online and multiplatform *Defiance* video game, which allows players to take on the roles of series characters or to create their own characters, and to lend their own (third-person-shooter) skills to the community's defense. The result, as reviewer Tim Surette describes, is the "first-ever fully realized television and video-game symbiotic relationship. Though the game and the show are set in the same universe, each project will inhabit a different part of the world, and events in one will be referenced in the other" (Surette). More signficantly, the show's producers claim that the show/game combination will result in a new sort of interactivity, with game players able to affect upcoming events in the series' narrative—an aim that could pose both technological challenges for the game designers and scripting challenges for the series. To date, a particularly adept game player's face has appeared on a wanted poster in the first season's final episode ("Everything is Broken"), and a contest has been announced to have a top-scoring player's character incorporated into the second season's narrative arc. Another announced effort at marrying the two media worlds sets up a game mission to stave off a plague that threatens the town of Defiance. If game players successfully combat this threat, the plots of several episodes are geared to reflect

Figure C.2 The post-apocalyptic world of Defiance's television and game narrative

the averted calamity, and if not, then the series' post-apocalyptic world will face one more grim challenge (see Grubb), thereby altering the narrative arc (Figure C.2). This goal of interactivity represents a major development for SFTV, one that suggests how the latest transmedia developments, along with a more "spreadable" approach to our texts, aims to produce more engaged fans, particularly ones who, as Jenkins, Ford, and Green put it, want to "have their voices heard" (303) within their SF texts.

But even if such a hoped-for level of interactivity remains something of an experimental process, there are other promising signs for our own and our SFTV's linked futures, other ways in which SFTV is generating new "texts" for our consideration. The slogan that has been used to advertise Defiance is "New Earth. New Rules," and that catchphrase also resonates for the genre's new level of cultural importance and its "spreadable" experience. A recent initiative by the Intel Corporation, long a leader in the information industry and the world's largest maker of semiconductor microchips—technology essential to creating the many new platforms on which we are mounting our SFTV—incorporates SF as part of its highly touted "Tomorrow Project." This multi-faceted and international effort at exploring "Futurism" and futuristic speculation involves a group of think tanks tasked with exploring the sort of future people would most like to live in, while also sponsoring some of the projects that are likely to get us there.

On its official website, the company's resident "Futurist" Brian David Johnson describes the impetus behind "The Tomorrow Project," while also hinting at its own SF dimension. As he notes,

> This is a unique time in history. Science and technology has [sic] progressed to the point where what we build is only constrained by the limits of our own imaginations. The future is not a fixed point in front of us that we are all hurtling helplessly towards. The future is built everyday by the actions of people. It's up to all of us to be active participants in the future and these conversations can do just that.

Of course, those "limits" of the imagination are precisely the stuff of SF; the "sense of wonder" the genre stages for us is symptomatic of the ways it tries to challenge conventional thinking. So it seems only fitting that Johnson and his cohorts have identified SF as a crucial contributor to this "conversation," one aimed at helping—with Intel's assistance—to design that better future. Thus the Project's official description suggests that the discussions surrounding issues like synthetic biology, robotics, computer security, DNA sequencing, virtual reality, and synthetic vision should function like a two-way street, with the public and scientists probing the best of contemporary SF—in literature, film, television, and elsewhere—to better understand the possibilities that are being conceived by those working quite practically at the imagination's "limits," and with the creators/authors of SF (noted SF author Cory Doctorow is one member of the Project's Board) in turn gaining better access to the latest research in these areas so that they might be further inspired, gain new ideas that will help us all "think about what the future will look like when these technologies affect our everyday lives" ("The Tomorrow Project").

Quite simply, with "The Tomorrow Project" Intel is asking its scientists and technicians to read SF, to view the best of SFTV, to mine the genre for ideas. And yet, this project is one in which, as a culture, many of us are already engaged. It is a conversation that is daily taking place on our blogs, an experience that is lived in our conventions, an exploration that is part of today's televisual experience—and indeed, one that has spurred the prolif-eration of ever more sophisticated SFTV series. As this book's Introduction suggested, we already inhabit a kind of SF world, one where we cannot help but encounter—stumble over, be challenged by—the many scientific and technological developments that are currently shaping our lives. Of course, it is helpful to have some guidance as we try to better understand those encounters, those developments, those new directions. The argument we have made throughout this book is that SFTV serves us as one of the most important of those guides, and the hope is that this text might itself work as a helpful introduction to the genre's many inviting visions.

SFTV: QUESTIONS FOR DISCUSSION

CHAPTER 1

1. Trace out the impact of the "space race" on a string of comic SF/fantasy series that appeared in the mid-1960s, shows such as *My Favorite Martian, My Living Doll, It's About Time,* and even *I Dream of Jeannie.*

2. The alien invasion theme has long been a concern of SF, both in film and on television. Compare the treatment of this motif across a variety of series over time, such as *The Invaders* (1967–68), *V* (1984–85), and the recent *Defiance* (2013–present).

3. How has the availability of relatively inexpensive digital effects altered our stories about space exploration? As examples of that impact, you might compare the use of special effects in the original *Star Trek* series to that in a show like *Battlestar Galactica.*

CHAPTER 2

1. As we have noted, the movie serials of the 1920s–50s had a strong impact on SFTV in its early days. Trace out the extent of that impact by comparing episodes of an early space film serial like *Flash Gordon* (1936) or *Buck Rogers* (1939) to *Rocky Jones, Space Ranger.*

2. SF historian Edward James suggests that one of the genre's most common types of stories is what he terms "the tale of science." Consider how a

fictional series like Eureka develops its narrative around this focus, and then compare it to a seemingly factual series such as Through the Wormhole with Morgan Freeman or Dark Matters: Twisted but True. Do they have any attitudes or narrative strategies in common? Why?

3. While categories like the marvelous, the fantastic, and the uncanny are very useful for helping us see a narrative's primary thrust, in practice SF series have often blurred such distinctions. For example, individual episodes of both The Twilight Zone and The Outer Limits appear to be uncanny, only to then reveal their marvelous dimensions. Describe how similar shifts drive any of the following series: The X-Files, Fringe, Lost. What do those shifts tell us about any of these series?

CHAPTER 3

1. View Joss Whedon's internet film Dr. Horrible's Sing-Along Blog (2008) and consider how it asks viewers to question traditional gender roles, particularly in its use of Nathan Fillion, who plays the lead role of Mal Reynolds in Whedon's Firefly series, as a somewhat questionable "superhero."

2. Can you identify some instances or shows where science and technology have been portrayed as "wacky" and have strained our credulity? How does that sort of presentation affect the tone of a series, and what does it say about our culture's attitudes towards science and technology?

3. Often SFTV has metaphorized contemporary racial or ethnic issues by using other or alien species to represent racial difference. Examine that metaphoric treatment of race/ethnicity in Alien Nation, Farscape, or Babylon 5.

CHAPTER 4

1. A number of SFTV series have been produced with a largely children's audience in mind. What kinds of accommodations or changes do you see in the SF elements of such series to accommodate that audience? Consider such series as Honey, I Shrunk the Kids, Phil of the Future, and Small Wonder.

2. Look at the websites for some of the SF-oriented or related conventions (or cons), such as DragonCon, Starfleet, Worldcon, TimeGate, or Comic-Con International. What SFTV series seem to be most commonly represented—with panel discussions, special guests, parade participation, and so forth—at these conventions? Does that representation tell us anything about their fandom?

3. A number of SFTV series have attained a cult status, marked especially by their fervent fan following. Among the most prominently mentioned "cult series" are *Star Trek*, *Farscape*, *Firefly*, *Stargate SG-1*, and *Doctor Who*. Is it possible to map the attractions and thus determine the typical characteristics of a "cult series" by comparing the features of some of these shows?

CHAPTER 5

1. One dimension of hybridity noted in the discussion of *Fringe* is its mixed tone, varying from the highly serious and even horrific to the whimsical. Consider how a very similar tonal mixture functions in series such as *Warehouse 13*, *Firefly*, or *Eureka*.
2. SF, we have suggested, seems to be a very welcoming host to other generic elements. How many different types of hybridity show up in episodes of even a relatively short-lived series such as the original *Star Trek*? Why did it accommodate such a formulaic variety?
3. Does animating SF produce another sort of hybridity—or at least alter how we perceive its science fictional context? As test cases, you might explore shows such as *Cowboy Bebop*, *Futurama*, or *Star Wars: The Clone Wars*.

A SELECT SFTV VIDEOGRAPHY

While the following listing does not presume to be an exhaustive compilation of English-language SFTV shows (i.e., one-shot presentations) or series, it brings together the titles and dates of many of the more prominent—and in some cases, simply curious—SFTV programs, with a particular emphasis on those cited throughout the text. In each case, I have appended production company and network information, in some cases the creators of the series, and a brief descriptive tag to let prospective viewers/students understand the primary focus or concern of the series, and thus to allow for ease of categorization and further research. More comprehensive listings, along with far more extensive credits, can easily be found at various on-line sites.

Adventure Time (2010–present). Frederator Studios/Cartoon Network. Created by Pendleton Ward. Post-apocalyptic animated children's adventure.

The Adventures of Brisco County, Jr. (1993–94). Boam/Cuse Productions/Warner Bros. TV/Fox. Created by Jeffrey Boam and Carlton Cuse. Steampunk adventures in the Wild West.

The Adventures of Superman (1951–58). National Productions, Inc./ABC. Based on the comic book character. Superhero adventures.

ALF (1986–90). Alien Productions Inc./NBC. Comic alien visitor.

Alias (2001–06). Bad Robot Productions/Touchstone TV/ABC. Created by J. J. Abrams. Female secret agent.

Alien Nation (1989–90). 20th Century Fox/Fox. Created by Kenneth Johnson and Rockne S. O'Bannon. Adapted from the feature film. Alien and human crime fighters.

Almost Human (2013–14). Bad Robot Productions/Warner Bros. TV/Fox. Created by J. H. Wyman. Robotic crime fighting.

Alphas (2011–12). BermanBraun/Universal/Syfy Channel. Superhuman crime fighters.

Angel (1999–2004). Mutant Enemy Productions/20th Century Fox/WB. Created by Joss Whedon. Vampire battles evil.

Ashes to Ashes (2008–10). BBC. Sequel to *Life on Mars*. Time travel police procedural.

Babylon 5 (1992–98). Babylonian Productions/Warner Bros. TV. Created by J. Michael Straczynski. Space travel/adventure.

Battlestar Galactica (1978–80). Glen A. Larson Productions/MCA/ABC. Created by Glen A. Larson. Space travel/adventure.

Battlestar Galactica (2004–09). British Sky Broadcasting/David Eick Productions/Syfy Channel. Based on the Glen A. Larson series. Space travel/adventure.

Being Human (2008–13). BBC. Created by Toby Whithouse. Fantastic figures try to fit in to human world.

The Bionic Woman (1976–78). Harve Bennett Productions/Universal TV/ABC. Female technological superhero.

Blake's 7 (1978–81). BBC. Created by Terry Nation. Space travel adventures.

Buck Rogers (1950–51). ABC. Based on the comic strip and serial. Futuristic adventure, space opera.

Buck Rogers in the 25th Century (1979–81). John Mantley Productions/Glen A. Larson Productions/Universal TV/NBC. Futuristic adventure, space opera.

Buffy the Vampire Slayer (1997–2003). Mutant Enemy Productions/20th Century Fox/WB/UPN. Created by Josh Whedon. Young woman fighting forces of evil.

Caprica (2010). Universal Cable Productions/Syfy Channel. Prequel to *Battlestar Galactica*.

Captain Midnight (1954–56). Screen Gems Television/CBS. Scientific action-adventure.

Captain Power and the Soldiers of the Future (1987–88). Canadian–American syndicated series. Created by Gary Goddard and Tony Christopher. Post-apocalyptic adventure.

Captain Video and His Video Rangers (1949–55). DuMont Televison. Created by Lawrence Menkin and James Caddigan. Space opera.

Captain Z-Ro (1951–56). W. A. Palmer Films/syndicated. Space opera/time travel.

Commando Cody: Sky Marshal of the Universe (1955). Republic Pictures/NBC. Based on the movie serial character. Superhero adventures/space opera.

Continuum (2012–14). Reunion Pictures/Showcase. Created by Simon Barry. Time travel adventures.

Cowboy Bebop (1998–99). Sunrise Productions/Bandai. Animated bounty hunter adventures in space.

Dark Angel (2000–02). Cameron/Eglee/20th Century Fox TV/Fox. Created by James Cameron and Charles H. Eglee. Genetically enhanced superhero adventures.

Dark Skies (1996–97). Bryce Zabel Productions/Columbia Pictures/NBC. Alien invasion.

Defiance (2013–present). Universal Cable Productions/Syfy. Created by Rockne S. O'Bannon, Kevin Murphy, and Michael Taylor. Post-alien invasion adventures.

Doctor Who (1963–89, 1996, 2005–present). BBC/BBC Wales/Canadian Broadcasting Corp. Time and dimensional travel adventure.

Dollhouse (2009–10). Mutant Enemy Productions/20th Century Fox/Fox. Created by Joss Whedon. Personality control.

Earth 2 (1994–95). Amblin Entertainment/Universal/NBC. Dystopian future space adventure.

Eureka (2006–12). Universal Cable Productions/NBC/Syfy Channel. Created by Andrew Cosby and Jaime Paglia. Secret government experiments in small town.

The Fades (2011). BBC. Created by Jack Thorne. Supernatural encounters.

Falling Skies (2011–present). Dreamworks Television/TNT. Created by Robert Rodat. Post-apocalyptic, alien invasion drama.

Farscape (1999–2003). Jim Henson Productions/Syfy Channel. Created by Rockne S. O'Bannon and Brian Henson. Space travel/adventure.

Firefly (2002–03). 20th Century Fox/Syfy Channel. Created by Joss Whedon. Space travel/adventure.

Flash Gordon (1954–55). Inter-Continental Television/King Features. Based on the comic strip and movie serial. Space opera.

Fringe (2008–13). 20th Century Fox/Bad Robot Productions/Warner Bros./Fox. Created by J. J. Abrams, Alex Kurtzman, and Roberto Orci. Paranormal investigations and dimensional travel.

Futurama (1999–2003, 2010–13). Curiosity Company/20th Century Fox/Fox. Created by Matt Groening. Animated futuristic comedy.

Galaxy High (1986). CBS. Created by Chris Columbus. Animated teen adventures in an intergalactic high school.

Grimm (2011–present). Universal Television/NBC. Police procedural investigation of fantastic events.

Hard Time on Planet Earth (1989). Demos-Bard/Shanachie Productions/CBS. Alien superhero on Earth.

Heroes (2006–10). Universal Television/NBC. Created by Tim Kring. Common people with unusual powers.

The Hitchhiker's Guide to the Galaxy (1981). BBC. Created by Douglas Adams. Comic space adventures.

Honey, I Shrunk the Kids (1997–2000). Buena Vista Television/Disney Channel. Based on the feature film. Fantastic inventions.

The Invaders (1967–68). Quinn Martin Productions/ABC. Created by Larry Cohen. Alien invasion narrative.

Invasion (2005–06). Warner Bros./Shaun Cassidy Productions/ABC. Created by Shaun Cassidy. Alien invasion narrative.

It's About Time (1967–68). United Artists Television/CBS. Comic time travel.

Jeremiah (2002–04). Platinum Studios/Lionsgate Television/Showtime. Post-apocalyptic adventures.

Jericho (2006–08). Paramount TV/Junction Entertainment/CBS. Post-apocalyptic adventures.

The Jetsons (1962–63, 1985–87). Screen Gems/World Vision Enterprises/Warner Bros./ABC. Created by Hanna-Barbera Productions. Animated futuristic sit-com.

Jimmy Neutron: Boy Genius (2002–06). O Entertainment/DNA Productions/Nickelodeon. Created by John A. Davis. Animated comedy adventure.

Johnny Jupiter (1953–54). DuMont TV Network. Puppet and live-action interplanetary adventures.

Jonny Quest (1964–65). Screen Gems/Hanna-Barbera Productions/ABC. Created by Doug Wildey. Scientific adventures.

Knight Rider (1982–86). MCA/Universal/NBC. Created by Glen A. Larson. Technologically empowered crime fighting.

Kolchak: The Night Stalker (1974–75). ABC. Created by Jeff Rice. Journalist investigates unusual phenomena.

Land of the Giants (1968–70). 20th Century Fox/Irwin Allen Productions/ABC. Created by Irwin Allen. Space travel adventure.

Legend (1995). UPN. Created by Michael Piller and Bill Dial. Steampunk adventures in the Wild West.

Life on Mars (2006–07, US version, 2008–09). BBC. Time travel police procedural.

Logan's Run (1977–78). MGM Television/CBS. Based on the feature film. Dystopian world.

The Lone Gunmen (2001). Fox. Spin-off of *The X-Files*. Conspiracy investigations.

Lost (2004–10). Touchstone/Bad Robot Productions/ABC. Castaways in mysterious adventures.

Lost Girl (2010–14). Prodigy Pictures/Showcase. Created by Michelle Lovretta. Supernatural crime drama.

Lost in Space (1965–68). 20th Century Fox/Irwin Allen Productions/CBS. Created by Irwin Allen. Space travel/adventure.

Mary Shelley's Frankenhole (2010–present). Shadowmachine/Starburns Industries/Cartoon Network. Created by Dino Stamatopoulos. Animated time and dimensional travel adventure.

Millennium (1996–99). Fox. Created by Chris Carter. Psychic crime fighting.

Misfits (2009–14). Clerkenwell Films/E4 (England). Created by Howard Overman. Adolescents with supernatural powers.

Mork and Mindy (1978–82). Paramount TV/Henderson Productions/ABC. Comic alien visitor.

My Favorite Martian (1963–66). Jack Chertok Productions/CBS. Created by John L. Greene. Comic alien visitor.

My Living Doll (1964–65). Jack Chertok Productions/CBS. Robot/android tale.

Night Gallery (1970–73). Universal TV/NBC. Created by Rod Serling. Anthology series.

Orphan Black (2013–14). Bell Media/BBC America/Space Channel. Investigation of cloning conspiracy.

Out There (1951–52). CBS. Anthology show.

The Outer Limits (1963–65, 1995–2002). Villa Di Stefano/Daystar Productions/MGM/ABC. Created by Leslie Stevens. Anthology show.

Painkiller Jane (2007). Global (Canada)/Syfy Channel. Created by Gil Grant, based on the comic book character. Female superhero's adventures.

Paradox (2009). BBC. Police procedural investigation of fantastic events.

Person of Interest (2011–present). Bad Robot Productions/Kilter Films/Warner Bros. TV/CBS. Created by Jonathan Nolan. Crime fighting with use of supercomputer

Phil of the Future (2004–06). Disney Channel. Created by Tim Maile and Douglas Tuber. Comic time travel.

Planet of the Apes (1974). 20th Century Fox Television/CBS. Based on the feature film. Post-apocalyptic adventures.

Planet Sheen (2010–13). Omation Animation/Nickelodeon. Created by John A. Davis, Keith Alcorn, and Steve Oedekerk. Animated space adventure.

The Powers of Matthew Star (1982–83). Paramount Television/NBC. Created by Harve Bennett. Teenage alien on Earth.

Primeval (2007–11). Impossible Pictures/ITV. Investigation of temporal anomalies.

Primeval: New World (2012–13). Impossible Pictures/Space Channel. Canadian spin-off of Primeval. Investigation of temporal anomalies.

The Prisoner (1967–68). Everyman Films/Associated TV/ITV. Dystopian prison escape drama.

Project UFO (1978–79). Mark VII Limited/Worldvision Enterprises/NBC. Created by Jack Webb. Investigating UFO encounters.

Quantum Leap (1889–93). Belisarius Productions/Universal TV/NBC. Created by Donald P. Bellisario. Time travel adventures.

Ray Bradbury Theater (1985–92). Alberta Filmworks/Atlantic Films/Ellipse/Granada TV/Showtime/HBO/USA. Created by Ray Bradbury. Anthology series.

Red Dwarf (1988–93, 1997–99, 2009, 2012–13). BBC/Grant Naylor Productions/Paul Jackson Productions/BBC2. Created by Rob Grant and Doug Naylor. Comic space adventures.

Revolution (2012–present). Bad Robot Productions/Warner Bros./NBC. Created by Eric Kripke. Post-apocalyptic adventure.

Rocky Jones, Space Ranger (1954). Roland Reed Productions/Space Ranger Enterprises. Created by Roland D. Reed. Space opera.

Rod Brown of the Rocket Rangers (1953–54). CBS. Space opera adventure.

Roswell (1999–2002). 20th Century Fox/Regency Television/WB/UPN. Created by Jason Katims. Alien teenagers in hiding.

Sanctuary (2007–11). Syfy Channel. Created by Damian Kindler. Group hunts and preserves abnormal life forms.

The Sarah Jane Adventures (2007–11). CBBC/BBC. Created by Russell T. Davies. Spin-off of Doctor Who. Investigative journalist's adventures.

Science Fiction Theatre (1955–57). Ziv Television. Creator/Producer: Ivan Tors. Anthology series.

Seaquest DSV (1993–96). NBC. Created by Rockne S. O'Bannon. Fantastic submarine adventures.

The Secret World of Alex Mack (1994–98). Nickelodeon. Created by Thomas W. Lynch and Ken Lipman. Adventures of a teen with super powers.

The Sentinel (1996–99). Pet Fly Productions/Paramount/UPN. Created by Danny Bilson and Paul De Meo. Crime fighting through hyperactive senses.

The Six Million Dollar Man (1974–78). Harve Bennett Productions/Universal/ABC. Technological superhero.

Smallville (2001–11). Tollin/Robbins Productions/WB/CW. Based on the Superman comics figure. Young superhero adventures.

Space: 1999 (1975–77). Group 3 Productions/RAI/ITC Entertainment/ITV. Created by Gerry and Sylvia Anderson. Space adventures.

Space Angel (1962–64). Cambria Productions. Created by Dick Darley. Animated space adventures.

Space Patrol (1950–55). Tower Productions/Mike Moser Enterprises/ABC. Created by Mike Moser. Space opera adventures

Space Rangers (1993). Trilogy Entertainment/CBS. Created by Pen Densham. Space opera adventure.

Star Trek (1966–69). Desilu/Paramount TV/NBC. Created by Gene Roddenberry. Space travel/adventure.

Star Trek: Deep Space Nine (1993–99). Paramount TV/UPN. Spin-off of *Star Trek*. Space station encounters.

Star Trek: Enterprise (2001–05). Braga Productions/Paramount TV/Rick Berman Productions/UPN. Space travel/adventure.

Star Trek: The Next Generation (1987–94). Paramount TV/CBS. Spin-off of *Star Trek*. Space travel/adventure.

Star Trek: Voyager (1995–2001). Paramount TV/UPN. Spin-off of *Star Trek*. Space travel/adventure.

Star Wars: The Clone Wars (2008–13). CGCG Inc./Lucasfilm/Cartoon Network. Animated continuation of the *Star Wars* saga. Created by George Lucas. Space adventures.

Stargate: Atlantis (2004–09). Sony/MGM/SyFy Channel. Spin-off of *Stargate SG-1*. Time/dimensional travel adventure

Stargate Infinity (2002–03). MGM/DIC Entertainment/Fox. Animated spin-off of *Stargate SG-1*. Time/dimensional travel adventure.

Stargate SG-1 (1997–2007). Sony/MGM/Showtime/Syfy Channel. Based on the feature film. Time/dimensional travel adventure.

Stargate: Universe (2009–11). Sony/MGM/Sydy Channel. Spin-off of *Stargate SG-1*. Time/dimensional travel adventure.

Starman (1986–87). Columbia Pictures/Henerson-Hirsch Productions/ABC. Based on the feature film. Alien on earth.

Superboy/The Adventures of Superboy (1988–92). Viacom/Warner Bros. TV/CBS. Based on characters from the *Superman* comics. Superhero adventures.

Taken (2002). Syfy Channel. Created by Leslie Bohem and Steven Spielberg. Extraterrestrial kidnappings.

Tales of Tomorrow (1951–53). George F. Foley Productions/ABC. Anthology series.

Terminator: The Sarah Connor Chronicles (2008–09). C2 Pictures/Warner Bros./Fox. Based on the *Terminator* film series. Time travel and technological threats.

3rd Rock from the Sun (1996–2001). Carsey-Werner/YBYL Productions/NBC. Created by Bonnie and Terry Turner. Comic aliens on earth.

The Time Tunnel (1966–67). 20th Century Fox/Irwin Allen Productions/ABC. Created by Irwin Allen. Time travel.

Tom Corbett, Space Cadet (1950–55). Rockhill Productions/CBS/ABC/NBC/Dumont. Based on the Robert A. Heinlein novel. Space opera, space adventuring.

Torchwood (2006–11). BBC/Starz Entertainment. Created by Russell T. Davies. Spin-off of *Doctor Who*. Secret service alien hunters.

The Tripods (1984–85). Fremantle International/7 Network/BBC. Alien invasion narrative.

Tron: Uprising (2012–13). Disney/ABC/Disney XD. Based on the *Tron* feature films. Animated adventures inside a computer.

The Twilight Zone (1959–64, 1985–89, 2002–03). Cayuga Productions/CBS. Created by Rod Serling. Anthology series.

V (1984–85). Warner Bros. TV/NBC. Created by Kenneth Johnson. Alien invaders.

Voyage to the Bottom of the Sea (1964–68). 20th Century Fox/Irwin Allen Productions/ABC. Created by Irwin Allen. Fantastic machine adventures.

The Walking Dead (2010–14). AMC. Based on the graphic novel. Post-apocalyptic zombie adventures.

Warehouse 13 (2009–present). Universal/Syfy Channel. Created by Jane Espenson and D. Brent Mote. Investigation of paranormal events.

War of the Worlds (1988–90). Hometown Films/Paramount TV. Adapted by Greg Strangis from the novel and feature film. Alien invaders.

Welcome to Paradox (1998). Chelser/Perlmutter Productions/Syfy Channel. Created by Lewis Chesler and Jeremy Lipp. Anthology series.

The X-Files (1993–2002). Ten Thirteen Productions/20th Century Fox/Fox. Created by Chris Carter. Alien conspiracy and investigation.

A SELECT SFTV BIBLIOGRAPHY

The following listing serves two purposes. It provides citations for the various works parenthetically noted throughout the text, and also serves as a guide to further readings in the area of media SF. Those looking to do additional research in this area might also consult the bibliographies in several of the other books listed here, particularly Telotte and Duchovnay's *Science Fiction Film, Television, and Adaptation*, and Geraghty's *American Science Fiction Film and Television*.

BIBLIOGRAPHY

Alvey, Mark. "'Too Many Kids and Old Ladies': Quality Demographics and 1960s U.S. Television." *Television: The Critical View.* 7th ed. Ed. Horace Newcomb. Oxford: Oxford UP, 2007. 15–36.

Amesley, Cassandra. "How to Watch Star Trek." *Cultural Studies* 3.3 (1989): 323–39.

Anderson, Porter. "Bonnie Hammer: She is Sci Fi." CNN.com. Feb. 5, 2001. www.articles.cnn.com/2001-02-05/business/hammer_1_bonnie-hammer-sci-fi-channel-alec-newman?_s=PM:CAREER#popup=. Accessed Aug. 15, 2012.

Anon. "25 Best Cult TV Shows from the Past 25 Years." *Entertainment Weekly*, Aug. 3, 2012. 39–40.

Badmington, Neil. "*Roswell High*, Alien Chic and the In/Human." *Teen TV: Genre, Consumption and Identity.* Eds. Glyn Davis and Kay Dickinson. London: BFI, 2004. 166–75.

Banks, Miranda J. "A Boy for All Planets: *Roswell, Smallville* and the Teen Male Melodrama." *Teen TV: Genre, Consumption and Identity.* Eds. Glyn Davis and Kay Dickinson. London: BFI, 2004. 17–28.

Barbour, Alan G. *Cliffhangers: A Pictorial History of the Motion Picture Serial.* Secaucus, NJ: Citadel, 1977.

Barnouw, Erik. *Tube of Plenty: The Evolution of American Television.* New York: Oxford UP, 1975.

Barrett, Michele, and Duncan Barrett. *Star Trek: The Human Factor.* London: Polity Press, 2001.

Battis, Jes. *Investigating* Farscape: *Uncharted Territories of Sex and Science Fiction.* London: I.B. Tauris, 2007.

Beeler, Stan, and Lisa Dickson. *Reading* Stargate SG-1. London: I.B. Tauris, 2006.

Bennett, Eve. "Techno-Butterfly: Orientalism Old and New in *Battlestar Galactica.*" *Science Fiction Film and Television* 5.1 (2012): 23–46.

Bernardi, Daniel Leonard. *Star Trek and History: Race-ing Toward a White Future.* New Brunswick: Rutgers UP, 1998.

Bianculli, David. *Teleliteracy: Taking Television Seriously.* Syracuse: Syracuse UP, 2000.

Bignell, Jonathan, and Stephen Lacey, eds. *Popular Television Drama: Critical Perspectives.* Manchester: Manchester UP, 2005.

Boddy, William. *Fifties Television.* Champaign: U of Illinois P, 1990.

———. *New Media and Popular Imagination: Launching Radio, Television, and Digital Media in the United States.* Oxford: Oxford UP, 2004.

Booker, M. Keith. "The Politics of Star Trek." *The Essential Science Fiction Television Reader.* Ed. J. P. Telotte. Lexington, KY: UP of Kentucky, 2008. 195–208.

———. *Science Fiction Television.* Westport, CT: Praeger, 2004.

Bould, Mark. "Film and Television." *The Cambridge Companion to Science Fiction.* Eds. Edward James and Farah Mendlesohn. Cambridge: Cambridge UP, 2003. 79–95.

———. *Science Fiction.* London: Routledge, 2012.

Boyer, Paul. *By the Bomb's Early Light: American Thought and Culture at the Dawn of the Atomic Age.* Chapel Hill, NC: U of North Carolina P, 1994.

Braun, Beth. "The X-Files and Buffy the Vampire Slayer: The Ambiguity of Evil in Supernatural Representations." *Journal of Popular Film and Television* 28.2 (2000): 88–94.

Britton, Piers D. and Simon J. Barker. *Reading Between Designs: Visual Imagery and the Generation of Meaning in* The Avengers, The Prisoner, *and* Doctor Who. Austin, TX: U of Texas P, 2003.

Brooks, Tim, and Earle Marsh. *The Complete Directory to Prime Time Network and Cable TV Shows, 1946–Present.* 8th ed. New York, NY: Ballantine, 2003.

Buchanan, Ginjer. "Who Killed Firefly?" *Finding Serenity: Anti-Heroes, Lost Shepherds and Space Hookers in Joss Whedon's Firefly.* Ed. Jane Espenson. Dallas, TX: BenBella Books, 2004. 47–53.

Bukatman, Scott. *Terminal Identity: The Virtual Subject in Post-Modern Science-Fiction.* Durham, NC: Duke UP, 1993.

Burns, Christy L. "Erasure: Alienation, Paranoia, and the Loss of Memory in The X-Files." *Camera Obscura* 15.3 (2000): 195–224.

Buxton, David. *From The Avengers to Miami Vice: Form and Ideology in Television Series.* Manchester: Manchester UP, 1990.

Casetti, Francesco. *Eye of the Century: Film, Experience, Modernity.* Trans. Erin Larkin and Jennifer Pranolo. New York, NY: Columbia UP, 2008.

Cawelti, John G. *Adventure, Mystery, and Romance: Formula Stories as Art and Popular Culture.* Chicago, IL: U of Chicago P, 1976.

Certeau, Michel de. "The Jabbering of Social Life." *On Signs.* Ed. Marshall Blonsky. Baltimore, MD: Johns Hopkins UP, 1985. 146–54.

Cheng, John. *Astounding Wonder: Imagining Science and Science Fiction in Interwar America.* Philadelphia, PA: U of Pennsylvania P, 2012.

Clareson, Thomas D. *Many Futures, Many Worlds: Theme and Form in Science Fiction.* Kent, OH: Kent State UP, 1977.

Corn, Joseph J., and Brian Horrigan. *Yesterday's Tomorrows: Past Visions of the American Future.* Baltimore, MD: The Johns Hopkins UP, 1996.

Csicsery-Ronay, Istvan, Jr. "Marxist Theory and Science Fiction." *The Cambridge Companion to Science Fiction.* Eds. Edward James and Farah Mendlesohn. Cambridge: Cambridge UP, 2003. 113–24.

Davenport, Misha. "'Fringe' Blinds Viewers with Science." *Chicago Sun-Times,* Sept. 9, 2008. www.suntimes.com/entertainment/television/1152182,CST-FTR-fringe09.article. Accessed May 30, 2013.

Davidson, Joy. "Whores and Goddesses." *Finding Serenity: Anti-Heroes, Lost Shepherds and Space Hookers in Joss Whedon's Firefly.* Ed. Jane Espenson. Dallas, TX: BenBella Books, 2004. 113–29.

Dery, Mark. *Escape Velocity: Cyberculture at the End of the Century.* New York, NY: Grove, 1996.

Dixon, Wheeler Winston. "Tomorrowland TV: The Space Opera and Early Science Fiction Television." *The Essential Science Fiction Television Reader.* Ed. J. P. Telotte. Lexington, KY: UP of Kentucky, 2008. 93–110.

Duncan, Andy. "Alternate History." *The Cambridge Companion to Science Fiction*. Eds. Edward James and Farah Mendlesohn. Cambridge: Cambridge UP, 2003. 209–18.

Eco, Umberto. *Travels in Hyperreality*. Trans. William Weaver. New York, NY: Harcourt Brace, 1986.

Ellington, Jane Elizabeth, and Joseph W. Critelli. "Analysis of a Modern Myth: The Star Trek Series." *Extrapolation* 24.3 (1983): 241–50.

Ellis, John. *Seeing Things: Television in the Age of Uncertainty*. London, I.B.: Tauris, 2000.

———. *Visible Fictions: Cinema: Television: Video*. Rev. ed. New York, NY: Routledge, 1992.

Erickson, Hal. *Syndicated Television: The First Forty Years, 1947–1987*. Jefferson, NC: McFarland, 1989.

Erisman, Fred. "Stagecoach in Space: The Legacy of *Firefly*." *Extrapolation* 47.2 (2006). 249–58.

Espenson, Jane. "Introduction." *Finding Serenity: Anti-Heroes, Lost Shepherds and Space Hookers in Joss Whedon's Firefly*. Ed. Jane Espenson. Dallas, TX: BenBella Books, 2004. 1–3.

Feldman, Leslie Dale. *Spaceships and Politics: The Political Theory of Rod Serling*. New York, NY: Lexington Books, 2010.

Feuer, Jane. "Genre Study and Television." *Channels of Discourse: Television and Contemporary Criticism*. Ed. Robert C. Allen. Chapel Hill, NC: U of North Carolina, NC, 1987. 113–33.

Foster, Amy. "Girls and 'Space Fever.'" *1950s "Rocketman", TV Series and Their Fans*. Eds. Cynthia J. Miller and A. Bowdoin Van Riper. New York, NY: Palgrave Macmillan, 2012. 67–82.

Freedman, Carl. *Critical Theory and Science Fiction*. Hanover, NH: UP of New England, 2000.

Fulton, Roger. *The Encyclopedia of TV Science Fiction*. 2nd ed. London: Boxtree, 2000.

Garcia, Frank. "*Crusade*: The Doomed Sequel Series to *Babylon 5* Premieres on TNT." *Cinefantastique* 31.7 (1999): 56–58.

George, Susan. "Fraking Machines: Desire, Gender, and the (Post)Human Condition." *The Essential Science Fiction Television Reader*. Ed. J. P. Telotte. Lexington, KY: UP of Kentucky, 2008. 159–75.

Geraghty, Lincoln. "The American Jeremiad and *Star Trek*'s Puritan Legacy." *Journal of the Fantastic in the Arts* 14.2 (2003): 228–45.

———. *American Science Fiction Film and Television*. Oxford: Berg, 2009.

———. "Homosocial Desire on the Final Frontier: Kinship, the American Romance, and *Deep Space Nine*'s 'Erotic Triangles.'" *Journal of Popular Culture* 36.3 (2003): 441–65.

————. *Living with Star Trek: American Culture and the Star Trek Universe*. London: I.B. Tauris, 2007.

Gitlin, Todd. *Inside Prime Time*. Rev. ed. London: Routledge, 1994.

Gould, Jack. "Television in Review." *The New York Times*, Nov. 20, 1949: 9.

Grubb, Jeffrey. "Plague Coming to *Defiance* TV Show—But You Can Stop It in the Game." *Gamesbeat*, June 3, 2013. www.venturebeat.com/2013/06/03/defiance-gets-new-tv-tie-in-content-will-impact-upcoming-episode/. Accessed July 10, 2013.

Haraway, Donna. "The Actors are Cyborg, Nature is Coyote, and the Geography is Elsewhere: Postscript to 'Cyborgs at Large.'" *Technoculture*. Eds. Constance Penley and Andrew Ross. Minneapolis, MN: U of Minnesota P, 1991. 21–26.

————. *Simians, Cyborgs, and Women: The Reinvention of Nature*. New York, NY: Routledge, 1991.

Hardy, Sarah, and Rebecca Kukla. "A Paramount Narrative: Exploring Space on the Starship *Enterprise*." *Journal of Aesthetics and Art Criticism* 57.2 (1999): 177–92.

Helford, Elyce Rae, ed. *Fantasy Girls: Gender in the New Universe of Science Fiction and Fantasy Television*. London: Rowman & Littlefield, 2000.

Heller, Lee E. "The Persistence of Difference: Postfeminism, Popular Discourse, and Heterosexuality in *Star Trek*." *Science-Fiction Studies* 24.2 (1997): 226–44.

Hill, Rodney. "'I Want to Believe the Truth Is Out There': *The X-Files* and the Impossibility of Knowing." *Science Fiction Film, Television, and Adaptation: Across the Screens*. Eds. J. P. Telotte and Gerald Duchovnay. New York, NY: Routledge, 2012. 115–26.

————. "Mapping *The Twilight Zone*'s Cultural and Mythological Terrain." *The Essential Science Fiction Television Reader*. Ed. J. P. Telotte. Lexington, KY: UP of Kentucky, 2008. 111–26.

Hills, Matt. *Fan Cultures*. London: Routledge, 2002.

Hollinger, Veronica. "Feminist Theory and Science Fiction." *The Cambridge Companion to Science Fiction*. Eds. Edward James and Farah Mendlesohn. Cambridge: Cambridge UP, 2003. 125–36.

Huddleston, Kathie. "J. J. Abrams, Alex Kurtzman and Roberto Orci Dig Deep to Discover 'the Pattern' in Their New Fox Series, *Fringe*." *Sci Fi Weekly* 608 (Dec. 15, 2008). www.scifi.com/sfw/interviews/sfw19440.html. Accessed June 6, 2013.

Hurd, Denise Alessandra. "The Monster Inside: 19th Century Racial Constructs in the 24th Century Myths of *Star Trek*." *Journal of Popular Culture* 31.1 (1997): 23–36.

Iaccino, J. F. "Babylon 5's Blueprint for the Archetypal Heroes." *Journal of Popular Culture* 34.4 (2001): 109–20.

Jackson, Rosemary. *Fantasy: The Literature of Subversion*. London: Methuen, 1981.

James, Edward. *Science Fiction in the Twentieth Century*. New York, NY: Oxford UP, 1994.

———, and Farah Mendlesohn, eds. *The Cambridge Companion to Science Fiction*. Cambridge: Cambridge UP, 2003.

Jameson, Fredric. "Towards a New Awareness of Genre." *Science-Fiction Studies* 9 (1982): 322–34.

Jancovich, Mark, and Derek Johnston. "Film and Television, the 1950s." *The Routledge Companion to Science Fiction*. Eds. Mark Bould, Andrew M. Butler, Adam Roberts, and Sherryl Vint. London: Routledge, 2009. 71–79.

Javna, John. *The Best of Science Fiction TV*. New York, NY: Harmony Books, 1987.

Jenkins, Henry. *Textual Poachers: Television Fans and Participatory Culture*. New York, NY: Routledge, 1992.

———, Sam Ford, and Joshua Green. *Spreadable Media: Creating Value and Meaning in a Networked Culture*. New York, NY: New York UP, 2013.

Johnson, Catherine. *Telefantasy*. London: BFI, 2005.

Johnson-Smith, Jan. *American Science Fiction TV: Star Trek, Stargate and Beyond*. Middletown, CT: Wesleyan UP, 2005.

Kapell, Matthew. "'Speakers for the Dead': Star Trek, the Holocaust, and the Representation of Atrocity." *Extrapolation* 41.2 (2000): 104–14.

Kellner, Douglas. "The X-Files and the Aesthetics and Politics of Postmodern Pop." *Journal of Aesthetics and Art Criticism* 57.2 (1999): 161–76.

Kuhlman, Martha. "The Uncanny Clone: The X-Files, Popular Culture, and Cloning." *Studies in Popular Culture* 26.3 (2004): 75–88.

Kuhn, Annette. "Introduction: Cultural Theory and Science Fiction Cinema." *Alien Zone*. Ed. Annette Kuhn. London: Verso, 1990. 1–12.

———, ed. *Alien Zone II: The Spaces of Science Fiction Cinema*. London: Verso, 1999.

LaFollette, Marcel Chotkowski. *Science on the Air: Popularizers and Personalities on Radio and Early Television*. Chicago, IL: U of Chicago P, 2008.

Lancaster, Kurt. "Web of Babylon." *Liquid Metal: The Science Fiction Film Reader*. Ed. Sean Redmond. London: Wallflower Press, 2004. 308–12.

Landon, Brooks. *Science Fiction After 1900: From the Steam Man to the Stars*. New York, NY: Routledge, 2002.

Lavery, David, Angela Hague, and Maria Cartwright. "Introduction: Generation X—The X-Files and the Cultural Moment." *"Deny All Knowledge": Reading The X-Files*. Eds. Lavery, Hague, and Cartwright. Syracuse, NY: Syracuse UP, 1996. 1–21.

Leopold, Todd. "Sci Fi Channel Becomes Syfy: Will Viewers Tune in or Drop Out?" CNN,com. July 6, 2009, www.cnn.com/2009/SHOWBIZ?TV/07/06/scifi.syfy.change. Accessed Sept. 26, 2013.

Lucanio, Patrick. *Them or Us: Archetypal Interpretations of Fifties Alien Invasion Films.* Bloomington, IN: Indiana UP, 1987.

———, and Gary Coville. *American Science Fiction Television Series of the 1950s: Episode Guides and Casts and Credits for Twenty Shows.* Jefferson, NC: McFarland, 1998.

———. *Smokin' Rockets: The Romance of Technology in American Film, Radio and Television, 1945–1962.* Jefferson, NC: McFarland, 2002.

Lyotard, Jean-Francois. *The Postmodern Condition: A Report on Knowledge.* Trans. Geoff Bennington and Brian Massumi. Minneapolis, MN: U of Minnesota P, 1984.

Mains, Christine. "Dreams Teach": (Im)possible Worlds in Science Fiction Television." *The Essential Science Fiction Television Reader.* Ed. J. P. Telotte. Lexington: up of Kentucky, 2008. 143–58.

Marling, Karal Ann. *As Seen on TV: The Visual Culture of Everyday Life in the 1950s.* Cambridge, MA: Harvard UP, 1994.

McNeil, Alex. *Total Television: The Comprehensive Guide to Programming from 1948 to the Present.* 8th ed. New York, NY: Penguin Books, 2003.

Miller, Cynthia J., and A. Bowdoin Van Riper, eds., *1950s "Rocketman" TV Series and Their Fans.* New York, NY: Palgrave Macmillan, 2012.

Miller, Mark Crispin. *Boxed In.* Evanston, IL: Northwestern UP, 1988.

Mittell, Jason. "A Cultural Approach to Television Genre Theory." *Cinema Journal* 40.3 (2001): 3–24.

———. *Genre and Television: From Cop Shows to Cartoons in American Culture.* London: Routledge, 2004.

Morton, Alan. *The Complete Directory to Science Fiction, Fantasy, and Horror Television Series: A Comprehensive Guide to the First 50 Years, 1946 to 1996.* Peoria, IL: Other Worlds Books, 1997.

Murray, Janet. *Hamlet on the Holodeck: The Future of Narrative in Cyberspace.* Cambridge, MA: MIT Press, 1997.

Neale, Steve. *Genre.* London: BFI, 1980.

Nelson, Robin. *TV Drama in Transition: Forms, Values, and Cultural Change.* Basingstoke: Macmillan, 1997.

Newcomb, Horace. "From Old Frontier to New Frontier." *The Revolution Wasn't Televised: Sixties Television and Social Conflict.* Eds. Lynn Spigel and Michael Curtin. London: Routledge, 1997. 287–304.

Nishime, Leilani. "Aliens: Narrating U. S. Global Identity Through Transnational and Interracial Marriage in *Battlestar Galactica*." *Critical Studies in Media Communication* 28.5 (2011): 450–65.

Palmer, Lorrie. "She's Just a Girl: A Cyborg Passes in *The Sarah Connor Chronicles*." *Science Fiction Film, Television, and Adaptation: Across the Screens*. Eds. J. P. Telotte and Gerald Duchovnay. New York, NY: Routledge, 2012. 84–98.

Pank, Dylan, and John Caro. " 'Haven't You Heard? They Look Like Us Now!': Realism and Metaphor in the New *Battlestar Galactica*." *Channeling the Future*. Ed. Lincoln Geraghty. Lanham, MD: Scarecrow, 2009. 199–215.

Peary, Danny, ed. *Omni's Screen Flights/Screen Fantasies*. Garden City, KS: Doubleday, 1984.

Penley, Constance, and Andrew Ross. "Cyborgs at Large: Interview with Donna Haraway." *Technoculture*. Eds. Penley and Ross. Minneapolis, MN: U of Minnesota P, 1991. 1–20.

Pierson, Michele. *Special Effects: Still in Search of Wonder*. New York, NY: Columbia UP, 2002.

Porter, Lynette, and David Lavery. *Unlocking the Meaning of Lost: An Unauthorized Guide*. Naperville, IL: Sourcebooks, 2006.

Potter, Tiffany, and C. W. Marshal. *Cylons in America: Critical Studies in Battlestar Galactica*. New York, NY: Continuum, 2008.

Reid, Robin Anne. "Fan Studies." *The Routledge Companion to Science Fiction*. Eds. Mark Bould, Andrew M. Butler, Adam Roberts, and Sherryl Vint. New York, NY: Routledge, 2009. 204–13.

Roberts, Robin. "Performing Science Fiction: Television, Theater, and Gender in *Star Trek, the Experience*." *Extrapolation* 42.4 (2001): 340–56.

———. "Rape, Romance, and Consent in *Star Trek: the Next Generation*." *Extrapolation* 40.1 (1999): 21–35.

Robinson, Murray. "Planet Parenthood." *Collier's* 129 (Jan. 5, 1952): 31, 63–64.

Ross, Sharon Marie, and Louisa Ellen Stein. "Introduction." *Teen Television: Essays on Programming and Fandom*. Eds. Ross and Stein. Jefferson, NC: McFarland, 2008. 3–25.

Roush, Matt. "Fantastic Voyages: The 60 Greatest Sci-Fi Shows of All Time." *TV Guide* 61.29 (2013): 14–15.

Rovin, Jeff. *The Great Television Series*. Cranbury, NJ: Barnes, 1977.

Ryan, Maureen. "Sex, Secrets and *Dollhouse*: Joss Whedon Talks About the End of His Fox Show." *Chicago Tribune*, Dec. 3, 2009. www.chicagotribune.com/entertainment_tv/2009/12/dollhouse-fox-joss-whedon.html. Accessed Dec. 4, 2012.

Said, Edward. *Orientalism*. New York, NY: Random House, 1978.

San Miguel, Renay. "Web Support for *Farscape* Out of This World." CNN.com/Sci-Tech. Sept. 18, 2002. www.cnn.com/2002/TECH/09/17/hln.wired. farscape/index.html. Accessed April 22, 2013.

Sander, Gordon F. *Serling: The Rise and Fall of Television's Last Angry Man*. New York, NY: Plume, 1994.

Scheibach, Michael. *Atomic Narratives and American Youth: Coming of Age with the Atom, 1945–1955*. Jefferson, NC: McFarland, 2003.

Sconce, Jeffrey. *Haunted Media: Electronic Presence from Telegraphy to Television*. Durham, NC: Duke UP, 2000.

Sharp, Patrick B. "Starbuck as 'American Amazon': Captivity Narrative and the Colonial Imagination in *Battlestar Galactica*." *Science Fiction Film and Television* 3.1 (2010): 57–78.

Silbergleid, Robin. "The Truth We Both Know': Readerly Desire and Heteronarrative in *The X-Files*." *Studies in Popular Culture* 25.3 (2003): 49–62.

Sobchack, Vivian. "Images of Wonder: The Look of Science Fiction." *Liquid Metal: The Science Fiction Film Reader*. Ed. Sean Redmond. London: Wallflower Press, 2004. 4–10.

———. "The Virginity of Astronauts: Sex and the Science Fiction Film." *Alien Zone: Cultural Theory and Contemporary Science Fiction Cinema*. Ed. Annette Kuhn. London: Verso, 1990. 103–15.

Sontag, Susan. "The Imagination of Disaster." *Against Interpretation*. New York, NY: Dell, 1966. 212–28.

Stanyard, Stewart T. *Dimensions Behind The Twilight Zone*. Toronto: ECW Press, 2007.

Stark, Steven D. "*The Twilight Zone*: Science Fiction as Realism." *Glued to the Set*. New York, NY: Free Press, 1997.

Stewart, Garrett. "The 'Videology' of Science Fiction." *Shadows of the Magic Lamp*. Eds. George E. Slusser and Eric S. Rabkin. Carbondale, IL: Southern Illinois UP, 1985. 159–207.

Storm, Jo. *Approaching the Possible: The World of Stargate SG-1*. Ontario: ECW Press, 2005.

Surette, Tim. "*Defiance* Series Premiere Review: Familiarity in an Unfamiliar World." *TV.Com*, April 16, 2013. www.tv.com/news/defiance-series-premiere-review-familiarity-in-an-unfamiliar-world-136569961425/. Accessed July 10, 2013.

Suvin, Darko. *Metamorphoses of Science Fiction: On the Poetics and Discourse of a Literary Genre*. New Haven, CT: Yale UP, 1979.

Taylor, Robert B. "The Captain May Wear the Tight Pants, but It's the Gals Who Make *Serenity* Soar." *Finding Serenity: Anti-Heroes, Lost Shepherds and Space Hookers in Joss Whedon's Firefly*. Ed. Jane Espenson. Dallas, TX: BenBella Books, 2004. 131–37.

Telotte, J. P. "Disney in Science Fiction Land." *Journal of Popular Film and Television.* 33.1 (2005): 12–21.

———. "The Detective as Dreamer: The Case of *The Lady in the Lake.*" *Journal of Popular Film and Television* 12.1 (1984): 4–15.

———, ed. *The Essential Science Fiction Television Reader.* Lexington, KY: UP of Kentucky, 2008.

———. "Lost in Space: Television as Science Fiction Icon." *The Essential Science Fiction Television Reader.* Ed. J. P. Telotte. Lexington, KY: UP of Kentucky, 2008. 37–54.

———. *Replications: A Robotic History of the Science Fiction Film.* Champaign, IL: U of Illinois P, 1995.

———. *Science Fiction Film.* Cambridge: Cambridge UP, 2001.

———, and Gerald Duchovnay, eds. *Science Fiction Film, Television, and Adaptation: Across the Screens.* New York, NY: Routledge, 2012.

Todorov, Tzvetan. *The Fantastic: A Structural Approach to a Literary Genre.* Trans. Richard Howard. Ithaca, NY: Cornell UP, 1975.

"The Tomorrow Project." Intel Corporation. www.tomorrow-projects.com. Accessed August 15, 2012.

Tulloch, John. *Television Drama: Agency, Audience, and Myth.* London: Routledge, 1990.

———, and Manuel Alvarado. *Doctor Who: The Unfolding Text.* London: Macmillan, 1983.

———, and Henry Jenkins. *Science Fiction Audiences: Watching Doctor Who and Star Trek.* London: Routledge, 1995.

"*TV Guide* Names the Top Cult Shows Ever." www.tvguide.com/news/top-cult-shows-40239.aspx. Accessed March 1, 2012.

Variety Television Reviews, 1946–1956. Vol. 1. London: Garland Science, 1990.

Vint, Sherryl. "Babylon 5: Our First, Best Hope for Mature Science Fiction Television." *The Essential Science Fiction Television Reader.* Ed. J. P. Telotte. Lexington, KY: UP of Kentucky, 2008. 247–65.

Virilio, Paul. *The Art of the Motor.* Trans. Julie Rose. Minneapolis, MN: U of Minnesota P, 1995.

———. *The University of Disaster.* Trans. Julie Rose. Cambridge: Polity Press, 2010.

———. *War and Cinema: A Logistics of Perception.* Trans. Patrick Camiller. London: Verso, 1989.

Wakefield, Sarah R. "'Your Sister in St. Scully': An Electronic Community of Female Fans of *The X-Files.*" *Journal of Popular Film and Television* 29.3 (2001): 130–37.

Weinstein, D. "*Captain Video:* Television's First Fantastic Voyage." *Journal of Popular Film and Television* 30.3 (2002): 148–57.

Westfahl, Gary. *Hugo Gernsback and the Century of Science Fiction*. Jefferson, NC: McFarland, 2007.

———. *The Mechanics of Wonder: The Creation of the Idea of Science Fiction*. Liverpool: Liverpool UP, 1999.

———. "Space Opera." *The Cambridge Companion to Science Fiction*. Eds. Edward James and Farah Mendlesohn. Cambridge: Cambridge UP, 2003. 197–208.

Whitfield, Stephen E., and Gene Roddenberry. *The Making of Star Trek*. New York, NY: Ballantine Books, 1968.

Wilcox, Rhonda V., and Tanya R. Cochran, eds. *Investigating Firefly and Serenity: Science Fiction on the Frontier*. London: I. B. Tauris, 2008.

Wildermuth, Mark. "The Edge of Chaos: Structural Conspiracy and Epistemology in *The X-Files*." *Journal of Popular Film and Television* 26.4 (1999): 146–57.

Williams, Raymond. *Television: Technology and Cultural Form*. London: Routledge, 2003.

Wolfe, Peter. *In the Zone: The Twilight World of Rod Serling*. Bowling Green, KY: Bowling Green UP/Popular Press, 1996.

Woodman, Brian J. "Escaping Genre's Village: Fluidity and Genre Mixing in Television's *The Prisoner*." *Journal of Popular Culture* 38.5 (2005): 939–56.

Woolery, George W. *Children's Television: The First Thirty-Five Years, 1946–1981; Part II: Live, Film and Tape Series*. Metuchen, NJ: Scarecrow, 1989.

Worland, Rick. "Sign-Posts Up Ahead: *The Twilight Zone, The Outer Limits*, and TV Political Fantasy, 1959–1965." *Science-Fiction Studies* 23.1 (1996): 103–22.

INDEX